365 Ways to Cook Vegetarian

365 Ways to Cook Vegetarian

Kitty Morse

BARNES
&NOBLE
BOOKS
NEW YORK

This book is dedicated with love to my mother Nicole,
who taught me the value of good nutrition.

Acknowledgments

I would like to thank all the friends who shared some of their favorite
meatless recipes with me for this book. Much of the credit goes to
my husband Owen, my chief food critic, who in the course of sampling
and tasting innumerable dishes, became a "meatless" eater.

2000 Barnes & Noble Books

ISBN 0-7607-2015-0

Printed and bound in the United States of America

00 01 02 03 04 MC 9 8 7 6 5 4 3 2 1

DYNE

Contents

Enticing appetizers and hors d'oeuvres offer a range from Watercress Asparagus Roll-Ups and Spinach Pâté to Roquefort Strudel and Mexican Flautas with Mole Verde.

Try a bowlful of goodness as a starter with Chilly Dilled Beet Borscht, Pumpkin and Carrot Bisque, Quick Gazpacho Olé. Or spoon up a meal with Smoky Wild Rice and Corn Soup, Moroccan Vegetable Tagine, Green on Green Gumbo.

Satisfaction is guaranteed with recipes like Black Bean Pistachio Burgers with Guacamole and Sweet Pickled Onions, Indian Garbanzo Beans with Fried Garlic and Peanuts, Meatless Cassoulet au Vin, and Red Lentil Pie with Cucumber Yogurt Sauce.

What's not here won't be missed when you offer your family dishes like Corn and Chili Pie, Eggplant Enchiladas, Mushroom Ravioli Divan, Quick Brown Rice Paella, Roasted Vegetables with Teriyaki Vinaigrette.

Here's everyone's vegetarian favorite: Easy Overnight Lasagne, Egg Noodles with Artichoke Hearts in Whiskey Saffron Sauce, Asparagus and Olive Linguine, Four-Cheese Macaroni au Gratin, Spaghetti and No-Meat Balls, and much more.

Pizza Primavera, California Artichoke Pie, Vegetable Potpie, Moroccan-Style B'steeya, and Fresh Tomato Tart are just a few of the easy ways with prepared dough and pastry presented in this chapter.

Light salads, starter salads, side salads, and main-course salads all star here in such tempting recipes as Taco Bean Salad with Chili Yogurt Dressing, Celery Root Rémoulade, Indonesian Gado-Gado with Peanut Sauce, Roasted Potato Salad with Capers and Balsamic Vinegar, Crunchy Vietnamese Salad.

Introduction

For "Vegetarian" in the title of this book, read "Vegetables." Although the volume is full of all kinds of recipes featuring pasta, rice, grains, eggs, and cheese, vegetables are the stars of this cookbook.

Fresh produce, as well as an increasing number of grains, is taking up more and more space on our collective dinner plate, pushing aside the hefty portions of meat once thought of as necessary to a well-rounded diet. The visible proof of this gradual change in American eating habits lies no further than the produce sections of most supermarkets. The common zucchini squash, ubiquitous iceberg lettuce, and traditional curly-leafed parsley now share shelf space with dozens of varieties of fruits and vegetables, some of which were almost unheard of barely a decade ago. Adding to the cornucopia, weekly farmers' markets are beginning to dot the urban and suburban landscapes from downtown Hollywood to rural Wisconsin, to satisfy increased consumer insistence for produce fresh from the source. Growers, in turn, are busy rediscovering heirloom varieties of fruits and vegetables and experimenting with produce items once strictly bound for a diminutive ethnic market. Culinarily speaking, America has turned into an even greater melting pot, offering a fragrant stew of ethnic cuisines simmering squarely on everyone's kitchen stove.

The increasing selection has fueled consumer awareness on the subject of a healthful diet and has translated into the consumption of more fresh fruits, vegetables, and grains. Indeed, recent research based on scientific evidence suggests that incorporating larger amounts of these staples into daily meals, while decreasing consumption of red meats, helps forestall the incidence of cancer and heart disease. The United States Department of Agriculture, the United States Department of Health and Human Services, and the National Institutes of Health all make similar recommendations through such programs as 5-a-Day for Better Health, which recommends at least five daily helpings of fresh fruits or vegetables.

The USDA's Dietary Guidelines are another indicator of the way daily food intake ought to go. According to this nutritional recommendation, breads, cereals, rice, and pasta should figure most prominently on everyone's daily menu, followed closely by generous helpings of fruits and vegetables and more modest amounts of meat, poultry, fish, eggs, and dairy products. The government agency's Food Guide Pyramid defines a serving as ½ cup of fruit or vegetables, 1 average piece of fruit, ¾ cup of vegetable or fruit juice, at least 1 cup of salad greens, or ¼ cup of dried fruit. The agency gives an even stronger recommendation for a meatless or almost meatless diet, placing at the bottom, or widest part, of the pyramid the starchy, carbohydrate-rich foods that should be consumed on a daily basis, such as breads (preferably whole grain) and cereals. Fiber-rich vegetables and fruits, on the next level of the pyramid, provide the vitamins, minerals, and fiber necessary to a person's well-being. The pyramid narrows with meat, poultry, fish, and dairy products, which are an important source of protein, calcium, iron, and zinc. A well-planned meatless diet will compensate for the lack of animal products with starches and legumes (beans, lentils, and peas) as well as other protein-rich foods. The tip of the pyramid belongs to fats, which should account for a scant one third of our daily calories. Finally, last, and preferably least, sweets should ideally be used only as condiments or flavorings.

For some, excluding meat or animal products from their daily fare is linked to ecological and moral concerns. For others, keeping the meat intake to a minimum is strictly a matter of health. For whatever reason, over twelve million Americans now consider themselves vegetarians, according to well-informed sources. Several levels of vegetarianism define the varying degrees of "meatless" eaters to be found in this country: Lacto-ovo vegetarians include eggs and dairy products in their diet; lacto-vegetarians eat dairy products but no eggs, while ovo-vegetarians do just the opposite. The strictest vegetarians of all are the vegans, who eat no food of animal origin. For those not quite ready to make such a drastic transition, less severe variations on the same theme include semi-vegetarians, who enjoy eggs, dairy products, chicken, and fish, and pesco-vegetarians, who opt for fish and seafood exclusively rather than meat. In *365 Ways to Cook Vegetarian*, home cooks have the opportunity to make up their own individual menus featuring nutritious meatless dishes. Some call for eggs or dairy products. Others are based exclusively on vegetables or grains. The choice is entirely an individual one.

The recipes in *365 Ways to Cook Vegetarian* reflect my international background. It includes a French mother, who taught me the rudiments of French home-style cooking, an English father, and a childhood spent in Morocco, where I was born. My extensive travels around the world introduced me to a host of exotic cuisines from Tunisia to Thailand. My passionate interest in fresh vegetables is due to this upbringing, and to the bountiful crops of farm-fresh products available almost year round in southern California, where I have resided for the past twenty years.

Because of this background, many of the dishes in *365 Ways to Cook Vegetarian* were inspired by the cuisines of other lands. Indeed, we have much to learn from a host of cultures where the cost of meat is often prohibitive. Witness the American passion for all things Italian, from traditional or designer-style pizzas to the once-lowly spaghetti, metamorphosed into "pasta" almost overnight. Endless variations on the pasta, pizza, and risotto themes are delicious proof that anyone can cut down on meat consumption without sacrificing good nutrition or delicious taste. The same goes for the ever-increasing numbers of Chinese, Thai, and Vietnamese restaurants. They introduced Americans to the culinary delights of the Far East, where crisp, stir-fried vegetables, or a bowl of broth brimming with chopped greens, flavorful noodles, and a few cubes of tofu account for the day's main meal. The cuisines of North Africa and the Middle East, where healthful grains, such as bulgur wheat and couscous are staples, also offer enticing choices. In many of these countries, economic constraints usually dictate that fresh fruits and vegetables, legumes, and nuts provide all the ingredients necessary for a well-rounded diet.

A funny thing happened as I was writing *365 Ways to Cook Vegetarian*. As a meat eater, my perception of eating a "vegetarian" diet, and more specifically, of "meatless dining," changed radically. Vegetarian cuisine need not lack in taste. On the contrary, the challenge lies in cooking for flavor, using fresh or dried herbs, and experimenting with the wide assortment of condiments available on the market. Another transformation occurred when my husband and I went from a diet that included moderate amounts of meat to one practically meat-free. We significantly reduced our fat intake, and we increased our consumption of whole grains and fresh vegetables in the bargain. Our appetite for red meat has decreased dramatically, although we do still enjoy poultry or fresh fish on occasion.

Those who are about to embark on this new taste adventure will find the experience rewarding on more than the culinary front. The ethnic foods sections of supermarket shelves now hold a wealth of ethnic staples, such as flavor-packed sauces and condiments. (Did you know, for instance, that the sale of fresh Mexican-style salsa has surpassed that of ketchup in the United States?) Many of the product labels, geared to an American audience, usually provide descriptions and recipes. Experimenting is part of the fun of eating meatless. Not only does minimizing meat consumption hold many a health benefit, but just as important, meatless meals tend to be easier on the wallet.

The following tips will provide a few guidelines when preparing healthful meatless dishes:

- Use heavy, nonstick cookware to minimize the use of oil. Olive oil, a monounsaturated fat that some studies indicate helps lower bad cholesterol counts and raise the good ones, should be a staple in your pantry, not only for its health benefits but also for its fruity flavor. Using an ozone-friendly cooking spray or a food-safe spray bottle filled with the oil of your choice further reduces calories.
- Steaming vegetables or cooking them in a minimal amount of broth, a little wine, or low-sodium tomato juice will eliminate even more calories from your diet.
- Save greens and fronds from bunches of celery, beets, and fennel to make a vitamin-packed fresh vegetable broth. You will find a recipe for a basic vegetable broth on page 30. For the majority of cooks who are not strictly vegetarian, all recipes calling for broth list reduced-sodium chicken broth as an alternative to a totally meatless vegetable broth. Canned vegetable broth is now sold alongside chicken broth in most supermarkets.
- Add low-fat or nonfat milk where milk or cream is called for in a

recipe. Canned evaporated skim milk lends a silken texture to cream sauces.

- Use plain yogurt instead of sour cream. Add it at the end of cooking time to prevent curdling.
- Use fresh herbs whenever possible. Most garden-variety culinary herbs are now commonly found in supermarkets. If you grow your own, snip them with scissors and freeze them. Purchase dried herbs in bulk from specialized food stores whenever possible. Not only is that a cheaper way to go, but a larger turnover indicates a fresher supply. Crush the herbs a little between your fingers before using them.
- Grinding spices and seeds in a mortar and pestle before adding them to a dish will bring out the fragrance.
- Read food labels before purchasing canned goods. Most processed foods already contain high levels of sodium. Add salt and pepper at the end of cooking time to prevent oversalting. Using generous amounts of herbs such as parsley, dill, cilantro, basil, or a few drops of lemon juice will often compensate for salt.
- Use frozen egg substitutes if you do not want to make whole eggs part of your diet.

Most recipes in *365 Ways to Cook Vegetarian* are suggested as individual dishes. Make sure to combine them with others to obtain a correct nutritional balance. For more detailed information, consult a good book on nutrition. Happy meatless cooking!

Chapter 1

Vegetables from the Start

Sometimes, when my husband and I have no desire for a dinner involving a salad, a main dish, and a dessert, we elect to have one made up entirely of appetizers. In Spain, for example, entire meals are made of an array of savory little dishes called *tapas*. Like the Spanish, we "graze" on enticing hot or cold little tidbits, dip an array of fresh vegetables in a savory sauce, or lather a thick slice of bread with a delicious spread. Not only is it a welcome change from preparing a regular meal, but it is often easier on the pocketbook.

When planning a party, I like to offer a selection of hot and cold hors d'oeuvres—some hearty, some light, yet all meant to add excitement to the occasion. This chapter includes an array of cold appetizers such as the lovely layered Avocado Pie and the ready-in-a-jiffy Stuffed Pita Wedges. Flavorful spreads such as Green Bean "Chopped Liver," Cashew Mushroom Pâté, and Sesame Sweet Pea Spread are a real taste treat when spread on crackers or slices of freshly baked baguette. The stunning Sourdough Brie Loaf provides a beautiful edible centerpiece where the hollowed loaf of bread is filled with warm melted cheese.

Tasty egg rolls stuffed with a variety of fillings are always a hit. Although they can be prepared days and even weeks ahead of time and frozen, egg rolls must be fried or baked at the last minute to retain their crispness. In this chapter, you will find an adaptation of traditional vegetable-filled Filipino-Style Egg Rolls, Crisp Feta Cheese and Dried Cranberry Won Tons with Jalapeño Pepper Jelly, and Crunchy Gyoza Potstickers, all easy to assemble with the ready-made egg roll and won ton wrappers commonly available in the frozen food or produce section of many supermarkets.

In recent years, south-of-the-border specialties such as crisp little tortilla rolls like Potato Taquitos with Tomatillo Sauce and Flautas with Mole Verde have gone mainstream, ranking among the most popular hot appetizers to serve at parties. Dipped in chunky Mexican salsa or in a smooth guacamole, for which you'll find the recipes on page 260 and page 257 respectively, these crunchy little cigar-shaped appetizers can become positively addictive.

Appetizers wrapped in filo always imply you have spent hours making them, yet you will be surprised at how easy they are to assemble. Filo-dough pastries such as Roquefort or Cabbage Strudel, Nutty Baked Brie in Filo, or flaky Spinach Filo Triangles are all crowd pleasers. The strudels, in fact, can easily double as a first course or as an entree for a light meal. Often, appetizers make full use of the season's produce. Such is the case for the dainty Watercress Asparagus Roll-Ups and for the Eggplant Pizzas, where slices of eggplant, tomato, and cheese make for a delectable broiled sandwich.

Whether you are planning an intimate hors d'oeuvre dinner for two or a more formal cocktail party, be sure to use your prettiest dishes to show off your creations. That's all part of the fun! Happy grazing!

1   CAPONATA

Prep: 15 minutes   Stand: 30 minutes   Cook: 26 to 28 minutes
Serves: 4

This classic Italian specialty keeps well for several days in the refrigerator. Use it as a spread or dip, as a topping for pasta, or as a filling for sandwiches.

1 **medium eggplant, peeled and cut into ½-inch cubes**
2 **teaspoons salt**
2 **tablespoons olive oil**
1 **medium onion, chopped**
3 **ripe tomatoes, peeled, seeded, and coarsely chopped**
3 **celery ribs, diced**

1 **tablespoon pine nuts**
1 **bay leaf**
2 **tablespoons balsamic vinegar**
⅓ **cup chopped green olives**
1 **tablespoon capers, drained**
1 **teaspoon salt**
2 **drops of Tabasco**

1. In a colander, toss eggplant cubes with salt. Let stand 30 minutes. Rinse under running water. Drain and pat dry.

2. In a large frying pan, heat oil over medium heat. Add eggplant cubes and cook until they soften, 4 to 5 minutes. Add onions and cook, stirring occasionally, until softened, 2 to 3 minutes. Add tomatoes, celery, pine nuts, and bay leaf. Reduce heat to low. Cover and cook 15 minutes.

3. Add vinegar, olives, capers, salt, and Tabasco. Cook 5 minutes. Discard bay leaf. Transfer caponata to a serving bowl. Serve at room temperature or chilled.

2   ARUGULA WALNUT PÂTÉ WITH BELGIAN ENDIVE

Prep: 20 minutes   Cook: none   Makes: about 2 cups

Use this pâté as a dip or as a spread for sandwiches. Arugula, also called roquette, is a delicate and spicy green usually tossed into mesclun, or young lettuce mix. You can substitute watercress for the arugula. Serving it with crisp and dainty endive leaves adds a festive touch to your dish.

3 cups arugula leaves, stemmed, rinsed, and patted dry
4 hard-boiled eggs, shelled and coarsely chopped
¼ cup plain yogurt
¼ cup mayonnaise
½ cup walnut pieces

1 teaspoon Dijon mustard
2 garlic cloves, minced
½ teaspoon lemon pepper
2 tablespoons lemon juice
3 scallions, coarsely chopped
2 Belgian endives, separated into leaves

1. In a blender or food processor, combine arugula, eggs, yogurt, mayonnaise, walnut pieces, mustard, garlic, lemon pepper, lemon juice, and scallions. Puree until fairly smooth.

2. On a serving platter, arrange endive leaves like flower petals around edge of plate. Mound pâté in center and use whole leaves as scoops.

3   AVOCADO PIE

Prep: 10 minutes   Cook: none   Chill: 1 hour   Serves: 6 to 8

1½ cups Mexican salsa, prepared or homemade
2 large ripe avocados
1 envelope ranch-style salad dressing mix
2 teaspoons lemon juice
½ cup sour cream
½ cup mayonnaise

1 bunch of scallions, chopped
1 (4-ounce) can chopped black olives, drained
1 cup shredded Monterey Jack cheese
¼ cup coarsely chopped cilantro or parsley
Tortilla chips

1. Place salsa in a colander to drain.

2. Meanwhile, cut avocados in half, remove pits, and scoop avocados into a medium bowl. Mash with a fork until fairly smooth. Add dressing mix and lemon juice. Stir to blend well.

3. In a small bowl, mix sour cream and mayonnaise.

4. To assemble, spread mashed avocado on bottom of an 8-inch pie plate. With a spatula, cover evenly with sour cream mixture. Spread drained salsa over sour cream. Cover with scallions, then chopped olives, then Monterey Jack cheese. Sprinkle cilantro or parsley leaves over top. Refrigerate up to 1 hour before serving. Serve with tortilla chips for dipping.

4   GREEN BEAN "CHOPPED LIVER"

Prep: 15 minutes   Cook: 28 to 35 minutes   Makes: about 2 cups

Grace Kirschenbaum, publisher of the *World of Cookbooks* newsletter, has been enjoying this vegetarian chopped liver since childhood: "Some people make it with eggplant, some add chopped walnuts to it. I always found this version to be the most delicious." She recommends making it with freshly picked green beans, if possible. Use this as an appetizer or as a spread. The flavor of pepper should be quite pronounced. Serve with crackers.

1 **pound fresh green beans, trimmed and cut into 1-inch pieces**	2 **hard-boiled eggs, shelled and quartered**
2 **tablespoons vegetable oil**	½ **teaspoon salt**
2 **large onions, chopped**	½ **to ¾ teaspoon freshly ground pepper**

1. In a large pan filled with lightly salted boiling water, cook green beans until very soft, 25 to 30 minutes; drain. Set aside.

2. Meanwhile, in a large frying pan, heat oil over medium-high heat and cook onions, stirring occasionally, until golden, 3 to 5 minutes. Remove from heat. Let cool.

3. In a blender or food processor, chop green beans, onions, and eggs in batches until finely chopped but not pureed. Season with salt and pepper. Transfer to a serving bowl. Serve chilled.

5   SESAME SWEET PEA SPREAD

Prep: 5 minutes   Cook: 10 to 13 minutes   Makes: 2 cups

This delicious spread acquires extra flavor from the addition of nutritional yeast, which is available in bulk in health food stores.

¼ **cup sesame seeds**	¼ **cup dry sherry**
2 **tablespoons butter**	1 **teaspoon salt**
1 **large onion, diced**	1 **tablespoon nutritional yeast (optional)**
1 **garlic clove, minced**	2 **teaspoons lemon juice**
1 **(10-ounce) package frozen petite peas, thawed**	

1. In a dry nonstick small frying pan, toast the sesame seeds over medium-high heat, stirring, until golden, 3 to 4 minutes. Transfer to a plate.

2. In a medium saucepan over medium heat, melt butter and cook onion and garlic until softened, 3 to 4 minutes. Add peas, sherry, and salt. Cover, reduce heat to low, and cook until peas are soft, 4 to 5 minutes. Stir in nutritional yeast and lemon juice. Let cool 5 minutes.

3. In a blender or food processor, puree peas. Add sesame seeds and process until well blended. Serve chilled with crackers or as a dip for vegetables.

6   EGGPLANT PIZZAS

Prep: 10 minutes   Stand: 10 minutes   Cook: 8 to 9 minutes
Serves: 4

My friend Doris Deakins recommends choosing tomatoes that have approximately the same circumference as the eggplant for best results.

1   medium eggplant
1   teaspoon salt
     Olive oil cooking spray
2   large tomatoes, sliced ¼ inch
       thick

2   teaspoons herbes de
       Provence
1   cup shredded Jarlsberg
       cheese

1. Preheat broiler. Wash eggplant, but do not peel. Cut crosswise into round slices ¼ inch thick. Sprinkle both sides of eggplant with a little salt. Let stand 10 minutes, then pat dry.

2. Set eggplant slices on a lightly greased baking sheet. Lightly spray eggplant with olive oil. Broil about 4 inches from heat until light brown, about 2 minutes. Carefully with tongs turn over and broil until light brown on second side, about 2 minutes.

3. Remove eggplant from broiler. Reduce oven temperature to 350°F. Top each eggplant slice with a tomato slice of equal size. Sprinkle with herbs. Top with shredded cheese.

4. Return slices to oven and bake 4 to 5 minutes until cheese melts. Serve immediately.

7   POTATO WEDGES WITH GUACAMOLE

Prep: 10 minutes   Cook: 25 to 30 minutes   Serves: 8

Serve the hot wedges with guacamole or fresh salsa.

8   medium russet potatoes
       (about 4 pounds)
¼   cup olive oil
1   envelope taco, fajita, or
       burrito seasoning mix

2   cups guacamole (page 257)
       or your favorite prepared
       brand

1. Preheat oven to 425°F. Scrub potatoes under running water. Cut into ½- to ¾-inch wedges. Set aside.

2. Line a baking sheet with foil. In a small bowl, mix olive oil with seasoning mix. Set potato wedges on baking sheet and generously paint with oil mixture on both sides.

3. Bake potato wedges until tender, 25 to 30 minutes. With tongs, transfer wedges to paper towels to drain briefly. Serve hot, with guacamole on the side for dipping.

8 LETTUCE NAPOLEON WITH TERIYAKI MAYONNAISE

Prep: 15 minutes   Cook: none   Serves: 4

I owe this idea to my friend Nicole Peyrafitte, an accomplished chef who hails from France. The layered presentation brings to mind a napoleon pastry, hence the name.

12 **large leaves of Boston lettuce**	6 **scallions, chopped**
1 **medium cucumber, peeled, seeded, and diced**	¼ **teaspoon pepper**
	1 **tablespoon lemon juice**
½ **red bell pepper, finely diced**	½ **cup mayonnaise**
2 **medium carrots, shredded**	½ **cup plain yogurt**
1½ **cups cooked whole-kernel corn**	1 **garlic clove, minced**
	2 **tablespoons teriyaki sauce**

1. Wash lettuce leaves under running water and pat dry. In a large bowl, combine diced cucumber, red pepper, carrots, corn, and 3 chopped scallions. Toss with pepper and lemon juice.

2. In a blender or food processor, make dressing by blending 3 remaining scallions with mayonnaise, yogurt, garlic, and teriyaki sauce until smooth. Reserve ¼ cup dressing for decoration. Toss remainder with diced vegetables.

3. To serve, set 1 leaf of lettuce on an individual plate. Top with ½ cup vegetables. Cover with second leaf. Spoon another ½ cup vegetables over leaf and top with final lettuce leaf. Decorate each napoleon with a dollop of dressing. Serve chilled.

9 MELON WITH PORT WINE

Prep: 5 minutes   Cook: none   Chill: 2 hours   Serves: 2

This super-simple way of enjoying a sweet chilled cantaloupe is to me the best indication that summer has arrived. Serve as a refreshing first course.

1 **ripe cantaloupe**	**Mint leaves**
½ **cup port wine**	

Cut cantaloupe in half and scoop out seeds. Pour ¼ cup port into each melon half. Cover and refrigerate until well chilled, at least 2 hours. Decorate with mint leaves and serve ice cold.

10   PESTO NACHOS
Prep: 10 minutes   Cook: 4 to 5 minutes   Serves: 4

1 (7-ounce) package round
    tortilla chips
3 tablespoons finely chopped
    sun-dried tomatoes

4 ounces fontina cheese,
    shredded
½ cup prepared basil pesto

1. Preheat oven to 400°F. Top each tortilla chip with a pinch of sun-dried tomato and about 1 teaspoon grated cheese. Set on a baking sheet.

2. Bake 4 to 5 minutes, until cheese melts. Top each chip with a dab of pesto and serve hot.

11   CASHEW MUSHROOM PÂTÉ
Prep: 15 minutes   Cook: 10 to 12 minutes   Chill: 2 hours
Makes: 2 cups

This mouth-watering pâté can be prepared a day ahead. Serve with crackers or toasted slices of French baguette.

½ pound white button
    mushrooms, wiped clean
    and coarsely chopped
1 small onion, peeled and
    quartered
1 medium carrot, peeled and
    cut into chunks

2 tablespoons butter
1 teaspoon lemon juice
1 garlic clove, minced
½ teaspoon dried tarragon
    leaves
1 tablespoon dry sherry
1 cup cashew pieces

1. In a food processor, chop mushrooms by pulsing on and off until mushrooms are coarsely ground. Transfer to a medium bowl. Process onion and carrot in same manner. Transfer to a small bowl. Rinse out processor.

2. In a large frying pan, melt butter over medium heat. Add onion and carrot and cook until softened, about 3 minutes. Add ground mushrooms, lemon juice, garlic, tarragon, and sherry. Cook, stirring occasionally, until most of liquid in pan has evaporated, 4 to 5 minutes. Transfer to medium bowl.

3. In a dry medium frying pan, toast cashew pieces over high heat, shaking pan back and forth to prevent scorching, until nuts turn golden, 3 to 4 minutes. Transfer to a plate and let cool 5 minutes. In processor, pulse nuts until finely ground.

4. Add ground nuts to mushroom mixture. Mix well. Cover and refrigerate 2 hours or overnight.

12   SPINACH PÂTÉ

Prep: 10 minutes   Cook: 5 to 6 minutes   Makes: about 2 cups

Serve this pâté with wedges of pita bread or crackers.

2 (10-ounce) packages frozen
    chopped spinach
⅔ cup pine nuts
1 small onion, finely diced
2 teaspoons celery seed
2 teaspoons dill weed

1 teaspoon sweet paprika
½ teaspoon garlic salt
1 tablespoon lemon juice
1 (3-ounce) package cream
    cheese, softened

1. In a medium saucepan filled with 1 cup water, cook spinach over medium-high heat, breaking up with a large fork to separate, for 3 minutes. Drain into a colander and rinse under cold running water to cool. With your hands, squeeze out as much liquid as possible. Transfer to a medium bowl.

2. In a dry nonstick medium frying pan, toast pine nuts over medium heat, tossing occasionally until nuts turn golden brown, 2 to 3 minutes. Watch closely to avoid scorching. Transfer to a plate.

3. In a blender or food processor, combine toasted pine nuts, onion, celery seed, dill weed, paprika, garlic salt, lemon juice, and cream cheese. Puree to a paste. Add spinach and process until blended. Transfer to a serving bowl, cover, and refrigerate until serving time.

13   SPINACH PUFFS

Prep: 20 minutes   Cook: 4 minutes per batch   Makes: about 25

Peggy Diamant lived in Korea for many years, and she adapted this local specialty for her family and for her friends at home.

2 (10-ounce) packages frozen
    chopped spinach
2 eggs, lightly beaten
1 medium onion, finely diced
1½ teaspoons baking powder
1 to 1½ cups Wondra flour
½ teaspoon pepper

½ cup soy sauce or tamari
6 tablespoons rice vinegar
3 tablespoons sugar
1 garlic clove, minced
½ teaspoon minced fresh
    ginger
    Vegetable oil, for frying

1. Preheat oven to 200°F. Cook spinach according to package directions. Drain into a colander and rinse under cold running water. With your hands, squeeze out as much liquid as possible.

2. In a medium bowl, with your hands or with a wooden spoon, mix spinach with eggs, onion, baking powder, 1 cup flour, and pepper. Blend in enough of remaining flour until mixture holds its shape without being too dry.

3. In a small bowl, mix soy sauce, vinegar, sugar, garlic, and ginger. Set sauce aside.

4. Line a baking sheet with a double layer of paper towels. In a medium frying pan or medium saucepan, pour vegetable oil to a depth of 1 inch. Heat over medium-high heat until a little piece of batter dropped in oil sizzles and floats to surface. Drop spinach mixture by scant tablespoons into oil. Fry puffs in batches without crowding, about 2 minutes on each side, until lightly browned. With a slotted spoon, transfer cooked puffs to paper-lined baking sheet to drain. Keep warm until ready to serve.

5. Serve puffs hot, with sauce for dipping.

---

14   SPINACH FILO TRIANGLES
Prep: 30 minutes   Stand: 2 hours   Cook: 15 to 20 minutes
Makes: about 60

When working with filo dough, make sure to keep the sheets covered to prevent their contact with the air, or they will turn brittle.

1 **(16-ounce) package frozen filo dough**	1 **tablespoon rosemary leaves, crushed**
3 **(10-ounce) packages frozen chopped spinach, thawed**	3 **scallions, finely chopped**
1 **pound Greek kasseri or feta cheese, finely crumbled**	1 **tablespoon lemon pepper**
⅓ **cup ricotta cheese**	2 **cups melted butter**
⅓ **cup seasoned bread crumbs**	1 **egg, lightly beaten**
	Wedges of lemon

1. Preheat oven to 375°F. Thaw filo dough 2 hours at room temperature or overnight in refrigerator. With your hands, squeeze spinach to remove as much liquid as possible.

2. In a medium bowl, mix spinach with kasseri cheese, ricotta, bread crumbs, rosemary, scallions, and lemon pepper.

3. Unwrap filo dough and place on a damp kitchen towel. With short side of filo facing you, cut a strip 3 inches wide. Keep remaining filo covered with a damp towel. With a small pastry brush, generously butter first strip of filo.

4. Place 1 tablespoon filling in bottom right-hand corner of first strip. Take bottom right-hand corner and fold over to form a triangle. Continue folding at right angles as you would a flag. Moisten edge with a little beaten egg to seal. Repeat with remaining filo and filling. At this point, triangles can be frozen. (To freeze, line a baking sheet with wax paper. Place triangles in a single layer on baking sheet and freeze; then store in an airtight container for up to 3 months.)

5. Arrange triangles in a single layer on 2 large ungreased baking sheets. Bake 15 to 20 minutes, until golden brown. Serve immediately, with a squeeze of lemon juice. (If baking frozen triangles, do not thaw. Allow 5 to 6 minutes additional baking time.)

15 CHERRY TOMATOES FILLED WITH CURRIED PEAS

Prep: 30 minutes   Cook: none   Makes: about 48

Garam masala is an Indian blend of spices. It is available in specialty markets and health food stores and in the spice section of some supermarkets.

48 cherry tomatoes
 1 cup frozen petite peas,
      thawed (about 5 ounces)
 2 scallions, minced
 1 cup salted roasted peanuts,
      crushed

¼ cup mayonnaise
¼ cup plain yogurt
½ teaspoon garam masala
    Grated zest of ½ lemon
 1 teaspoon lemon juice
    Parsley leaves, for garnish

1. To prepare cherry tomatoes for filling, cut off tops. With a grapefruit knife or pointed spoon, scoop out tomato pulp, leaving a ¼-inch shell. On a flat surface, invert tomatoes to drain.

2. In a medium bowl, combine peas, scallions, peanuts, mayonnaise, yogurt, garam masala, lemon zest, and lemon juice. Stir to mix well.

3. Fill each tomato with 1 to 2 heaping teaspoons of peanut mixture. Decorate each with a parsley leaf. Refrigerate until ready to serve.

16 WATERCRESS ASPARAGUS ROLL-UPS

Prep: 20 minutes   Cook: 8 to 10 seconds   Makes: 16

The slightly bitter flavor of radicchio, a red-leafed "gourmet" salad green commonly found in supermarkets, lends itself well to this simple appetizer. If radicchio isn't available, substitute tender leaves of red leaf lettuce, for instance.

 1 head of radicchio, separated
      into leaves
 8 ounces whipped cream
      cheese with herbs
 1 tablespoon chopped sun-
      dried tomatoes

 1 pound fresh asparagus tips,
      lightly cooked and
      drained
 1 bunch of watercress

1. Carefully separate 16 leaves of radicchio. In a medium saucepan filled with boiling water, blanch radicchio leaves until pliable, 8 to 10 seconds. Immediately drain, then rinse under cold running water. Drain again.

2. In a small bowl, mix cream cheese with sun-dried tomatoes.

3. With a teaspoon, place some cream cheese inside each radicchio leaf. Top with an asparagus tip. Add a sprig of watercress. Roll up to form a dainty "bouquet." Place on serving platter.

4. Proceed in similar fashion until all ingredients are used. Refrigerate until ready to serve.

17   DÉLICES AU FROMAGE

Prep: 10 minutes   Cook: 18 to 20 minutes   Serves: 4

Use the removable bottom of a springform pan for easier handling of this cheesy pastry.

1 (17¼-ounce) package frozen puff pastry dough, thawed
2 tablespoons chopped chives
1 cup diced Emmenthaler cheese

2 tablespoons imitation bacon bits
2 tablespoons chopped olives
1 egg, lightly beaten

1. Preheat oven to 350°F. On a floured surface, unfold puff pastry rectangles. Lightly roll dough flat to even thickness. Using 9-inch pan as a template, cut out 2 large rounds of dough.

2. Lightly grease removable bottom of a 9-inch springform pan. Set one circle of dough on bottom of pan. Top with chives, cheese, bacon bits, and olives, leaving a ½-inch border around edges. Brush border with beaten egg. Top with second circle of dough, pressing edges to seal. (Pie will look flat in pan.)

3. With a sharp knife, lightly score top of pie. Bake 18 to 20 minutes, until pie is puffy and brown. Serve immediately.

18   SOURDOUGH BRIE LOAF

Prep: 10 minutes   Cook: 12 to 15 minutes   Makes: 1 (1-pound) loaf

Set this amusing appetizer in the center of the table so that everyone can break off pieces of the cheese-filled loaf. The loaf also makes a good accompaniment to soups.

1 (1-pound) round loaf of unsliced sourdough bread
3 tablespoons butter, melted
3 garlic cloves, crushed in a press

8 ounces firm Brie cheese, cubed
⅛ teaspoon dried thyme leaves
⅛ teaspoon dried marjoram leaves
Dash of cayenne

1. Preheat oven to 350°F. With a sharp knife, cut a lid off top of loaf. Carefully remove insides, leaving 1-inch crust.

2. In a small bowl, mix butter with garlic. Brush garlic butter inside loaf. Add cubed Brie. Sprinkle with thyme, marjoram, and cayenne. Top with reserved lid.

3. Set filled loaf on a baking sheet and bake until cheese is melted and loaf is crusty, 12 to 15 minutes. Serve hot.

19   ROQUEFORT STRUDEL

Prep: 25 minutes   Cook: 20 to 25 minutes   Serves: 6 to 8

A savory strudel, hot out of the oven, is always a hit. You can prepare this one up to a day ahead and bake it just before serving. Always keep the filo dough covered with a damp towel so it doesn't turn brittle upon contact with the air. This will yield two medium strudels

8 sheets frozen filo dough (½ of a 16-ounce package), thawed	2 eggs, lightly beaten
¾ cup mashed potatoes	1 teaspoon curry powder
¾ cup milk	¼ teaspoon salt
¾ cup ricotta	1 stick (4 ounces) butter, melted
6 ounces Roquefort cheese, crumbled	½ cup bread crumbs

1. Preheat oven to 375°F. Lay filo sheets on a flat surface and cover with a damp towel or plastic wrap.

2. In a large bowl, combine mashed potatoes, milk, ricotta, Roquefort, eggs, curry powder, and salt. Beat until well blended.

3. With a small brush, paint 1 sheet of filo with melted butter. Set a second sheet on top and paint with butter. Repeat with 2 more sheets. Sprinkle ¼ cup bread crumbs over top sheet of filo. With narrow end of filo facing you, spread half of potato mixture close to bottom edge, leaving 2 inches clear on the sides. Fold sides over and roll up strudel away from you, jelly-roll style, buttering generously as you roll. Carefully transfer strudel to a nonstick baking sheet. Proceed in similar fashion for second strudel.

4. Bake 20 to 25 minutes, until strudel is crisp and golden. Serve hot.

20   CABBAGE STRUDEL

Prep: 25 minutes   Cook: 42 to 58 minutes   Serves: 6 to 8

This recipe yields two medium strudels.

2 tablespoons vegetable oil	¾ cup shelled pecans
1 medium onion, thinly sliced	½ (16-ounce) package frozen filo dough, thawed (8 sheets)
1 small head of cabbage, shredded	1 stick (4 ounces) butter, melted
½ teaspoon caraway seeds	
½ teaspoon salt	
¼ teaspoon pepper	

1. In a large frying pan or flameproof casserole, heat oil. Add onion and cook over medium heat, stirring occasionally, until soft, 2 to 3 minutes. Add cabbage, caraway seeds, salt, and pepper. Cover tightly and cook over medium-low heat, stirring occasionally, until cabbage turns a golden caramel color, 20 to 30 minutes. Remove from heat and let cool 10 minutes.

2. Preheat oven to 375°F. In a blender or food processor, coarsely chop pecans; set aside. Lay filo sheets on a flat surface and cover with a damp towel or plastic wrap.

3. With a small brush, paint 4 sheets of filo with butter and place them one atop the other. Sprinkle final sheet with ¼ cup ground pecans. With narrow end of filo facing you, spread half cabbage mixture close to bottom edge, leaving 2 inches clear on sides. Fold sides over and roll up strudel away from you, jelly-roll style, buttering generously as you roll. Carefully transfer strudel to a nonstick baking sheet. Proceed in similar fashion for second strudel.

4. Bake 20 to 25 minutes, until strudel is crisp and golden. Serve hot.

---

21   CHEESE AND ARTICHOKE PUFFS

Prep: 30 minutes   Cook: 2 to 3 minutes per batch
Makes: 30 to 32

4 tablespoons butter
1 teaspoon dried tarragon
   leaves
1 cup flour
4 eggs
1 cup grated fontina cheese
½ teaspoon salt
⅛ teaspoon cayenne

1 tablespoon sweet hot
   mustard
¼ cup canned artichoke hearts,
   drained and finely
   chopped
   Vegetable oil, for frying
½ cup grated Parmesan cheese

1. In a heavy medium saucepan, bring 1 cup water, butter, and tarragon to a boil. Remove from heat and add flour in a stream, stirring with a wooden spoon to blend thoroughly.

2. Add eggs, one at a time, stirring to incorporate each one thoroughly, until batter forms a sticky mass. Mix in cheese, salt, cayenne, mustard, and artichoke hearts. (Batter can be prepared a day ahead up to this point. Cover and refrigerate; let return to room temperature before proceeding.)

3. In a deep medium frying pan or saucepan, pour vegetable oil to depth of 1 inch. Heat over medium-low heat until a bit of batter dropped into oil floats to surface.

4. Preheat oven to 200°F. Line a baking sheet with a double layer of paper towels. Drop batter into hot oil, 2 teaspoonfuls at a time, taking care to keep puffs as round as possible. This can be accomplished by scraping batter off a teaspoon with a spatula. Fry puffs in batches without crowding until golden brown all over, 2 to 3 minutes.

5. With a slotted spoon, transfer puffs to towel-lined sheet to drain. Keep warm in oven while frying remaining puffs. When all are cooked, roll puffs in grated Parmesan cheese. Serve warm.

22   NIÇOISE PIZZA

Prep: 20 minutes   Cook: 41 to 50 minutes   Serves: 4 to 6

Pissaladière is a thin-crust pizza specialty from Nice, in the south of France. It simply calls for a topping of cooked onions, tomatoes, and black olives. The Gruyère cheese and roasted peppers give it a more colorful appearance.

1 **red bell pepper**	1 **teaspoon sugar**
1 **green bell pepper**	1 **cup shredded Gruyère**
1 **cup flour**	**cheese**
4 **tablespoons butter**	2 **medium tomatoes, thinly**
½ **teaspoon salt**	**sliced**
2 **tablespoons olive oil**	2 **teaspoons dried thyme**
2 **medium onions, very thinly**	**leaves**
sliced	12 **kalamata olives**

1. Preheat broiler. Line a small baking sheet with aluminum foil. Place peppers on baking sheet and broil as close to heat as possible, turning with tongs, until skin blisters, all over, 8 to 10 minutes. Transfer peppers to a paper or plastic bag, seal, and set aside to cool for about 10 minutes. Reduce oven temperature to 375°F. Peel and seed peppers and cut into ½-inch-wide strips.

2. In a food processor, combine flour, butter, salt, and 3 tablespoons water. Pulse on and off 10 times, or until mixture resembles coarse crumbs. Add 1 more tablespoon water if necessary. Transfer dough to a bowl and shape into a ball. Cover and refrigerate 10 minutes.

3. Meanwhile, in a large frying pan, heat olive oil. Add onions, sprinkle with sugar, and cook over medium heat, stirring occasionally until soft and golden brown, 8 to 10 minutes. Remove from heat.

4. Roll out dough to a round about ⅛ inch thick. Carefully transfer dough to a 9-inch pie plate, lining bottom and sides. Trim dough to size. With tines of fork, prick crust a dozen times.

5. To assemble, spread onions over bottom of pie crust. Sprinkle shredded cheese over onions. Top with tomatoes and season with thyme. Arrange pepper strips in a lattice pattern over top and decorate with olives.

6. Bake 25 to 30 minutes, until crust is golden. Serve warm, cut into wedges.

23   CHILEAN EMPANADAS

Prep: 30 minutes   Chill: 30 minutes
Cook: 34 to 45 minutes   Makes: 18 to 20

Empanadas are savory little turnovers, which are a popular Latin American snack food. The following potato-filled empanadas could just as easily serve as picnic fare. In this recipe, I use frozen hash brown potatoes for convenience.

2 tablespoons vegetable oil
1 medium green bell pepper, diced
1 small onion, diced
1 medium carrot, shredded
1½ cups frozen hash brown potatoes, thawed
⅓ cup pitted green olives, diced

1 tablespoon ground cumin
½ teaspoon salt
¼ teaspoon pepper
3 cups sifted flour
6 tablespoons butter
2 eggs

1. In a large frying pan, heat oil over medium heat. Add green pepper and cook, stirring occasionally, until soft, 4 to 5 minutes. Add onion, carrot, and potatoes. Reduce heat to medium-low. Cover and cook until potatoes are tender, 10 to 15 minutes. Stir in olives, cumin, salt, and pepper. Set potato filling aside to cool.

2. Meanwhile, place flour and butter in a food processor. Pulse until mixture resembles coarse crumbs. Or in a large bowl, using 2 knives scissor fashion, cut butter into flour. Add ¾ cup cold water, a little at a time, mixing until dough is evenly moistened. Add 1 egg and incorporate until well mixed.

3. Transfer dough to a lightly floured work surface. With your hands, knead dough 2 to 3 minutes, until fairly smooth. Do not overknead, or dough will become tough. Shape into a ball. Transfer to a lightly oiled bowl, turn to coat, cover with plastic wrap, and refrigerate 30 minutes.

4. Preheat oven to 375°F. Separate chilled dough into 4 equal parts. On a lightly floured surface, roll out 1 piece of dough to ⅛ inch thick. Using a 5-inch bowl or saucer as template, cut out circles of dough. Gather up dough scraps. Repeat procedure with remaining dough and scraps.

5. In a small bowl, beat remaining egg with 1 tablespoon water. Fill each circle with 1 tablespoon potato filling. Brush edges of pastry with some beaten egg. Fold over dough to enclose filling. With tines of fork, press edges to seal empanada. Prick top with tines of fork in 2 or 3 places. Transfer empanadas to 1 or 2 greased baking sheets. Brush tops with beaten egg.

6. Bake 20 to 25 minutes, until empanadas are golden brown. Serve hot or warm.

24   BEAN BOQUITAS
Prep: 10 minutes   Cook: 2 to 4 minutes per batch   Makes: 24

Boquitas means "little mouthfuls" in Spanish. These crisp, fan-shaped little treats are a great way to use up leftover beans. Serve them with salsa or with your favorite guacamole.

1 **(15-ounce) can refried beans**
    with onions
1 **dozen (6-inch) flour tortillas**
1 **cup grated Cheddar cheese**
    (about 4 ounces)

Vegetable oil, for frying
2 **cups salsa (page 260) or your**
    favorite bottled brand

1. In a medium bowl, mash refried beans with a fork to loosen them. Cut tortillas in half. Fill each half with 1 heaping teaspoon refried beans. Sprinkle with 1 teaspoon grated cheese. Fold tortilla over to form a fan shape.

2. In a large frying pan, heat 1 inch vegetable oil until thermometer registers 350°F.

3. Fry boquitas in batches without crowding, squeezing edges closed with tongs when you turn them, until golden brown, 1 to 2 minutes on each side. With slotted spoon, transfer boquitas to paper towels to drain. Serve hot, with salsa on the side.

25   FLAUTAS WITH MOLE VERDE
Prep: 20 minutes   Cook: 2 to 3 minutes per batch   Serves: 4 to 6

For these slender *flautas* (the Spanish word for flute) you can use corn or flour tortillas. However, corn tortillas have more crunch.

1 **(15-ounce) can black beans**
2 **garlic cloves, minced**
¼ **teaspoon ground cumin**
1 **small onion, diced**
1 **(5-ounce) can whole-kernel**
    corn, drained

12 **(6-inch) corn tortillas**
    Vegetable oil, for frying
1 **cup prepared green**
    enchilada sauce, heated

1. In a medium bowl, mash beans and their liquid with garlic, cumin, and onion to form a chunky puree. Stir in drained corn kernels.

2. Spoon about ¼ cup bean mixture on lower edge of each tortilla and roll up like a fat cigar.

3. Preheat oven to 200°F. Line a baking sheet with a double layer of paper towels. In a large frying pan, heat vegetable oil over medium heat to depth of 1 inch. Fry flautas in batches without crowding, seam side down, turning them carefully with tongs, until crisp, 2 to 3 minutes. Transfer to prepared baking sheet to drain. Keep warm in oven while cooking remaining flautas.

4. Serve hot, with warm enchilada sauce for dipping.

26   NUTTY BAKED BRIE IN FILO

Prep: 15 minutes   Cook: 25 to 30 minutes   Serves: 4 to 6

This appetizer looks much more difficult to assemble than it really is. Simply remember to keep the filo covered if you let it sit at room temperature more than 10 minutes. If not, the dough will turn brittle in contact with the air.

6 **sheets filo dough, thawed**
1 **stick (4 ounces) butter,**
   melted

½ **cup shelled pistachio nuts,**
   crushed
8 **ounces firm Brie cheese with**
   herbs, thinly sliced

1. Preheat oven to 375°F. Set filo sheets on a flat surface covered with a damp towel or plastic wrap. Cut each sheet in half vertically. Cover with a second damp towel or plastic wrap.

2. With a pastry brush, generously butter a 9-inch tart pan with a removable bottom. Butter first layer of filo and set in pan; ends will extend over edge of pan. Butter second piece of filo and set in pan perpendicular to first sheet. Continue in similar fashion with remaining filo sheets.

3. Sprinkle crushed pistachios over filo and arrange Brie slices to cover dough in pan. Fold sides of filo over to enclose cheese. Cover with 6 additional layers of buttered filo pieces. Carefully fold all sheets under filo pie as you would a bedsheet. Generously butter outside layer. Set pie on a baking sheet.

4. Bake 25 to 30 minutes, until golden brown. Let stand 10 minutes. Cut into wedges to serve.

27   STUFFED PITA WEDGES

Prep: 15 minutes   Cook: none   Makes: 24 to 36

2 **(7-ounce) jars diced red**
   pimientos
1 **medium Bermuda onion,**
   finely chopped
2 **tablespoons minced parsley**
2 **tablespoons chopped black**
   olives

Juice of ½ lemon
½ **teaspoon pepper**
1 **(10-ounce) container cream**
   cheese with herbs, at
   room temperature
6 **(6-inch) pita pockets**
4 **ounces alfalfa sprouts**

1. In a blender or food processor, puree pimientos with their liquid. Place mixture in a medium bowl and add onion, parsley, olives, lemon juice, and pepper. Fold in cream cheese and blend well.

2. Carefully slice pita open just enough to be able to spread mixture on lower half. Top with sprouts. Close pita by pressing both halves together gently. Refrigerate until ready to serve.

3. To serve, cut each pita into 4 to 6 wedges.

28   TIPSY FONDUE

Prep: 20 minutes   Cook: 18 to 22 minutes   Serves: 4 to 6

A fondue calls for a roaring fire, good wine, and hours of conversation with friends. You will need a fondue dish and long fondue forks to further set the atmosphere. Choose a good-quality dry white wine as your base.

1 **garlic clove**	1 **tablespoon cornstarch**
1 **cup cauliflower florets**	2 **teaspoons paprika**
1 **cup broccoli florets**	½ **cup heavy cream**
2 **cups dry white wine**	1 **cup small button**
1½ **cups shredded**	**mushrooms, stems**
Jarlsberg cheese	**removed**
2 **cups shredded Gruyère**	4 **cups 2-inch cubes crusty**
cheese	**French bread**

1. Rub inside of fondue dish with cut garlic clove. Discard garlic.

2. In a medium saucepan filled with lightly salted boiling water, boil cauliflower and broccoli florets for 3 minutes; drain. Rinse under cold water and drain well.

3. In a medium nonreactive saucepan, bring wine to a simmer over medium heat, but do not boil. Gradually add shredded cheeses one third at a time, stirring constantly over low heat until cheeses melt, 10 to 12 minutes.

4. In a small bowl, whisk cornstarch and paprika with cream. Stir into hot cheese mixture and continue cooking until fondue thickens slightly, 5 to 7 minutes.

5. Transfer cheese to fondue dish set atop warming tray or burner with low flame. Serve with prepared vegetables and bread cubes on the side. Use fondue forks, long toothpicks, or skewers to dip into cheese fondue.

29 POTATO TAQUITOS WITH TOMATILLO SAUCE

Prep: 20 minutes   Cook: 27 to 36 minutes   Makes: 24

Taquitos are tightly wound little cigars made of corn tortillas and then fried. They can become addictive, especially when they are served hot from the pan. Instead of making your own sauce, you can use the prepared tomatillo sauce available in the Mexican section of supermarkets.

¼ cup olive oil	8 fresh tomatillos, husks removed, quartered
1 large onion, finely diced	
1 small green bell pepper, finely diced	⅔ cup vegetable or reduced-sodium chicken broth
1 large potato, peeled and cut into 1-inch chunks	1 (4-ounce) can diced green chiles
2 garlic cloves, minced	¼ cup chopped cilantro
1 teaspoon oregano	2 drops of Tabasco
1 teaspoon chili powder	24 (6-inch) corn tortillas
1½ teaspoons salt	Vegetable oil, for frying
4 scallions, chopped	

1. Preheat oven to 200°F. In a large frying pan, heat 2 tablespoons oil. Add onion and green pepper and cook over medium-high heat until onion is golden, 4 to 5 minutes. Add potato, garlic, oregano, and chili powder. Cover and cook, stirring occasionally, until potato is tender, 15 to 20 minutes. Add 1 teaspoon salt. Set aside to cool 10 minutes. Mash with a fork.

2. Meanwhile, in a medium nonreactive saucepan, heat remaining olive oil. Add scallions and cook over medium-high heat until soft, 2 to 3 minutes. Add tomatillos and ⅓ cup broth. Cover and cook over medium heat until tomatillos are soft, 4 to 6 minutes. Remove from heat and let cool in broth 5 minutes.

3. In a blender or food processor, puree scallions and tomatillos with their broth until fairly smooth. Add remaining broth, 2 tablespoons diced chiles, cilantro, remaining ½ teaspoon salt, and Tabasco. Return to pan.

4. Fill each tortilla with 1 to 2 tablespoons of potato mixture and roll up into a cigar shape. Line a baking sheet with a double layer of paper towels.

5. In a large frying pan, pour oil to a depth of 2 inches and heat until a piece of tortilla dropped in oil sizzles. Fry taquitos in batches without crowding, turning occasionally with tongs, until crisp and golden, 2 minutes. Transfer to baking sheet and keep warm in the oven. Reheat tomatillo sauce and serve taquitos hot with warm tomatillo sauce for dipping.

30   EGG ROLLS WITH PEANUT SAUCE
Prep: 30 minutes   Cook: 8 to 11 minutes per batch   Makes: 24

3 dried Chinese mushrooms
2 tablespoons vegetable oil
1 small onion, finely diced
4 garlic cloves, minced
2 celery ribs, finely diced
½ cup water chestnuts, finely diced
½ cup bamboo shoots, finely diced
1 medium carrot, shredded
1 cup finely shredded Chinese cabbage
1 cup bean sprouts, coarsely chopped

2 tablespoons soy sauce or tamari
¼ cup plus 2 tablespoons peanut butter
1 tablespoon oyster sauce (see Note)
24 egg roll skins
Vegetable oil, for deep-frying
½ cup vegetable or reduced-sodium chicken broth
2 teaspoons honey
1 teaspoon lime juice

1. Preheat oven to 200°F. In a small bowl, soak Chinese mushrooms in 1 cup hot water for 10 minutes, or until soft, then drain. Cut off woody stems and discard. Cut mushroom caps into thin slivers.

2. In a wok or a large skillet, heat 2 tablespoons vegetable oil over high heat. Add onion, 3 minced garlic cloves, celery, water chestnuts, bamboo shoots, and carrot. Stir-fry 2 minutes. Add Chinese cabbage, a handful at a time, and stir-fry until cabbage wilts, 3 to 4 minutes. Add sliced mushroom caps and bean sprouts. Stir in 1 tablespoon soy sauce, 2 tablespoons peanut butter, and oyster sauce. Remove from heat. Set mixture in a colander to drain and cool to room temperature.

3. Place 1 egg roll skin on a flat surface, with points at 12, 3, 6, and 9 o'clock. Place 1 heaping tablespoon cooled filling in center of egg roll skin. Fold in points at 3 and 9 o'clock and roll up skin to form a cigar-shaped roll. Moisten top point with a little water to adhere. Repeat procedure with remaining egg roll skins until all filling is used.

4. Line a baking sheet with paper towels. In a wok or a large skillet, heat vegetable oil to a depth of 1 inch until a thermometer registers 350°F. Deep-fry rolls in batches, turning once with tongs, until golden brown on all sides, 2 to 3 minutes. With tongs, transfer egg rolls to prepared baking sheet. Keep warm in oven.

5. In a small saucepan, bring broth to a simmer. Whisk in remaining ¼ cup peanut butter, honey, lime juice, and remaining soy sauce and garlic. Cook, stirring, until hot, 1 to 2 minutes. Serve warm as a dip for egg rolls.

NOTE: *Oyster sauce is available in Chinese markets and in the Asian foods section of many supermarkets.*

31 CRISP FETA CHEESE AND DRIED CRANBERRY WON TONS WITH JALAPEÑO PEPPER JELLY

Prep: 20 minutes   Cook: 2 to 3 minutes per batch   Makes: 24

These crisp little mouthfuls must be served when they are hot. Any uncooked won tons can be frozen for later use. You can substitute any other tangy jelly for the pepper jelly.

4 ounces feta cheese
2 tablespoons dried
    cranberries
2 scallions, chopped
½ teaspoon minced fresh
    ginger

Flour, for dusting
24 (2½-inch) square won ton
    wrappers
1 egg white, lightly beaten
    Vegetable oil, for frying
½ cup hot pepper jelly

1. Preheat oven to 200°F. In a small bowl, mix together feta cheese, dried cranberries, scallions, and ginger. Set filling aside.

2. Dust a baking sheet with flour. With fingertips, brush edges of won ton wrappers with egg white. Place 1 heaping teaspoon filling in center of each wrapper. Fold over to form triangular shape. Press edges to seal while pushing filling toward center of won ton. Transfer filled won tons onto floured baking sheet.

3. In a wok or a large frying pan, pour oil to depth of 1 inch. Heat oil until it registers 375°F on a thermometer or until a piece of won ton wrapper starts to sizzle. Fry won tons in batches until golden brown, about 1 minute. With a slotted spoon, transfer won tons to paper towels to drain. Keep warm in oven.

4. In a small saucepan, combine jelly with 2 tablespoons water. Cook over medium heat, stirring, until melted and hot, 1 to 2 minutes. Transfer to a bowl and serve as a dip with hot won tons.

32   FILIPINO-STYLE EGG ROLLS
Prep: 30 minutes   Cook: 23 to 31 minutes   Makes: about 20

Lumpia are the Filipino version of Chinese egg rolls. Round lumpia wrappers, similar to a very thin pancake, are available in some supermarkets or Asian markets. If they are unavailable, substitute egg roll skins. Any store-bought Asian marinade will make a good dipping sauce.

2 tablespoons vegetable oil	2 cups finely shredded
1 large onion, finely diced	Chinese cabbage
2 garlic cloves, minced	1½ cups prepared honey
2 small potatoes, peeled and	teriyaki marinade
finely diced (about 1 cup)	2 cups fresh bean sprouts,
1 cup green beans, cut into	chopped
1-inch pieces	20 (8-inch) lumpia wrappers
1 large carrot, shredded	Vegetable oil, for frying

1. Preheat oven to 200°F. In a large frying pan, heat 2 tablespoons vegetable oil. Add onion and cook over medium-high heat until soft and golden, 4 to 5 minutes. Add garlic and potatoes. Cover, reduce heat to medium-low, and cook until potatoes are tender, 10 to 15 minutes.

2. Add green beans, carrot, cabbage, and ½ cup marinade. Cook, covered, 5 minutes. Add bean sprouts and remove from heat. Transfer vegetable mixture to a colander to drain. Let cool completely.

3. Meanwhile, unwrap lumpia wrappers. Place 1 heaping tablespoon cooled filling along bottom quarter of wrapper. Cover filling, fold over sides, and roll up lumpia to form a cigar about 5 inches long and ½ inch in diameter. (At this point, lumpia can be frozen in an airtight container for up to 3 months.)

4. To cook, line a baking sheet with paper towels. In a wok or deep skillet, heat 1 inch vegetable oil until thermometer registers 350°F. With tongs, carefully set each lumpia, seam side down, into hot oil. Deep-fry in batches, turning once, until golden brown, 2 to 3 minutes on each side. With a slotted spoon, transfer lumpia to baking sheet to drain. Keep warm in oven until ready to serve. Serve with remaining honey teriyaki marinade warmed as a dip.

33   CRUNCHY GYOZA POTSTICKERS

Prep: 40 minutes   Cook: 6 to 9 minutes per batch   Makes: 24

Chinese chili paste and Chinese five-spice powder are available in the Asian food section of supermarkets or in ethnic markets. Gyoza wrappers are usually available in Asian markets. If you do not have access to gyoza wrappers, use the more commonly available won ton wrappers, fold them into triangles, and trim the edges to form a semicircle.

⅓ cup sliced water chestnuts, drained
3 scallions
1 cup fresh bean sprouts, coarsely chopped
1 medium carrot, grated
4 garlic cloves, minced
¼ teaspoon Chinese chili paste
⅛ teaspoon Chinese five-spice powder
2 teaspoons Asian sesame oil
¼ cup plus 1 tablespoon soy sauce

½ teaspoon minced fresh ginger
1 tablespoon wheat germ Flour, for dusting
24 (2½- to 3-inch) round gyoza wrappers (see head note)
1 egg white, lightly beaten
3 tablespoons vegetable oil
1 tablespoon rice wine vinegar
2 teaspoons sugar
1 teaspoon lemon juice

1. Preheat oven to 200°F. With a sharp knife, coarsely chop water chestnuts and scallions. Transfer to a medium bowl. Add chopped bean sprouts, carrot, half of minced garlic, chili paste, five-spice powder, sesame oil, 1 tablespoon soy sauce, minced ginger, and wheat germ. Mix well. Set filling aside.

2. Dust a baking sheet with flour or cornstarch. Carefully unwrap 2 dozen gyoza wrappers. Reseal rest for later use. With finger, brush edges of each wrapper with egg white. Place 1 heaping teaspoon filling in center of each wrapper. Fold over to form a half moon. Press and crimp edges to seal. Transfer to a baking sheet. Proceed in similar fashion until all filling is used.

3. To cook, heat vegetable oil in a large nonstick frying pan. Add 8 to 12 potstickers and fry over medium-low heat until golden, 1 to 2 minutes on each side. Add ¼ cup water to pan. Reduce heat to low. Cover and let potstickers steam until bottom is crusty brown, 4 to 5 minutes. With a slotted spoon, transfer potstickers to paper towels to drain. Then transfer to a baking sheet and keep warm in oven while you cook remaining potstickers.

4. To serve, in a small bowl, mix ¼ cup soy sauce with vinegar, remaining minced garlic, sugar, and lemon juice. Serve potstickers warm, with dipping sauce on the side.

34 HALLOWEEN FRITTERS
Prep: 10 minutes   Cook: 4 to 6 minutes per batch   Serves: 4

I like to use pumpkin or any kind of yellow-fleshed winter squash, such as butternut and the sweet delicata or hubbard squashes. To cook squash, bake it, steam it, boil it, or cook it in the microwave. I prefer to mash it by hand rather than in a food processor for a more interesting texture.

2 **pounds pumpkin or squash, cooked and mashed**
2 **eggs, lightly beaten**
2 **scallions, chopped**
½ **cup chopped parsley**
3 **tablespoons Italian bread crumbs**

2 **tablespoons flour**
¼ **teaspoon paprika**
½ **teaspoon lemon pepper**
   Vegetable oil, for frying

1. Preheat oven to 200°F. Line a baking sheet with paper towels.

2. Place mashed squash in a medium bowl. Add eggs, scallions, parsley, bread crumbs, flour, paprika, and lemon pepper. Stir to blend.

3. In a frying pan over medium heat, heat vegetable oil to a depth of 1 inch until a drop of batter sizzles. Drop batter by heaping tablespoons into hot oil. Flatten gently with back of a spoon. Fry in batches until golden brown, turning over carefully with spatula, 2 to 3 minutes on each side.

4. With a slotted spoon, transfer to prepared baking sheet to drain. Keep warm in oven until serving time.

Chapter 2

Savory Soups and Stews

To me, an overcast day automatically calls for a steaming pot of soup or a hearty stew. There is nothing I like better when rain is predicted than to head for my refrigerator to pull out the makings for minestrone, chili, or vegetable stew. I often make double the quantity of a favored recipe and freeze the leftovers for another day.

No other element of a meal is quite so versatile as soup. It can be hearty or light, according to the inspiration of the cook. Most soups are served hot, although a bowl of chilled soup, such as Chilly Dilled Beet Borscht or a cold bowl of Herbed Vichyssoise, is a refreshingly cool alternative on a sweltering day, and so is the Quick Gazpacho Olé. Clear broths or consommés, such as the Elegant Consommé à l'Orientale, make for a light and flavorful first course. So does a cupful of sherry-spiked Roasted Eggplant Soup with Garlic Croutons.

Since I prefer to entertain informally, hearty soups are an essential part of my repertoire. Dinner may consist of steaming bowls of Albóndigas Soup, a traditional Mexican soup where I have substituted *albóndigas*, or meatballs, made of ground nuts instead of meat; or I will bring from the oven to the table pretty, ovenproof dishes bubbling with French Onion Soup au Vin and their topping of Jarlsberg Garlic Toast. My husband Owen's Sweet and Sour Cabbage Borscht, a holdover from his college days, has become standard fare at our house. When in the mood for more exotic flavors, I prepare Spicy Mulligatawny, a curry-flavored soup brimming with vegetables, or else the fragrant Green Chile and Potato Soup with Tortilla Cheese Floats from Mexico. One of my all-time favorites is the Soupe au Pistou, a specialty from the south of France where a tablespoon or two of pesto is placed in the bottom of each bowl to stir into the hot soup.

Serving a stew is also a great way to entertain, for many stews only gain in taste if they are prepared a day ahead. This leaves you free almost until serving time, since all that is needed is to reheat the evening's feast. Half the fun of making the Barbecued Argentinean Pumpkin Stew is to watch your guests' delight when presented with the whole pumpkin that serves as an edible container.

Of course, the stock used as the base for your soup or stew will greatly affect the flavor of the finished dish. A basic recipe for vegetable broth is included in the beginning of this chapter. The broth can be further seasoned according to individual tastes with additional salt, dried herbs, or soy sauce, for instance. A canned vegetarian broth now available on the market makes a good substitute if time is a factor. Powdered vegetable broth mix is also available in health food stores. For convenience, canned chicken broth is offered as an alternative in every recipe.

35 BASIC VEGETABLE BROTH

Prep: 15 minutes   Cook: 2¼ to 2¾ hours   Makes: about 2 quarts

Roasting the vegetables before adding them to the soup pot yields a more flavorful broth. Omit the beet if you prefer a clearer liquid. Save all your leafy greens to add to your broth.

2 **medium onions, unpeeled and halved**	½ **cup olive oil**
3 **medium carrots, cut into chunks**	1 **whole head of garlic, papery husk removed**
3 **small turnips, halved**	1 **bunch of parsley, cleaned and tied with string**
4 **celery ribs, with leaves, chopped**	8 **whole cloves**
1 **parsnip, cut into chunks**	12 **peppercorns**
1 **beet, scrubbed and quartered**	2 **bay leaves**
2 **tart apples, cored and quartered**	3 **tablespoons soy sauce or tamari**

1. Preheat oven to 400°F. In a large bowl, toss onions, carrots, turnips, celery, parsnip, beet, and apples with olive oil. Drizzle a little oil over unpeeled head of garlic. Place vegetables in a single layer on a baking sheet lined with aluminum foil. Roast, turning occasionally with tongs, for 35 to 40 minutes.

2. When vegetables are roasted, in a large soup pot, bring 10 cups water to a boil over high heat. Add roasted vegetables, parsley, cloves, peppercorns, and bay leaves. Cook, uncovered, 10 minutes. Reduce heat to medium. Partially cover and simmer until broth reduces by one third, 1½ to 2 hours.

3. Strain broth through a fine-mesh strainer into a large bowl, pressing down on cooked vegetables to extrude all liquid. Discard vegetables and spices. Season with tamari. Refrigerate or freeze broth until ready to use.

36 CHILLY DILLED BEET BORSCHT
Prep: 10 minutes   Cook: 10 minutes   Chill: 2 hours   Serves: 4

2 (14½-ounce) cans vegetable
 or reduced-sodium
 chicken broth
1 cup dry red wine
1 (16-ounce) can whole baby
 beets

½ teaspoon pepper
1 tablespoon chopped fresh
 dill or 1½ teaspoons dried
½ cup plain yogurt

1. In a medium saucepan, combine broth and wine. Bring to a boil. Reduce heat to low and simmer 10 minutes. Remove from heat and let cool.

2. In a blender or food processor, puree beets and their liquid with broth in batches if necessary until smooth. Transfer to a serving bowl and season with pepper and dill. Cover and refrigerate until well chilled, 2 hours or overnight.

3. Serve with yogurt on the side.

37 SWEET AND SOUR CABBAGE BORSCHT
Prep: 20 minutes   Cook: 45 to 60 minutes   Serves: 6 to 8

This borscht contributed to my husband Owen's reputation as a good cook during his college days. It has since turned into a family favorite.

5 medium onions, chopped
1 small head of cabbage,
 shredded
1 (28-ounce) can crushed
 tomatoes
1 (16-ounce) can tomato sauce
6 cups vegetable or reduced-
 sodium chicken broth
1 cup ketchup

¼ cup lemon juice
2 tablespoons Worcestershire
 sauce
¾ cup firmly packed brown
 sugar
1 teaspoon salt
½ teaspoon pepper
Sour cream and wedges
 of lemon

1. In a large soup pot, combine onions, cabbage, tomatoes, tomato sauce, and broth.

2. Bring to a boil over medium heat. Cover and cook until cabbage turns soft, 25 to 30 minutes.

3. Add ketchup, lemon juice, Worcestershire, and brown sugar. Reduce heat to medium-low, cover, and simmer 20 to 30 minutes to blend flavors. Add salt and pepper.

4. Serve hot, with a bowl of sour cream and wedges of lemon on the side.

38   WISCONSIN-STYLE CHEESE SOUP
Prep: 15 minutes   Cook: 17 to 25 minutes   Serves: 4

2 tablespoons vegetable oil
1 small onion, chopped
1 celery rib, chopped
1 small green bell pepper, diced
¼ cup flour
1 (14½-ounce) can vegetable broth or reduced-sodium chicken broth

1 (12-ounce) can beer
2 cups shredded sharp Cheddar cheese
1 cup finely diced smoked Gouda cheese
3 tablespoons white wine Worcestershire sauce
2 cups half-and-half
1 teaspoon paprika

1. In a large saucepan or soup pot, heat oil over medium heat. Add onion, celery, and green pepper and cook, stirring occasionally, until softened, 4 to 5 minutes.

2. Add flour and stir to blend. Whisk in broth and beer. Bring to a boil until liquid thickens, 3 to 5 minutes.

3. Add Cheddar and Gouda cheeses, Worcestershire, and half-and-half. Stir to blend. Reduce heat to low. Cover and cook, stirring occasionally, until cheeses melt, 10 to 15 minutes. Gouda may remain a little chunky.

4. Transfer soup to a serving bowl and sprinkle with paprika.

39   HERBED VICHYSSOISE
Prep: 10 minutes   Cook: 35 to 40 minutes   Serves: 4

3 medium leeks, green tops included
2 (14½-ounce) cans vegetable broth or reduced-sodium chicken broth
1 pound small red potatoes, peeled and quartered
6 medium Swiss chard leaves, coarsely chopped

½ small onion, chopped
2 tablespoons white wine Worcestershire sauce
2 teaspoons dried tarragon
1 teaspoon salt
¼ teaspoon white pepper
1 cup heavy cream
¼ cup chopped chives

1. Carefully wash leeks under running water, removing all grit from between leaves. Coarsely chop leeks and rinse again; drain in a colander.

2. In a large saucepan, bring broth to a boil. Add leeks, potatoes, chard, and onion. Cover and return to a boil. Reduce heat to medium-low and cook until potatoes are tender, 25 to 30 minutes. Remove from heat. Let cool 10 minutes.

3. In a blender or food processor, puree soup until smooth. Return to saucepan. Add Worcestershire, tarragon, salt, and white pepper. Cover and simmer 5 minutes. Add cream and heat through, stirring occasionally, 5 minutes longer.

4. At this point, if cold soup is desired, mixture can be refrigerated until serving time. If soup needs to be thinned, add more cream or broth. To serve, ladle soup into bowls and sprinkle with chives.

---

40 ALBÓNDIGAS SOUP

Prep: 20 minutes   Cook: 35 to 45 minutes   Serves: 4 to 6

Sopa de albóndigas, or meatball soup, is a traditional Mexican specialty where the meatballs are poached in a light, chili-scented broth. Here, nutty "no-meat" balls take the place of the classic albóndigas.

2 tablespoons olive oil	6 sprigs of parsley
3 celery ribs, chopped	2 eggs
1 carrot, peeled and sliced	1 cup walnut pieces
1 turnip, peeled and diced	1 cup plain dried bread
1 medium onion, diced	crumbs
1 (14½-ounce) can Mexican-	1 tablespoon butter, melted
style stewed tomatoes	2 teaspoons ground cumin
1 (1¼-ounce) envelope taco	1 teaspoon chili powder
seasoning mix	½ teaspoon salt
3 (14½-ounce) cans vegetable	2 limes, quartered
broth or reduced-sodium	
chicken broth	

1. In a large soup pot, heat olive oil over medium heat. Add celery, carrot, turnip, and half of onion. Cook, stirring occasionally, until carrot is lightly browned, 8 to 10 minutes. Add stewed tomatoes with their liquid. Cover and cook, stirring occasionally, until blended, 4 to 5 minutes.

2. Stir seasoning mix and broth into pot. Cover and cook over low heat until vegetables are tender, 15 to 20 minutes.

3. Meanwhile, prepare walnut balls. In a blender or food processor, place remaining onion, parsley, eggs, and walnut pieces. Process until smooth. Transfer to a medium bowl and stir in bread crumbs and melted butter. Season with cumin, chili powder, and salt.

4. To make albóndigas, with your hands, fashion balls about ¾ inch in diameter. With a large spoon, drop albóndigas gently into simmering soup. Cook until balls float to surface, 8 to 10 minutes. Serve soup immediately, with wedges of lime on the side.

41 ROASTED EGGPLANT SOUP WITH GARLIC CROUTONS

Prep: 10 minutes   Cook: 1¼ to 1½ hours   Serves: 4 to 6

2 medium eggplants
4 garlic cloves
2 tablespoons vegetable oil
1 small potato, peeled and cut
   into ½-inch dice
1 small onion, diced
4 tablespoons butter
2 cups bread cubes
2 (14½-ounce) cans vegetable
   or reduced-sodium
   chicken broth

½ cup dry sherry
2 tablespoons chopped fresh
   basil or parsley
½ teaspoon grated nutmeg
½ teaspoon salt
½ teaspoon pepper
1 cup light cream

1. Preheat oven to 350°F. Place whole eggplants on a baking sheet, poking holes in flesh with tines of fork. Bake until tender, 50 minutes to 1 hour. With a sharp knife slit eggplants open. Let cool 10 minutes. With a spoon, scoop out eggplant into a medium bowl; discard skins.

2. Meanwhile, mince 2 garlic cloves. In a medium frying pan, heat vegetable oil over medium heat. Add potato, onion, and minced garlic and cook until potato is tender, 15 to 20 minutes.

3. Slice remaining 2 garlic cloves. In a large frying pan, melt butter over medium heat. Add garlic and cook until soft and fragrant, about 1 minute. With a slotted spoon, discard garlic. In same pan, toast bread cubes, stirring until golden, 2 to 3 minutes. Set croutons aside.

4. In a blender or food processor, puree eggplant, potato mixture, and broth, in batches if necessary, until smooth. Transfer to a large saucepan.

5. Bring soup to a simmer over medium-low heat. Add sherry, basil, nutmeg, salt, and pepper. Simmer 5 minutes. Add cream and heat through, stirring, about 3 minutes.

6. Ladle into individual bowls, adding a little extra sherry to each if desired. Top with croutons.

42 ELEGANT CONSOMMÉ À L'ORIENTALE
Prep: 10 minutes   Cook: 16 to 20 minutes   Serves: 4

6 large dried Chinese mushrooms	2 teaspoons minced fresh ginger
6 cups vegetable or reduced-sodium chicken broth	⅓ cup unsweetened pineapple juice
½ cup white rice	½ cup dry sherry
2 tablespoons soy sauce or tamari	4 sprigs of cilantro or parsley

1. Rinse mushrooms in cold water. Drain.

2. In a large saucepan, bring broth to a boil over medium-high heat. Add rice and dried mushrooms and reduce heat to medium. Cover and cook until mushrooms turn soft, 8 to 10 minutes. With a slotted spoon, transfer mushrooms to a cutting board. Cut off tough stems and discard. Slice mushroom caps into thin slivers. Return sliced mushrooms to broth and reduce heat to a simmer.

3. Add soy sauce, ginger, pineapple juice, and sherry to simmering broth. Cook, covered, stirring occasionally, until rice is tender, 8 to 10 minutes.

4. Ladle soup into bowls and top with a few cilantro leaves. Serve with additional soy sauce on the side.

43 QUICK GAZPACHO OLÉ
Prep: 20 minutes   Cook: none   Chill: 1 hour   Serves: 4

This low-calorie gazpacho, lightly spiked with dry vermouth, is perfect for a summer evening. Serve it in pretty bowls with a few diced vegetables sprinkled over the top.

½ cup finely diced cucumber	1 tablespoon balsamic or rice vinegar
1 medium carrot, shredded	2 garlic cloves, minced
3 scallions, chopped	2 tablespoons chopped parsley
2 celery ribs, finely diced	½ teaspoon pepper
4 cups tomato or vegetable juice	
½ cup dry vermouth	
2 tablespoons Worcestershire sauce	

1. Reserve 1 teaspoon of each vegetable. In a large serving bowl, mix remaining cucumber, carrot, scallions, and celery with tomato juice, vermouth, Worcestershire, vinegar, garlic, chopped parsley, and pepper. Cover and refrigerate at least 1 hour, until chilled.

2. To serve, ladle soup into individual serving bowls and sprinkle with reserved vegetables.

44   POTAGE OF GREEN BEANS AMANDINE
Prep: 10 minutes   Cook: 25 minutes   Serves: 4

Canned green beans lend this soup a smoother consistency than fresh or frozen vegetables. A cupful of ground almonds gives it a rich, slightly crunchy texture.

2 tablespoons vegetable oil	1 cup whole almonds, ground
3 scallions, coarsely chopped	to a powder
2 (14½-ounce) cans vegetable	½ teaspoon salt
broth or reduced-sodium	½ teaspoon pepper
chicken broth	¼ teaspoon grated nutmeg
1 teaspoon dried marjoram	1 cup half-and-half
1 teaspoon dried tarragon	
1 (15-ounce) can French-cut	
green beans, drained and	
rinsed under running	
water	

1. In a large saucepan, heat oil over medium heat. Add scallions and cook, stirring occasionally, until golden, 3 to 4 minutes. Add broth, marjoram, and tarragon. Bring to a boil, then reduce heat to medium-low. Cover and cook, stirring occasionally, 10 minutes. Remove broth from heat and let cool 10 minutes.

2. In a blender or food processor, in batches if necessary, puree green beans and broth until smooth. (Cover blender lid with a clean cloth to prevent liquid from escaping.) Return puree to saucepan. Stir in ground almonds, salt, pepper, nutmeg, and half-and-half.

3. Simmer over low heat, stirring occasionally, 10 minutes. Serve hot.

45   MINTY NOODLE SOUP
Prep: 10 minutes   Cook: 32 to 39 minutes   Serves: 6

This soup gets its flavor from a generous pinch of freshly chopped mint placed in the bottom of each bowl before ladling in the hot broth.

4 (14½-ounce) cans vegetable	2 turnips, peeled and
broth or reduced-sodium	quartered
chicken broth	1 bay leaf
1 medium onion, quartered	½ teaspoon pepper
2 celery ribs, chopped	4 ounces wide egg noodles
1 large carrot, peeled and	1 tablespoon finely chopped
sliced	fresh mint leaves

1. In a large soup pot, combine broth, onion, celery, carrot, turnips, and bay leaf. Bring to a boil, cover, reduce heat to medium-low, simmer until vegetables are tender, 25 to 30 minutes. Season with pepper. With a slotted spoon, remove and discard onion and bay leaf.

2. Meanwhile, in a large saucepan filled with lightly salted water, cook egg noodles until tender, 5 to 6 minutes. Drain and rinse under cold water; drain again. Add noodles to simmering broth and heat through, 2 to 3 minutes.

3. To serve, place ½ teaspoon chopped mint in each of 6 bowls. Ladle in broth with vegetables and noodles and serve.

---

46 SPICY MULLIGATAWNY
Prep: 10 minutes   Cook: 27 to 33 minutes   Serves: 4 to 6

Coconut milk lends a rich texture to this Indian-inspired curry-flavored soup. Canned coconut milk, not to be confused with coconut cream, is available in many major supermarkets.

1 small leek (white and tender green), chopped	2 teaspoons minced fresh ginger
2 tablespoons vegetable oil	½ cup white rice
1 medium onion, chopped	1 (13½-ounce) can unsweetened coconut milk
2 tablespoons tomato paste	
2 garlic cloves, minced	
1 teaspoon curry powder	Grated zest of 1 lime
½ teaspoon turmeric	1 cup frozen mixed vegetables
6 cups vegetable broth or reduced-sodium chicken broth	1 teaspoon salt
	1 teaspoon pepper
	1 cup coarsely chopped spinach leaves, rinsed
2 teaspoons dried thyme leaves	1 cup plain yogurt

1. Swish chopped leek in a bowl of cold water to remove all grit. Lift out with your hands or a slotted spoon and drain in a colander.

2. In a large soup pot, heat oil over medium heat. Add leek and onion and cook until softened, 2 to 3 minutes. Add tomato paste, garlic, curry, and turmeric and stir to blend. Add broth, thyme, ginger, and rice. Cover and cook for 10 minutes.

3. Add coconut milk, lime zest, and frozen vegetables and bring to a boil. Reduce heat to medium-low. Cook until rice is tender, 12 to 15 minutes.

4. Add salt, pepper, and spinach leaves. Stir well. Cook until spinach wilts, 3 to 5 minutes. Serve hot with a swirl of yogurt in each soup bowl.

47 BOLIVIAN CORN CHOWDER
Prep: 10 minutes   Cook: 28 minutes   Serves: 6

Corn is one of the staples of Bolivian cuisine, and as can be imagined, Bolivians serve up corn, or *choclo*, in hundreds of different ways. This hearty chowder is made all the more unusual with a touch of chipotle in adobo sauce, a smoky-flavored hot Mexican pepper sauce. You can find it in the Mexican food section of many supermarkets.

2 tablespoons olive oil	1 (4-ounce) can diced green
1 medium onion, finely diced	chiles
2 medium potatoes, peeled	½ teaspoon chipotle in adobo
and shredded	sauce
1 (17-ounce) can whole-kernel	4 garlic cloves, minced
corn	½ teaspoon dried oregano
1 (17-ounce) can cream-style	½ teaspoon ground cumin
corn	1 cup half-and-half
1 (14½-ounce) can vegetable	½ teaspoon salt
broth or reduced-sodium	2 limes
chicken broth	

1. In a large saucepan or soup pot, heat olive oil over medium heat. Add onion and cook, stirring occasionally, until softened, about 3 minutes.

2. Add shredded potatoes, whole-kernel corn, cream-style corn, and broth. Reduce heat to medium-low. Cover and cook 15 minutes.

3. Add diced green chiles with any liquid from the can, chipotle sauce, garlic, oregano, and cumin. Continue cooking, covered, 10 minutes.

4. Shortly before serving time, add half-and-half and salt and heat through. With a sharp knife, cut half a lime in very thin slices and float on top of soup. Cut remaining limes into quarters and serve on the side.

48   VIETNAMESE NOODLE SOUP
Prep: 30 minutes   Cook: 21 minutes   Serves: 4

I once found myself early one morning in a Vietnamese restaurant in Los Angeles' Little Saigon, and I did as the locals did: enjoyed a steaming bowl of noodle soup for breakfast. This will warm you up at any time of the day, however. Rice noodles are available in the Asian section of supermarkets or in Asian markets.

12 ounces flat rice noodles or
    rice vermicelli
½ cup soy sauce or tamari
3 tablespoons lime juice
3 garlic cloves, minced
4 thin slices of fresh ginger
    plus 2 teaspoons minced
½ teaspoon crushed hot red
    pepper
1 tablespoon sugar
8 cups vegetable or reduced-
    sodium chicken broth
4 seeds of star anise

1 cinnamon stick
4 whole cloves
½ cup diced firm tofu
2 cups fresh bean sprouts,
    rinsed and coarsely
    chopped
¼ cup coarsely chopped
    cilantro
4 scallions, chopped
½ cup coarsely chopped fresh
    mint
    Chinese hot chili paste

1. In a large bowl, soak rice noodles in hot water for 20 minutes. In a small bowl, mix soy sauce, lime juice, garlic, minced ginger, red pepper, sugar, and 2 tablespoons water. Set soy-ginger-garlic sauce aside.

2. Meanwhile, in a large saucepan, bring broth to a simmer. Add star anise, cinnamon stick, sliced ginger, and cloves. Cover and cook over low heat 20 minutes. With a slotted spoon, remove and discard all spices. Add tofu to broth.

3. In another large saucepan, bring 8 cups water to a boil. Drain soaked rice noodles and immerse in boiling water for 1 minute. Drain immediately.

4. Divide noodles among 4 large, deep soup bowls. Ladle hot broth with tofu over noodles. Top with equal amounts of chopped bean sprouts, cilantro, scallions, and mint leaves. Serve with soy-ginger-garlic sauce and hot chili paste on the side.

49   PUMPKIN-TOMATO CREAM
Prep: 10 minutes   Cook: 12 to 13 minutes   Serves: 4

This soup has a subtler flavor when made with fresh pumpkin or winter squash, but you can easily substitute the canned variety for convenience's sake.

4 large tomatoes
2 tablespoons butter
½ medium onion, chopped
2 cups tightly packed cooked fresh pumpkin or butternut squash or 1¾ cups solid-pack canned pumpkin

1 (14½-ounce) can vegetable or reduced-sodium chicken broth
¾ cup dry sherry
1 teaspoon salt
½ teaspoon pepper
2 teaspoons dried tarragon
2 cups heavy cream

1. In a large pot filled with boiling water, blanch tomatoes for 10 seconds. With a slotted spoon, transfer tomatoes to colander to cool. Peel, seed, and quarter tomatoes.

2. In a medium frying pan, melt butter over medium heat, add onion, and cook, stirring occasionally, until golden, 4 to 5 minutes.

3. In a blender or food processor, puree tomatoes, onion, pumpkin, and broth until smooth. Transfer to a large saucepan.

4. Add sherry, salt, pepper, and tarragon. Cover and simmer, stirring occasionally, 5 minutes. Add cream and heat through, about 3 minutes. Serve hot.

50   PUMPKIN AND CARROT BISQUE
Prep: 15 minutes   Cook: 15 to 17 minutes   Serves: 4

Although pumpkin is most commonly used in pies for dessert in the United States, in many parts of the world it is better known as an ingredient for savory soup. This one is light in flavor, yet hearty enough to stand on its own. Fresh butternut squash or any sweet variety of yellow-fleshed winter squash can be substituted for the pumpkin.

3 carrots, peeled and sliced
2 cups cooked fresh or solid-pack canned pumpkin or cooked butternut squash (see Note)
1 (14½-ounce) can vegetable broth or reduced-sodium chicken broth

½ cup dry sherry
2 cups heavy cream
1 teaspoon salt
½ teaspoon white pepper
1 teaspoon curry powder

1. In a medium saucepan, cook carrot slices in ¼ cup water, covered, over medium heat until carrots are tender, 10 to 12 minutes.

2. Transfer carrots with any liquid remaining in pan to a blender or food processor. Add pumpkin and broth and puree until smooth. Return puree to saucepan.

3. Bring soup to a simmer and add sherry. Cook, stirring, 2 minutes. Add cream, salt, pepper, and curry powder. Heat through, stirring occasionally, about 3 minutes.

4. Ladle soup into bowls. Dust with a little curry powder and serve.

NOTE: *Preheat oven to 350°F. Place a 1½- to 2-pound squash in a baking pan and bake about 1 hour, until tender in center when tested with tip of a knife. Remove from oven and let cool. Cut cooled squash open. With a large spoon, scoop out seeds and discard. Scoop out enough squash to measure 2 cups.*

For convenience you can use canned 100 percent natural solid-pack pumpkin. Reduce the amount by ¼ cup.

---

51 GREEN CHILE AND POTATO SOUP WITH TORTILLA CHEESE FLOATS

Prep: 15 minutes   Cook: 45 to 48 minutes   Serves: 4 to 6

2 tablespoons olive oil
1 medium onion, chopped
2 medium tomatoes, coarsely chopped
1 pound potatoes, peeled and cut into ¼-inch dice
3 (14½-ounce cans) vegetable broth or reduced-sodium chicken broth
1 (7-ounce) can whole green chiles, drained and coarsely chopped

2 teaspoons dried marjoram
1 teaspoon dried rosemary
½ teaspoon salt
1 cup half-and-half
1 (7-ounce) package tortilla chips
1 cup shredded Cheddar cheese

1. Preheat oven to 350°F. In a soup pot or a large saucepan, heat olive oil over medium-high heat. Add onion and cook, stirring occasionally, until golden, 4 to 5 minutes. Add tomatoes and cook, uncovered, stirring occasionally, until liquid partially evaporates, 3 to 4 minutes. Add potatoes, broth, chopped chiles, marjoram, and rosemary. Reduce heat to medium-low, cover, and simmer 30 minutes.

2. Add salt and half-and-half to soup. Simmer, stirring occasionally, 5 minutes.

3. Meanwhile, on a baking sheet, make 4 to 6 piles of tortilla chips, counting on 1 cup of chips per person. Sprinkle with cheese. Bake 3 to 4 minutes, until cheese melts, as you would nachos.

4. To serve, ladle soup into bowls and top with individual tortilla chip floats.

52   VEGETABLE CHILI

Prep: 15 minutes   Cook: 40 to 43 minutes   Serves: 6 to 8

3 tablespoons olive oil
1 large onion, chopped
1 red or green bell pepper, chopped
2 garlic cloves, minced
2 celery ribs, diced
1 (14½-ounce) can Italian-style stewed tomatoes
2 tablespoons chili powder
2 teaspoons ground cumin
½ teaspoon dried basil
8 ounces mushrooms, sliced

2 medium zucchini, sliced
2 large carrots, sliced
1 (16-ounce) bag frozen corn kernels
2 (16-ounce) cans red kidney beans
1½ teaspoons salt
¼ teaspoon cayenne
¼ cup chopped parsley
1 (16-ounce) container sour cream

1. In a large soup pot, heat oil and cook onion over medium heat, stirring occasionally, until softened, 2 to 3 minutes. Add bell pepper, garlic, and celery. Cook, stirring, until soft, 3 to 5 minutes longer.

2. Add tomatoes, chili powder, cumin, basil, mushrooms, zucchini, and carrots. Cover, reduce heat to medium-low, and cook 25 minutes.

3. Add corn, kidney beans with their liquid, salt, and cayenne. Simmer, covered, 10 minutes. Sprinkle with parsley. Serve hot, with a dollop of sour cream.

53   SMOKY WILD RICE AND CORN SOUP

Prep: 10 minutes   Cook: 22 to 27 minutes   Serves: 4 to 6

I usually wait until I have leftover cooked wild rice to make this minestrone. To cook wild rice, place it in a saucepan containing triple the amount of water. Simmer, covered, until rice kernels burst open, 40 to 45 minutes. The texture will remain a little chewy. For this recipe, you'd need about ⅓ cup wild rice.

4 tablespoons butter
1 carrot, sliced
4 celery ribs, finely diced
½ medium onion, finely diced
2 (14½-ounce) cans vegetable broth or reduced-sodium chicken broth
2 imported bay leaves
1 cup cooked wild rice

1½ teaspoons dried thyme leaves
1 (17-ounce) can whole-kernel corn
½ teaspoon liquid smoke
1 teaspoon salt
2 cups buttermilk
½ cup chopped cilantro

1. In a medium frying pan, melt butter over medium heat, and cook carrot, celery, and onion, stirring occasionally, until carrot is lightly caramelized, 8 to 10 minutes.

2. Meanwhile, in a large saucepan or a soup pot, bring broth with bay leaves to a simmer over medium heat. Add cooked wild rice. Cover and keep simmering until vegetables are ready.

3. Add cooked vegetables, thyme, and undrained corn to broth. Cover and simmer until vegetables are heated through, 10 to 12 minutes.

4. Stir in liquid smoke, salt, and buttermilk. Heat through, stirring to blend, 4 to 5 minutes. Discard bay leaves. Pour into a soup tureen and sprinkle with cilantro leaves.

54   FRENCH ONION SOUP AU VIN WITH JARLSBERG GARLIC TOAST

Prep: 10 minutes   Cook: 37 to 47 minutes   Serves: 6

2 tablespoons olive oil	2 cups dry red wine
6 large Bermuda onions, sliced	½ teaspoon salt
1 garlic clove, minced	½ teaspoon pepper
1 teaspoon sugar	Jarlsberg Garlic Toast (recipe follows)
3 tablespoons flour	
4 (14½-ounce) cans vegetable broth or reduced-sodium chicken broth	

1. In a large flameproof casserole, heat oil over medium heat. Add onions and cook, stirring occasionally, until soft, 5 to 7 minutes. Add garlic and sugar. Continue to cook, stirring often, until onions turn an amber color, 20 to 25 minutes. Stir in flour to coat onions and cook, stirring, 2 to 3 minutes.

2. Gradually add broth, stirring constantly to prevent any lumps from forming. Bring to a boil, stirring occasionally, until soup thickens, 5 to 7 minutes. Add wine, salt, and pepper. Cover, reduce heat to low, and simmer 5 minutes.

3. Ladle soup into bowls and float Jarlsberg Garlic Toast on top.

JARLSBERG GARLIC TOAST

Prep: 10 minutes   Cook: 4 to 5 minutes   Serves: 6

2 garlic cloves, peeled	1½ cup shredded Jarlsberg or fontina cheese
12 slices of French baguette bread, cut ½ inch thick	

1. Preheat oven to 425°F. Cut garlic cloves in half. Rub bread slices with garlic. Top each bread slice with cheese. Set on an ungreased baking sheet.

2. Bake 4 to 5 minutes, until cheese melts.

55   SWEET POTATO AND RUTABAGA BISQUE
Prep: 10 minutes   Cook: 35 to 40 minutes   Serves: 4

Also known as swede or yellow turnip, rutabaga adds a distinctive flavor to this elegant soup.

4 small sweet potatoes, peeled
    and diced
1 large rutabaga, peeled and
    diced
1 bay leaf
1 cup dry white wine
2 (14½-ounce) cans vegetable
    or reduced-sodium
    chicken broth

½ teaspoon ground mace
½ teaspoon salt
¼ teaspoon pepper
1 cup heavy cream
1 tablespoon minced candied
    ginger (optional)

1. In a large nonreactive saucepan, combine sweet potatoes, rutabaga, bay leaf, white wine, and 2 cups of broth. Bring to a boil, reduce heat to medium-low, cover, and cook until sweet potatoes are tender, 25 to 30 minutes. Discard bay leaf.

2. Transfer to a blender or food processor and puree, in batches if necessary, until smooth. Return to saucepan. Stir in remaining broth, mace, salt, pepper, and cream. Simmer, stirring occasionally, 10 minutes.

3. Ladle into soup bowls and sprinkle candied ginger on top.

56   ELEGANT EGGPLANT CURRY
Prep: 15 minutes   Cook: 21 to 26 minutes   Serves: 4

2 medium eggplants
2 tablespoons vegetable oil
1 (16-ounce) package firm-
    style tofu, drained
2 tablespoons Asian sesame
    oil
½ green bell pepper, diced
½ pound mushrooms, sliced
1 tart apple, peeled, cored,
    and sliced
2 garlic cloves, minced

½ teaspoon minced fresh
    ginger
1 cup vegetable broth or
    reduced-sodium chicken
    broth
2½ teaspoons curry powder
½ cup plain yogurt
¼ teaspoon pepper
¼ cup chopped cilantro or
    parsley

1. Preheat broiler. Peel eggplants and cut lengthwise into ¼-inch-thick slices. Set on a kitchen towel to drain 5 minutes on each side. Pat dry.

2. Set eggplant slices in single layer on a lightly oiled baking sheet. Paint lightly with vegetable oil. Broil slices as close to heat as possible until light brown, turning over with tongs and watching carefully to prevent scorching, 2 to 3 minutes on each side. Transfer slices to a platter to cool. Cut each slice into ½-inch strips.

3. Drain tofu and cut in half horizontally. Cut each half into 8 squares. Drain well on paper towels.

4. In a large frying pan, heat sesame oil over medium heat. Add green pepper, mushrooms, and apple and cook, stirring occasionally, until soft, 4 to 5 minutes. Stir in garlic, ginger, eggplant strips, broth, and curry powder. Reduce heat to low. Cover and cook until slightly thickened, 8 to 10 minutes. Add tofu and simmer 5 minutes.

5. Just before serving, stir in yogurt. Season with pepper and garnish with cilantro.

---

57   WON TON SOUP AMANDINE
Prep: 30 minutes   Cook: 4 to 6 minutes   Serves: 4 to 6

The ingredients for won tons are available in Chinese markets or in the Asian food section of large supermarkets.

½ **cup water chestnuts, drained**
½ **cup slivered almonds**
3 **garlic cloves, minced**
⅛ **teaspoon Chinese chili paste**
1 **teaspoon Asian sesame oil**
10 **sprigs of cilantro**
1 **teaspoon minced fresh ginger**

1 **teaspoon soy sauce**
2 **teaspoons hoisin sauce**
24 **won ton wrappers**
1 **egg white, lightly beaten**
Flour or cornstarch, for dusting
8 **cups vegetable or reduced-sodium chicken broth**
3 **cups fresh spinach leaves, stemmed and rinsed**
3 **scallions, chopped**

1. In a blender or food processor, coarsely chop water chestnuts and almonds with minced garlic, chili paste, sesame oil, cilantro, ginger, soy sauce, and hoisin sauce. Transfer filling to a small bowl.

2. Brush edges of an individual won ton wrapper with lightly beaten egg white. Place 1 heaping teaspoon water chestnut filling in center of wrapper. Fold over to form a triangular shape, pressing to seal closed. Place a dab of egg white in triangle. Fold over 2 corners at base of triangle to touch in the center. Transfer to a baking sheet lightly dusted with flour or cornstarch. Proceed in similar fashion for remaining won tons.

3. Gently drop won tons into a large saucepan filled with boiling water. Cook until won tons float to surface, 1 to 2 minutes. With a slotted spoon, transfer won tons to bowl of cold water. This will stop cooking process and can be done up to 1 hour ahead.

4. In another large saucepan, bring vegetable broth to a simmer. Stir in spinach leaves. With a slotted spoon, transfer won tons from cold water to simmering broth. Cook until heated through, 3 to 4 minutes. Ladle into individual bowls. Top with chopped scallions.

58   POTATO CAULIFLOWER CURRY
Prep: 10 minutes   Cook: 24 to 30 minutes   Serves: 4

Serve with yogurt, steamed rice, pita bread, and chutney, for a completely meatless meal.

1   small head of cauliflower,
     broken into small florets
2   tablespoons vegetable oil
1   medium onion, chopped
1   green bell pepper, finely
     diced
4   garlic cloves, minced
1   teaspoon minced fresh
     ginger
1½   teaspoons ground cumin
⅛   teaspoon turmeric
⅛   teaspoon ground cardamom
2   medium tomatoes, cut into
     ¼-inch dice

6   small red potatoes, scrubbed
     and quartered
1   cup vegetable broth or
     reduced-sodium chicken
     broth
12   ounces fresh cleaned
     spinach leaves, torn into
     large pieces
½   teaspoon salt
⅛   teaspoon cayenne
½   cup frozen petite peas
     Wedges of lemon

1. In a large saucepan of boiling salted water, cook cauliflower until crisp-tender, about 3 minutes. Drain, rinse under cold running water, and drain again.

2. In a large flameproof casserole, heat oil. Add onion and cook over medium-high heat, stirring occasionally, until onion is lightly browned, 4 to 5 minutes. Add green pepper and garlic and cook until pepper is softened, 2 to 3 minutes. Add ginger, cumin, turmeric, and cardamom and cook, stirring, 1 to 2 minutes, to toast spices.

3. Add tomatoes, cauliflower, potatoes, and broth. Cover and cook over medium heat until potatoes are tender, 12 to 15 minutes. Add additional broth or water if mixture becomes too dry.

4. When potatoes are cooked, stir in spinach leaves, salt, cayenne, and peas. Cook until spinach is just wilted, about 2 minutes. Serve with wedges of lemon.

59 BARBECUED ARGENTINEAN PUMPKIN STEW

Prep: 20 minutes   Cook: 1¾ to 2 hours   Serves: 6

This festive stew is served in the baked pumpkin shell.

1 (3-pound) pumpkin
4 tablespoons butter, melted
2 garlic cloves, minced
2 tablespoons vegetable oil
1 medium onion, chopped
3 celery ribs, chopped
3 small potatoes, peeled and cut into ½-inch dice
1 small sweet potato, peeled and cut into ½-inch dice

10 dried apricot halves
½ cup hickory-flavored barbecue sauce
1 (14½-ounce) can vegetable broth or reduced-sodium chicken broth
1 cup frozen peas and carrots, thawed
½ teaspoon salt
½ teaspoon pepper

1. Preheat oven to 350°F. Carefully cut open top of pumpkin and reserve lid. With a large spoon, scoop out and discard seeds and stringy membrane.

2. In a small bowl, mix melted butter and garlic. Brush mixture inside pumpkin, covering bottom and sides. Replace lid. Place pumpkin snugly in an ovenproof baking dish. Bake 1 to 1¼ hours, until knife easily penetrates skin.

3. Meanwhile, in a large saucepan or a Dutch oven, heat oil. Add onion and celery and cook over medium heat until onion begins to color, 3 to 5 minutes. Add potatoes, sweet potato, apricot halves, barbecue sauce, and broth. Cover and cook until potatoes are tender, 35 to 40 minutes. Add peas and carrots, salt, and pepper. Cook 5 minutes longer. Remove from heat.

4. When pumpkin is cooked through, reduce heat to 200°F. Fill cooked pumpkin with vegetable stew. Replace lid. Keep warm in the oven until ready to serve.

60   LEBANESE-STYLE VEGETABLE RAGOUT
Prep: 15 minutes   Cook: 35 minutes   Serves: 6

I like to serve this savory stew over cooked bulgur wheat or couscous.

2 tablespoons olive oil
2 medium onions, chopped
10 garlic cloves, chopped
1 (14½-ounce) can diced
   stewed tomatoes
4 medium carrots, sliced
2 medium potatoes, peeled
   and cut into 1-inch cubes
½ bunch of parsley, cleaned
   and tied with string
1 tablespoon brown sugar

1½ teaspoons lemon pepper
½ teaspoon ground cinnamon
½ teaspoon ground coriander
2 medium zucchini, cut into
   ½-inch dice
1 (8½-ounce) can quartered
   artichoke hearts, drained
1 (15-ounce) can garbanzo
   beans
1 cup plain yogurt

1. In a medium flameproof casserole, heat olive oil over medium-high heat. Cook onions, stirring occasionally until golden, 4 to 5 minutes. Add garlic and cook, stirring, 1 minute. Add tomatoes, carrots, potatoes, and parsley. Reduce heat to medium. Cover and cook 20 minutes.

2. Add brown sugar, lemon pepper, cinnamon, coriander, zucchini, artichoke hearts, and garbanzo beans. Cover and cook 10 minutes.

3. To serve, discard parsley. Stir in yogurt. Heat through but do not boil.

61   GREEN ON GREEN GUMBO
Prep: 10 minutes   Cook: 33 to 42 minutes   Serves: 8

The base for this gumbo is a roux, a mixture of butter and flour that is cooked until it turns a deep golden color.

6 tablespoons butter
¼ cup flour
2 teaspoons Créole seasoning
2 medium onions, chopped
3 garlic cloves, minced
1 (16-ounce) package frozen
   okra slices, thawed
1 (14½-ounce) can vegetable
   broth or reduced-sodium
   chicken broth
1 teaspoon dried thyme leaves
2 tablespoons Worcestershire
   sauce

1 cup dry white wine
1 pound fresh spinach, rinsed
   and stemmed
1 pound Swiss chard, rinsed
   and coarsely chopped
2 cups coarsely chopped beet
   greens, rinsed
2 cups chopped celery leaves
1 teaspoon salt
   Hot pepper sauce

1. In a Dutch oven or large soup pot, melt butter over medium heat. Add flour and cook, stirring, until flour turns golden, 5 to 7 minutes; do not brown or soup will be bitter. Stir in Créole seasoning.

2. Add onions and garlic. Cook over medium heat, stirring occasionally, until onion softens, about 3 minutes. Stir in okra, cover, and cook, stirring occasionally, until okra is just tender, 5 to 7 minutes. Add broth, thyme, Worcestershire, and wine. Cook, stirring, 5 minutes.

3. Gradually add greens, stirring them gently into stew. Cover and cook until greens are tender, 15 to 20 minutes. Add salt.

4. Serve gumbo over cooked white rice with hot sauce on the side.

62   SOUPE AU PISTOU
Prep: 15 minutes   Cook: 50 to 62 minutes   Serves: 6 to 8

Soupe au pistou is the French counterpart to Italian minestrone. Pistou is the French version of pesto. Here, a spoonful of the condiment is placed at the bottom of each soup bowl to enhance the flavor of the broth. Serve this with plenty of warm, crusty bread and a green salad.

6 cups vegetable or reduced-sodium chicken broth	1 tablespoon dried basil
1 (16-ounce) can red kidney beans	1 teaspoon dried thyme leaves
	1 (17-ounce) can whole-kernel corn
1 (16-ounce) can diced tomatoes	1 teaspoon salt
4 small red potatoes, peeled and cut into ¼-inch dice	½ teaspoon pepper
2 large zucchini, sliced	1 cup broken-up vermicelli
2 large carrots, thinly sliced	1 cup Basil Pesto (page 262) or prepared pesto
1 large onion, diced	2 cups shredded Gouda or Edam cheese
3 small turnips, peeled and cut into ¼-inch dice	

1. In a large stockpot, combine broth, undrained beans and tomatoes, potatoes, zucchini, carrots, onion, turnips, basil, and thyme. Cook, covered, over medium heat until all vegetables are tender, 40 to 50 minutes.

2. Add undrained corn, salt, and pepper. Reduce heat to a simmer and cook 5 minutes longer.

3. Meanwhile, in a medium saucepan filled with lightly salted boiling water, cook vermicelli until tender but still firm, 4 to 5 minutes; drain. Add pasta to soup pot and heat through, 1 to 2 minutes.

4. To serve, place a dollop of pesto in bottom of each bowl. Ladle on hot soup. Serve with cheese on the side.

63   MOROCCAN VEGETABLE TAGINE

Prep: 10 minutes   Cook: 34 to 45 minutes   Serves: 4

Tagine is the Moroccan word to describe an exotic stew. It refers to the dish as well as to the earthenware cooking vessel in which it is prepared. This flavorful stew gets its zing from plenty of lemon juice and also from diced lemon zest. Serve it over rice or couscous.

2 tablespoons olive oil
1 medium onion, sliced
3 medium carrots, peeled and cut into 1-inch chunks
2 small turnips, peeled and quartered
1 pound small red potatoes, peeled and cut in half
1 cup vegetable broth or reduced-sodium chicken broth

½ cup chopped parsley
¼ cup chopped cilantro
1 tablespoon lemon juice
1 teaspoon paprika
Grated zest of ½ lemon
1 cup pitted green olives, drained and rinsed under running water
½ teaspoon salt
½ teaspoon pepper

1. In a Dutch oven, heat oil over medium heat. Add onion and cook, stirring occasionally, until golden, 4 to 5 minutes. Add carrots, turnips, potatoes, and broth. Cover and continue cooking, stirring occasionally, until turnips are fairly tender, 15 to 20 minutes.

2. Meanwhile, in a blender or food processor, combine parsley, cilantro, lemon juice, paprika, and ⅓ cup water. Process until fairly smooth.

3. Add herb mixture to vegetables on stove. Add lemon zest and olives. Reduce heat to a simmer. Cover and cook, stirring occasionally, until vegetables are tender, 15 to 20 minutes. Season with salt and pepper.

Chapter 3

From the Bean Pot

Dried beans, such as kidney beans, navy beans, and garbanzo beans, to name a few, have long been prized as an energy source. So have dried split peas and lentils. These soul-satisfying legumes, all complex carbohydrates, take longer to digest than many other foods, thus creating an impression of fullness even after relatively modest amounts are consumed. They are low in fat and sodium, high in fiber, and free of cholesterol. The average serving of ½ cup of cooked beans contains less than 120 calories.

According to the United States Department of Agriculture's (USDA) recently developed Food Guide Pyramid, which is meant as a daily dietary guide for a well-rounded diet, legumes stand on a par with meat, poultry, or fish, and the recommended amount, meant as a guideline to replace meat, is 2 to 3 servings a day. Another benefit of preparing bean-based dishes is that leftovers freeze well, so large amounts can be made ahead for later use.

Dried beans, lentils, and peas are also an important source of protein. They are rich in iron, calcium, and phosphorus. Pairing them with other grains or vegetables makes up for their lack of some of the important amino acids necessary for a complete diet. Rare are the natural foods that can boast of so many positive attributes. Most of the recipes included in this chapter rely on canned beans for convenience. When preparing dried beans from scratch, however, rinse them well and discard any grit. For best results, beans should be soaked before cooking. For quick soaking, bring at least 10 cups of water to a boil for each pound of dried beans, taking into account that they will plump up to twice their size. Let the beans cook for 2 to 3 minutes, then cover them and set aside for at least an hour. A longer soaking time will help to decrease beans' gas-causing properties. Whatever method you select, discard the soaking water and add fresh water before you proceed with the recipe, and remember that the older the beans, the longer they will take to cook. Lentils and split peas, unlike dried beans, require little or no advance soaking. Rinse them well and discard any impurities or grit; then drain them and proceed with your recipe.

In this chapter, you will find an assortment of international dishes that feature an array of legumes: Moroccan Lentil Soup is redolent of cilantro; a hearty meal-in-a-bowl Meatless Cassoulet au Vin has been adapted for meatless tastes while retaining a full-bodied flavor; Basque Sheepherder's Soup was inspired by one my husband and I enjoyed in the Basque community in Bakersfield, California. Often Chili con Wheat Berries elicits more compliments than the traditional meat-filled version I used to prepare. A cup of Smoky Green Split Pea and Lettuce Soup or one filled with Yellow Split Peas with Cashews is an ideal opener for a winter dinner. A steaming bowl of Farm Fresh Minestrone with Two Beans needs only warm slices of crusty bread as an accompaniment.

Beans and legumes, when cooked and lightly mashed, lend themselves to all sorts of creative substitutions. Consider the rising acceptance of meatless burgers made from a spiced bean puree instead of ground meat. You can now find them ready-made in the frozen foods section of supermarkets. Meatless burgers are also making inroads on restaurant menus. In this chapter, you can make your own Lentil Patties with Zingy Coconut Relish or the easy-to-assemble Black Bean Pistachio Burgers with Guacamole and Sweet Pickled Onions. Beans and lentils are also good cold, in salads. When left to marinate in a spice-accented dressing, the flavors of Black Bean Salad Santa Fe, Portuguese Garbanzo Bean Salad with Roasted Garlic, or multicolored Rainbow Bean Salad will only intensify.

64 SHERRIED BLACK BEAN BISQUE
Prep: 10 minutes   Cook: 10 minutes   Serves: 4 to 6

This smooth black bean bisque calls for canned beans, but if you have leftover cooked black beans so much the better. Plain yogurt is a good alternative to sour cream in this recipe.

2 (15-ounce) cans black beans	1½ teaspoons ground cumin
1 (14½-ounce) can vegetable broth or reduced-sodium chicken broth	⅛ teaspoon cayenne
	1 cup half-and-half
½ cup dry sherry	¼ cup sour cream
	2 scallions, thinly sliced

1. In a blender or food processor, puree beans with their liquid and broth until smooth. Transfer to a large saucepan.

2. Cook over medium heat, stirring, 5 minutes. Add sherry, cumin, and cayenne. Cover and simmer 5 minutes. Add half-and-half and heat through.

3. Ladle into bowls. Swirl 1 tablespoon sour cream into each bowl and garnish with sliced scallions.

65 VENEZUELAN BLACK BEANS AND RICE WITH FRIED PLANTAINS

Prep: 10 minutes   Cook: 25 to 34 minutes   Serves: 4 to 6

I once spent six months at the home of relatives in Venezuela to perfect my Spanish. Practically every meal we ate included *arroz y caraotas*, Venezuelan black beans with rice. Topped with fried plantains and a fried egg, this dish turns into a hearty dinner. Shopping tip: When plantains are ripe, their skin is heavily spotted with black.

¼ cup olive oil
1 medium onion, chopped
1 celery rib, finely diced
1 small red bell pepper, finely diced
1 cup long-grain white rice, rinsed and drained
1 (14½-ounce) can vegetable broth or reduced-sodium chicken broth
1 teaspoon turmeric

1 teaspoon oregano
1 teaspoon salt
½ cup vegetable oil
2 medium ripe plantains
2 tablespoons butter
4 eggs
1 (15-ounce) can black beans
1 teaspoon crushed hot red pepper
Lemon wedges and Tabasco

1. In a medium saucepan, heat 2 tablespoons olive oil over medium-high heat. Add onion and cook, stirring occasionally, until soft, 2 to 3 minutes. Add celery, bell pepper, and rice. Cook, stirring, until rice turns pale golden, 2 to 3 minutes. Reduce heat to low. Add broth, turmeric, oregano, and salt. Cover and cook until rice is tender and all liquid is absorbed, 15 to 20 minutes. Remove from heat and fluff with a fork.

2. Meanwhile, in a medium frying pan, heat vegetable oil over medium-high heat to 375°F. With a sharp knife, cut off ends of plantains and peel away skin. Slice each plantain crosswise on an angle to form elongated slices ½ inch thick. Fry plantain slices in batches, turning with tongs, until they are pale golden, 3 to 4 minutes on each side. Transfer to paper towels to drain.

3. Empty frying pan of oil and wipe clean with paper towels. Melt butter in frying pan over medium heat, and fry eggs according to individual taste. Heat black beans on top of stove or in a microwave oven. Drain off liquid.

4. To serve, mix rice with heated black beans. Mound on a large platter. Top with fried plantain and eggs. Sprinkle hot pepper flakes over top. Serve with lemon wedges and Tabasco on the side.

66   BLACK BEAN SALAD SANTA FE
Prep: 15 minutes   Cook: none   Serves: 4

This black bean salad is redolent of the flavors of the Southwest. You can also serve it rolled up in a flour tortilla.

1 (15-ounce) can black beans, drained and rinsed	1 tablespoon lemon juice
1 cup whole-kernel corn	1 tablespoon chopped cilantro
½ small onion, diced	½ teaspoon salt
2 garlic cloves, minced	1 avocado, cut into ½-inch dice
1 teaspoon chili powder	½ cup tomato, seeded and diced
½ teaspoon ground cumin	

1. In a serving bowl, place drained black beans and corn. Stir to blend. Add onion, garlic, chili powder, cumin, lemon juice, cilantro, and salt. Toss to mix well. At this point, salad can be refrigerated up to 1 hour.

2. Shortly before serving, toss salad with avocado and diced tomato.

67   BOOZY BLACK BEANS
Prep: 20 minutes   Soak: overnight   Cook: 2 to 3 hours
Serves: 8 to 10

Unsweetened chocolate is the surprise ingredient that lends a rich smoothness to this Latin American soup. Serve the beans over cooked rice or bulgur wheat for extra nutrition.

1 pound dried black beans, rinsed and picked over	1 cup light rum
6 cups reduced-sodium chicken broth or water	1 (1-ounce) square unsweetened chocolate
2 medium onions, chopped	1 teaspoon dried thyme leaves
1 medium carrot, peeled and sliced	1 teaspoon dried basil
1 tart apple, peeled, cored, and diced	2 garlic cloves, crushed through a press
12 sprigs of parsley tied together with kitchen string	2 teaspoons salt
	1 teaspoon pepper
	¼ cup chopped parsley, for decoration

1. In a large bowl, soak beans in water overnight. The next day, drain beans. (Or use the quick-soaking method on page 51.)

2. In a soup pot or a crockpot, combine drained beans, broth, onions, carrot, apple, parsley sprigs, rum, chocolate, thyme, basil, and garlic. Cover pot. For stovetop cooking, simmer until beans are tender, 2 to 3 hours. If using a crockpot, set on medium heat for 8 to 10 hours.

3. When beans are cooked, discard tied parsley. Season with salt and pepper. Sprinkle with chopped parsley and serve immediately.

68 BLACK BEAN PISTACHIO BURGERS WITH GUACAMOLE AND SWEET PICKLED ONIONS

Prep: 15 minutes   Cook: 15 to 17 minutes per batch
Chill: 8 hours   Serves: 6

You can prepare the pickled onions the day before, using any of the sweet onions now on the market: Walla Walla, Vidalia, or Maui. Bermuda onions will do in a pinch.

2 large sweet onions, very thinly sliced
½ cup cider vinegar
½ cup sugar
¼ teaspoon celery seed
2 (15-ounce) cans black beans, liquid reserved
2 medium yellow onions, quartered
½ cup chopped parsley
½ cup crushed pistachio nuts
1 egg

1 tablespoon olive oil
1 tablespoon chili powder
1 teaspoon salt
2 tablespoons wheat germ
1 tablespoon sweet-hot mustard
Vegetable oil, for frying
1 cup bread crumbs
6 hamburger rolls
2 medium tomatoes, sliced
2 cups prepared guacamole

1. Place sliced sweet onions in a medium heatproof bowl. In a small non-reactive saucepan, combine vinegar, 1 cup water, sugar, and celery seed. Bring to a boil, cover, and cook over medium heat 5 minutes. Pour over sliced onions. Let cool, then cover and refrigerate 8 hours or overnight.

2. In a food processor, gradually process beans with their liquid until coarsely pureed. Transfer to a medium bowl.

3. In food processor, chop yellow onions, parsley, and pistachio nuts a little at a time. Add to beans. Blend in egg, olive oil, chili powder, salt, wheat germ, and mustard. Mix well.

4. In a large frying pan over medium-high heat, heat enough oil to cover bottom. Place bread crumbs on small saucer next to pan. Shape a portion of bean mixture into a hamburger-sized patty. Dredge in bread crumbs on both sides. Repeat with rest of bean mixture. Set patties in frying pan and cook over medium-high heat for 5 to 6 minutes on each side.

5. To serve, set a hot black bean patty on a hamburger bun. Top with a tomato slice and pickled onions. Serve with guacamole on the side.

69   SOUTHWESTERN JUMBLE WITH BLACK-EYED PEAS

Prep: 15 minutes   Cook: none   Serves: 6

Chipotle in adobo is a smoky-flavored Mexican hot sauce available in many supermarkets. If it isn't available, use your favorite hot sauce instead.

1 (15-ounce) can white
  hominy, drained
1 (15-ounce) can black-eyed
  peas, drained
1 (4-ounce) can whole-kernel
  corn, drained
1 (4-ounce) jar diced red
  pimiento, drained
1 medium onion, chopped

1 (14½-ounce) can Cajun-style
  stewed tomatoes, drained
2 tablespoons chopped
  cilantro
2 tablespoons lemon juice
1 tablespoon chopped chives
½ teaspoon chipotle hot sauce
6 cherry tomatoes, cut in half

1. In a serving bowl. mix hominy, black-eyed peas, corn, pimiento, onion, tomatoes, cilantro, lemon juice, chives, and chipotle sauce. Toss to mix. Cover and refrigerate until ready to serve.

2. Before serving, decorate with tomato halves.

70   HARLEQUIN BAKED BEANS

Prep: 15 minutes   Cook: 1 hour 8 minutes   Serves: 10 to 12

My friend JoAnne Schlemmer often serves this sweet and spicy bean casserole at large gatherings, and people always ask her for the recipe. Serve it as a topping for rice or with warm pieces of cornbread. Tossed greens accented with a spicy vinaigrette dressing will make the meal complete.

¼ cup olive oil
3 large onions, thinly sliced
3 garlic cloves, minced
½ cup packed brown sugar
¼ cup dark molasses
¼ cup cider vinegar
1 tablespoon dry mustard

¼ teaspoon liquid smoke
1 (15-ounce) can kidney
  beans, liquid reserved
1 (15-ounce) can butter beans,
  drained
1 (15-ounce) can Boston baked
  beans

1. Preheat oven to 375°F. In a large frying pan, heat oil over medium-high heat. Add onions and cook, stirring occasionally, until golden, 4 to 5 minutes. Stir in garlic and remove from heat.

2. In a small nonreactive saucepan, combine brown sugar, molasses, vinegar, and mustard. Cook over medium heat, stirring occasionally, until sugar is dissolved, 4 to 5 minutes. Stir in liquid smoke.

3. In a large bowl, combine kidney beans with their liquid, butter beans, baked beans, and brown sugar sauce. Toss to mix.

4. Spoon beans into a generously oiled 9 x 13-inch baking dish. Bake 1 hour. Serve hot.

71   BASQUE CABBAGE AND BEAN SOUP
Prep: 10 minutes   Cook: 1 hour 20 to 1 hour 35 minutes   Serves: 6

This heartwarming cabbage and bean stew called *garbure* (gar-BOOR) is from the Pyrenees, the mountainous region that straddles France and Spain. A simple green salad with crusty bread and grated cheese provide the perfect accompaniments.

2 tablespoons olive oil	½ cup green split peas
2 medium onions, chopped	1 teaspoon dried thyme leaves
2 medium turnips, peeled and quartered	½ teaspoon dried marjoram
	¼ cup chopped parsley
1 bunch of scallions, chopped	1 small cabbage, shredded
10 garlic cloves, peeled	1 (15-ounce) can Great Northern beans, liquid reserved
5 peppercorns	
3 small carrots, sliced	
6 new potatoes, peeled and quartered	1 teaspoon salt
	1 French baguette bread
5 cups vegetable broth or reduced-sodium chicken broth	1 cup shredded Gruyère cheese

1. In a large soup pot, heat olive oil over medium-high heat. Add onion and cook, stirring occasionally, until golden, 2 to 3 minutes. Add turnips and continue cooking, stirring occasionally, until turnips are lightly browned, 8 to 10 minutes.

2. Add scallions, garlic, peppercorns, carrots, potatoes, broth, split peas, thyme, marjoram, and parsley and bring to a boil. Reduce heat to low. Cover and cook until all vegetables are tender, 40 to 45 minutes.

3. Add cabbage and beans with their liquid. Continue cooking until cabbage is tender, 20 to 25 minutes. Season with salt.

4. About 15 minutes before serving, preheat oven to 300°F. Cut baguette into ½-inch slices. Set slices on a cookie sheet and top each slice with a little cheese. Bake 10 to 12 minutes, until cheese melts.

5. To serve, ladle hot soup into a large soup bowl or tureen, top with cheese toasts, and serve immediately.

72   GARBANZO BEANS WITH ROASTED GARLIC
Prep: 10 minutes   Cook: 35 to 40 minutes   Serves: 6

The sweet, buttery flavor of roasted garlic can become positively addictive. Roast more garlic than you will need so you have plenty to squeeze onto slices of bread as a savory substitute for butter.

2 heads of garlic, papery outside husks removed	2 tablespoons rice wine vinegar
2 (15-ounce) cans garbanzo beans, drained	½ teaspoon salt
6 cherry tomatoes, cut in half	¼ teaspoon pepper
2 tablespoons chopped fresh basil or parsley	

1. Preheat oven to 400°F. Wrap garlic in foil. Place in a small baking dish and roast in oven 35 to 40 minutes, until garlic turns soft.

2. Place drained garbanzo beans in a medium bowl. As soon as garlic is cool enough to handle, separate cloves and gently squeeze roasted garlic into garbanzo beans. Mix well.

3. Add tomatoes, basil, vinegar, salt, and pepper. Toss and serve.

73   INDIAN GARBANZO BEANS WITH FRIED GARLIC AND PEANUTS
Prep: 10 minutes   Cook: 29 to 32 minutes   Serves: 4

Serve this stew over cooked brown rice and accompany with Indian-style condiments, such as chutney or yogurt.

3 tablespoons vegetable oil	2 tablespoons tomato paste
2 medium onions, thinly sliced	¼ teaspoon ground cardamom
½ red bell pepper, cut into ¼-inch strips	1 teaspoon dry mustard
½ green bell pepper, cut into ¼-inch strips	½ teaspoon salt
1 large tomato, diced	⅛ teaspoon cayenne
½ teaspoon minced fresh ginger	10 garlic cloves, finely diced
1 (15-ounce) can garbanzo beans, drained, with liquid reserved	1 cup unsalted dry-roasted peanuts

1. In a large saucepan or a small Dutch oven, heat 2 tablespoons of oil. Add onions and cook over medium heat, stirring occasionally, until softened, 2 to 3 minutes. Add red and green bell peppers, and cook, covered, until tender, 4 to 5 minutes. Reduce heat to low. Add tomato and ginger, cover, and cook 5 minutes.

2. In a small bowl, combine reserved garbanzo liquid, tomato paste, cardamom, mustard, and salt. Blend well. Stir into garbanzo beans and simmer, covered, 15 minutes. Season with cayenne.

3. Meanwhile, in a small, nonstick frying pan, heat remaining 1 tablespoon oil over medium heat. Add garlic and cook, stirring, until it turns pale golden, 2 to 3 minutes. Do not burn or garlic will turn bitter. With a slotted spoon, transfer garlic to a small bowl. In same pan, fry peanuts until golden brown, tossing pan back and forth to prevent scorching, 45 seconds to 1 minute. Add to garlic.

4. Serve garbanzo stew hot, garnished with fried garlic and peanuts.

---

74 PORTUGUESE GARBANZO BEAN SALAD WITH ROASTED GARLIC

Prep: 15 minutes   Cook: 30 to 40 minutes   Serves: 6

The subtle flavor of roasted garlic is an exotic alternative to butter or spreads. Roast several heads of garlic at a time. They will keep for several days in an airtight container in the refrigerator.

1 head of garlic, papery outside husks removed	3 medium tomatoes, cut into ½-inch dice
2 (15-ounce) cans garbanzo beans, drained	1 teaspoon ground cumin
1 tablespoon chopped fresh basil or 1 teaspoon dried	1 teaspoon salt
2 tablespoons balsamic vinegar	½ teaspoon pepper

1. Preheat oven to 425°F. Slice ¼ inch off top of head of garlic. Wrap garlic in foil. In a small baking dish, roast garlic until it turns buttery soft, 30 to 40 minutes. Let stand 10 minutes to cool.

2. Meanwhile, in a serving bowl, mix garbanzo beans with basil and vinegar. Set aside.

3. When garlic is cool enough to handle, squeeze out each clove into bean mixture. Stir well to coat beans.

4. Toss with diced tomatoes. Season with cumin, salt, and pepper. Serve at room temperature.

75   CREAMY GARBANZO BEAN STEW
Prep: 15 minutes   Cook: 1 hour 4 minutes   Serves: 4

You can substitute acorn or pumpkin for the butternut squash in this delectable stew. Thick slices of lightly toasted sourdough bread and a green salad are all that is needed as accompaniment.

3 medium tomatoes, diced	1 cup dry white wine
1 (15-ounce) can garbanzo	1 bay leaf
beans, undrained	10 garlic cloves, peeled
1 pound butternut squash,	1 teaspoon dried thyme leaves
peeled and cut into 2-inch	1 teaspoon seasoned salt
cubes	2 cups half-and-half
1 large onion, diced	1 cup shredded Cheddar
2 medium carrots, cut into	cheese (4 ounces)
1-inch chunks	

1. Preheat oven to 375°F. In a large saucepan or Dutch oven, combine tomatoes, garbanzo beans and their liquid, butternut squash, onion, carrots, wine, bay leaf, garlic cloves, and thyme. Cover tightly and bake 1 hour.

2. Transfer pan to stovetop. Discard bay leaf. Season with salt. Stir in half-and-half and Cheddar cheese. Cook over low heat, stirring, until cheese melts, 4 to 5 minutes; do not boil.

NOTE: *To make whole butternut squash easier to peel, prick with a fork in several places. Microwave on High for 6 minutes. Let cool completely. Cut squash into chunks and peel.*

76   BASQUE SHEEPHERDER'S SOUP
Prep: 15 minutes   Cook: 32 to 34 minutes   Serves: 4 to 6

Have plenty of warm sourdough bread on hand to accompany this hearty soup—an adaptation of one enjoyed by the Basque sheepherders in the California Sierras.

2 tablespoons olive oil	1 (16-ounce) can whole-kernel
1 medium onion, diced	corn
3 celery ribs, diced	1 (16-ounce) can crushed
2 tablespoons flour	tomatoes
1 cup vegetable or reduced-	1 cup grated Cheddar cheese
sodium chicken broth	1 teaspoon salt
1 cup milk	½ teaspoon pepper
1 (15-ounce) can lima beans	2 or 3 drops of Tabasco

1. In a large soup pot, heat oil. Add onion and celery and cook over medium heat, stirring occasionally, until softened, 2 to 3 minutes. Sprinkle in flour and cook, stirring, 1 minute. Stir in broth and milk. Bring to a boil and cook until mixture thickens slightly, 4 to 5 minutes.

2. Add undrained lima beans, undrained corn, and crushed tomatoes. Cover and simmer 20 minutes.

3. Reduce heat to medium-low and stir in grated cheese. Simmer 5 minutes, but do not let soup boil. Season with salt, pepper, and Tabasco. Serve at once.

---

77   MEATLESS CASSOULET AU VIN
Prep: 15 minutes   Stand: 1 hour   Cook: 2 to 3 hours   Serves: 6 to 8

Cassoulet is a traditional bean dish from southwestern France. This meatless version relies on a good dry white wine to give the beans a more intense flavor. When pureed, leftover cassoulet blended with a little milk will yield a delicious creamy bean soup.

1½ **cups dried small white navy beans, rinsed and drained**	1 **envelope dry mushroom soup mix**
10 **cloves garlic, peeled**	2 **cups dry white wine**
1 **small onion**	1 **bay leaf**
6 **whole cloves**	1 **teaspoon dried thyme leaves, crushed**
1 **large carrot, cut into chunks**	1 **teaspoon salt**
1 **medium tomato, diced**	½ **teaspoon pepper**
½ **pound mushrooms, chopped**	

1. In a large saucepan, bring navy beans, 6 cups water, and garlic to a rolling boil. Boil 2 to 3 minutes. Turn off heat. Let beans stand 1 hour; drain.

2. Stud onion with cloves. In a large soup pot, place onion, drained beans, carrot, tomato, mushrooms, mushroom soup mix, wine, 3 cups water, bay leaf, and thyme. Bring to a boil. Cover, reduce heat to medium-low, and cook until beans are tender, 2 to 3 hours. Season with salt and pepper. Discard bay leaf. Serve hot.

78   CHUCK'S MEXICAN PINTO BEANS

Prep: 15 minutes   Soak: 8 hours   Cook: 2 to 3 hours 12 minutes
Serves: 8 to 10

If you have beans left over, drain them and mash them gently with a fork to use as a filling for tortillas. A crockpot or a slow cooker is ideal for simmering these beans, although the cooking time will be longer.

1 **pound dried pinto beans, rinsed and picked over**	⅛ **teaspoon cayenne**
2 **bay leaves**	2 **teaspoons seasoned salt**
8 **whole red chili peppers**	2 **tablespoons rice wine vinegar**
¼ **cup molasses**	1 **cup salsa, prepared or homemade**
10 **garlic cloves, peeled**	1 **cup sour cream**
2 **medium onions, chopped**	1 **cup chopped cilantro**
2 **tablespoons ground cumin**	

1. Soak beans overnight in a large pot with enough water to cover by at least 2 inches. Or use quick-soaking method: Place beans in a large pot and cover with 2 inches of hot water. Boil for 2 to 3 minutes. Turn off heat and let beans stand for 1 hour; drain.

2. In a large soup pot, combine beans with 6 cups fresh water. Add bay leaves, chili peppers, molasses, garlic, and onions. Boil for 10 minutes. Reduce heat to a simmer. Cover and cook until beans are soft, 2 to 3 hours.

3. Discard bay leaves and chili peppers. Stir in cumin, cayenne, salt, and vinegar. Serve hot with salsa, sour cream, and chopped cilantro on the side.

79   FARM FRESH MINESTRONE WITH TWO BEANS

Prep: 20 minutes   Cook: 45 to 48 minutes   Serves: 6 to 8

3 **tablespoons olive oil**	1 **bay leaf**
2 **medium onions, chopped**	1 **teaspoon dried oregano**
1 **(16-ounce) can Italian-style stewed tomatoes**	1 **(16-ounce) can kidney beans**
3 **garlic cloves, minced**	1 **(8-ounce) can garbanzo beans, undrained**
1 **large carrot, sliced**	1 **teaspoon pepper**
2 **small turnips, diced**	½ **cup chopped Italian flat-leaf parsley**
2 **celery ribs, diced**	1 **cup elbow macaroni**
5 **cups vegetable or reduced-sodium chicken broth**	1 **cup grated Parmesan cheese**
1 **cup dry red wine**	

1. In a large soup pot, heat oil. Add onions and cook over medium-high heat, stirring occasionally, until golden 2 to 3 minutes. Add tomatoes and garlic and cook 2 minutes. Add carrot, turnips, and celery. Cook, stirring occasionally, 3 minutes.

2. Add broth, wine, bay leaf, and oregano. Bring to a boil. Cover and cook over medium heat 15 minutes. Add kidney beans and garbanzo beans with their liquid. Cover and simmer 10 minutes. Stir in pepper and parsley.

3. Meanwhile, in a medium saucepan of lightly salted boiling water, cook elbow macaroni until tender but still firm, 8 to 10 minutes. Drain well. Add to simmering minestrone.

4. Cook until pasta is heated through, 5 minutes. Serve with grated cheese on the side.

---

80 CHILI CON WHEAT BERRIES
Prep: 15 minutes   Cook: 1 hour   Serves: 6

This heartwarming chili takes on a festive appearance if you serve it inside individual hollowed-out crusty sourdough rolls.

2 tablespoons olive oil	1 tablespoon plus 1 teaspoon
2 medium onions, finely	chili powder
diced	1 tablespoon ground cumin
2 garlic cloves, minced	½ bunch fresh cilantro, rinsed
½ medium green bell pepper,	and tied with string
finely diced	2 bay leaves
1 (28-ounce) can crushed	1 cup sliced mushrooms
tomatoes	¼ cup chopped pitted green
½ cup wheat berries, rinsed	Spanish olives
and drained	2 teaspoons salt
1 cup dry red wine	1 cup sour cream
2 (14½-ounce) cans vegetable	6 scallions, finely chopped
broth or reduced-sodium	1 cup shredded Cheddar
chicken broth	cheese
1 (15-ounce) can kidney beans	

1. In a large soup pot, heat olive oil over medium-high heat. Add onions and cook, stirring occasionally, until soft, about 3 minutes. Add garlic, bell pepper, and crushed tomatoes. Cover and cook 5 minutes. Add wheat berries, wine, and broth. Stir to blend. Cook, covered, 5 minutes. Add kidney beans, chili powder, cumin, cilantro, and bay leaves. Cover and cook over medium-low heat 40 minutes.

2. Add mushrooms, olives, and salt. Simmer for 5 minutes. Discard bay leaves and cilantro.

3. Serve hot, with sour cream, chopped scallions, and grated cheese on the side.

81 MULTIBEAN AND SALSA STEW

Prep: 1 hour   Stand: 1 hour   Cook: 1½ hours   Serves: 6

This hearty multibean stew is made with the bean mixes found in bulk in health food stores or in some supermarkets. Any mixture will do.

2 cups multibean dried bean mix
2 (14½-ounce) cans vegetable or reduced-sodium chicken broth
1 (15-ounce) can diced stewed tomatoes
2 cups Mexican salsa, preferably fresh

1 medium onion, coarsely chopped
2 celery ribs, chopped
1 medium carrot, sliced
2 tablespoons soy sauce or tamari
1 teaspoon pepper

1. To quick-soak beans, in a large soup pot, bring beans and 5 cups water to a boil. Boil for 2 to 3 minutes. Remove from heat, cover, and let stand 1 hour.

2. Drain beans. Return beans to pot with broth, stewed tomatoes, salsa, onion, celery, carrot, and soy sauce. Cover and cook over medium-low heat until beans are tender and flavors are blended, 1½ hours.

3. Remove from heat. Season with pepper.

82 RAINBOW BEAN SALAD

Prep: 10 minutes   Cook: 15 to 20 minutes   Serves: 8 to 10

1 cup pink lentils, rinsed and picked over
1 (16-ounce) can red kidney beans, drained
1 (15-ounce) can whole-kernel corn, drained
2 sweet onions, cut into thin rings
1 (2-ounce) jar diced red pimiento, drained

1 small green bell pepper, finely diced
2 celery ribs, finely diced
1 (4-ounce) jar marinated artichoke quarters
2 tablespoons chopped fresh chives
1 teaspoon chili powder
1 (8-ounce) bottle oil and vinegar dressing

1. In a medium saucepan of boiling water, cook lentils until soft, 15 to 20 minutes. Drain well.

2. In a large serving bowl, combine lentils with kidney beans, corn, onions, diced pimiento, diced pepper, celery, marinated artichokes, chives, chili powder, and dressing. Toss to mix well. Cover and refrigerate until serving time. Serve chilled.

83 BARBECUED PINTO BEANS

Prep: 10 minutes   Stand: overnight
Cook: 2 hours 7 minutes to 2 hours 40 minutes   Serves: 6 to 8

These barbecued beans will acquire even more flavor if they are made the day before. Be aware, however, that the older the beans, the longer they will need to cook.

1 (16-ounce) package dried
    pinto beans, rinsed and
    picked over
2 tablespoons olive oil
2 medium onions, chopped
1 (28-ounce) can diced
    tomatoes, with juice
1 (12-ounce) can beer
¾ cup molasses

2 garlic cloves, minced
1 cup mesquite-flavored
    barbecue sauce
2 tablespoons soy sauce or
    tamari
1 cup vegetable broth or
    reduced-sodium chicken
    broth
½ teaspoon pepper

1. In a large bowl, soak pinto beans overnight in enough water to cover by a depth of 2 inches. Or use quick-soaking method suggested on page 51. Next day, drain beans.

2. In a large soup pot or a medium Dutch oven, heat oil over medium heat. Add onions and cook, stirring occasionally, until golden, 3 to 5 minutes. Increase heat to medium-high. Add pinto beans, tomatoes with their juice, beer, molasses, garlic, barbecue sauce, soy sauce, broth, and pepper. Stir to blend. Bring to a boil and cook, stirring occasionally, 4 to 5 minutes.

3. Reduce heat to medium-low. Cover and simmer until beans are tender, 2 to 2½ hours. If liquid evaporates during last hour of cooking, add a little water.

84 LENTIL PATTIES WITH ZINGY COCONUT RELISH

Prep: 25 minutes   Cook: 37 to 44 minutes   Serves: 2 to 3

You can shape these patties like burgers and serve them on a roll with all the trimmings, or fashion smaller versions and serve them as an accompaniment to another dish.

1¼ cups dried lentils, rinsed and picked over
1 egg
3 tablespoons wheat germ
1½ tablespoons Worcestershire sauce
⅛ teaspoon hot pepper sauce
2 tablespoons sliced black olives, drained
2 garlic cloves, minced
½ teaspoon ground cumin
1 teaspoon salt
⅛ teaspoon pepper
1 small onion, chopped
1 small carrot, shredded
1 cup seasoned bread crumbs
3 tablespoons butter
¾ cup fresh cilantro leaves
2 tablespoons fresh lemon juice
⅓ cup unsweetened shredded coconut
2 teaspoons minced ginger
1 teaspoon sugar

1. In a large saucepan, combine lentils with 4 cups water. Cook, covered, over medium heat, until lentils are tender, 25 to 30 minutes; drain.

2. In a blender or food processor, combine cooked lentils and egg. Pulse, turning machine quickly on and off 5 or 6 times, until lentils are coarsely mashed. Transfer to a large bowl.

3. Add wheat germ, Worcestershire, hot sauce, olives, garlic, cumin, salt, pepper, onion, and carrot. Mix well to blend.

4. Spread bread crumbs on a large plate. With hands, fashion lentil patties. Dredge in bread crumbs to coat both sides. In a large frying pan, melt butter over medium heat. With a wide spatula, carefully set lentil patties inside frying pan. Cook, turning once, until golden brown, 6 to 7 minutes on each side.

5. Meanwhile, in a blender or food processor, combine cilantro leaves with lemon juice, coconut, ginger, 2 tablespoons water, and sugar. Process until cilantro is chopped. Transfer to a small serving bowl.

6. Serve lentil patties hot, with coconut relish on the side.

85 MOROCCAN LENTIL SOUP

Prep: 30 minutes   Cook: 1 hour 39 minutes to 2 hours 10 minutes
Serves: 8

This is the traditional soup with which Moroccans break their daily fast during Ramadan, the Muslim month of fasting. It is ideally suited to making in a crockpot. Accompany with a salad and lots of crusty bread. It freezes very well.

2 tablespoons olive oil
2 medium onions, sliced
1 (28-ounce) can whole peeled tomatoes, juices reserved
¼ teaspoon ground ginger
¼ teaspoon turmeric
⅛ teaspoon saffron threads, crushed
½ cup chopped cilantro
1 cup lentils, rinsed and picked over

½ cup wheat berries
6 cups vegetable broth or water
1 (15-ounce) can garbanzo beans
1 egg, lightly beaten
2 lemons
2 teaspoons salt
1 teaspoon pepper

1. In a large nonreactive soup pot, heat olive oil. Add onions and cook over medium-high heat, stirring occasionally, until golden, 4 to 5 minutes.

2. Meanwhile, in a blender or food processor, combine tomatoes with their liquid, ginger, turmeric, saffron, and cilantro. Puree until fairly smooth. Add tomato puree to onions in soup pot. Bring to a boil, cover, and cook over medium heat 5 minutes.

3. Add lentils, wheat berries, and broth. Cover tightly. If using a crockpot, set on medium heat for 8 to 10 hours, or on low heat overnight. For stovetop cooking, simmer soup until wheat berries are tender, 1½ to 2 hours.

4. About 15 minutes before serving, add garbanzo beans with their liquid to soup.

5. About 10 minutes before serving, in a small bowl, beat egg with juice from 1 lemon. Reduce heat under soup to a simmer. Stir egg mixture into soup until egg forms strands. Season soup with salt and freshly ground pepper.

6. To serve, squeeze juice of remaining lemon into 8 bowls before ladling in soup.

86 PUREED PUMPKIN AND LENTIL SOUP WITH ORANGE JUICE

Prep: 15 minutes   Cook: 52 to 58 minutes   Serves: 6

Orange juice (preferably freshly squeezed) lends a citrusy-sweet flavor to this interesting soup. I like to use any variety of winter squash such as butternut, acorn, or even pumpkin. You can also use canned pumpkin puree, provided it is unsweetened.

1 cup dried lentils	Grated zest of 1 orange
2 tablespoons vegetable oil	1 cup cooked and mashed
2 medium onions, diced	pumpkin or butternut
½ teaspoon cinnamon	squash or solid-pack
1 teaspoon honey	canned pumpkin
1 small carrot, sliced	½ cup orange juice
1 celery rib, finely diced	Chopped fresh dill or
8 cups vegetable or reduced-	parsley
sodium chicken broth	1 cup sour cream
1 teaspoon chopped fresh dill	
or ½ teaspoon dried	

1. In a medium bowl, soak lentils for 15 minutes and discard any impurities. Drain.

2. In a soup pot or heavy Dutch oven, heat oil over medium-high heat and cook onion, stirring occasionally, until softened, 2 to 3 minutes. Stir in cinnamon and honey. Add carrot, celery, and broth. Cover and bring to a rolling boil. Add drained lentils, dill, and orange zest. Lower heat to medium. Cover and cook until lentils are tender, 40 to 45 minutes. Stir in cooked squash and orange juice and simmer 10 minutes.

3. To serve, ladle soup into bowls, sprinkle with dill, and serve with sour cream on the side.

87 RED LENTIL PIE WITH CUCUMBER YOGURT SAUCE

Prep: 10 minutes   Cook: 58 minutes to 1 hour 11 minutes   Serves: 4

The lovely red lentils now available everywhere inspired me to concoct this healthful bake. It is even more flavorful and nutritionally balanced when served with a topping of Cucumber Yogurt Sauce. Red lentils cook faster than brown or green lentils, so be sure to check them after the minimum cooking time suggested below.

½ cup red lentils, rinsed and picked over
2 tablespoons olive oil
4 scallions, chopped
1½ cups broccoli florets, chopped
2 eggs
2 tablespoons wheat germ

1 cup cottage cheese
⅓ cup crumbled goat cheese
½ teaspoon ground cumin
½ teaspoon dried basil
2 tablespoons bread crumbs
1 cup Cucumber Yogurt Sauce (recipe follows)

1. Preheat oven to 350°F. In a medium saucepan, combine lentils with 2½ cups water. Cook over medium heat, covered, until lentils are tender, 15 to 20 minutes; drain.

2. Meanwhile, in a large frying pan, heat olive oil over medium heat. Add scallions and cook, stirring occasionally, until softened, 2 to 3 minutes. Add chopped broccoli. Cover, reduce heat to medium-low, and cook, stirring several times, until soft, 6 to 8 minutes. Remove from heat.

3. In a medium bowl, coarsely mash cooked lentils with a fork. Add eggs, wheat germ, cottage cheese, goat cheese, cumin, and basil. Blend well.

4. Sprinkle bread crumbs over bottom of a generously oiled 9-inch pie plate. Spoon half of lentil mixture evenly over crumbs. Cover with broccoli. Top with remaining lentils.

5. Bake 35 to 40 minutes, until golden and puffy. Serve hot or at room temperature, with Cucumber Yogurt Sauce on the side.

CUCUMBER YOGURT SAUCE

Prep: 15 minutes   Cook: none   Makes: about 2 cups

1 medium cucumber, peeled, seeded, and finely diced
1½ cups plain yogurt
1 garlic clove, minced
1 teaspoon lemon juice

1 tablespoon chopped chives
1 teaspoon chopped fresh mint or ½ teaspoon dried
¼ teaspoon salt

In a medium bowl, mix all sauce ingredients. Serve chilled.

88   SMOKY GREEN SPLIT PEA AND LETTUCE SOUP

Prep: 10 minutes   Cook: 58 minutes to 1 hour 10 minutes   Serves: 6

Beer is the secret ingredient in this savory soup. A dash of liquid smoke adds a rich, smoky flavor.

2 tablespoons vegetable oil
1 medium leek (white and tender green), well rinsed and thinly sliced
2 medium carrots, sliced
1 pound dried green split peas, rinsed and drained
3 (14½-ounce) cans vegetable or reduced-sodium chicken broth

1 (12-ounce) can beer
10 leaves of Boston lettuce, shredded
2 bay leaves
10 fresh mint leaves, chopped, or 1 teaspoon dry mint, crushed
1½ teaspoons liquid smoke
½ cup sour cream

1. In a large saucepan or a soup pot, heat oil over medium heat. Add leek and carrots and cook, stirring occasionally, until leeks are very soft and beginning to color, 8 to 10 minutes.

2. Add split peas, broth, beer, lettuce, bay leaves, and mint. Bring to a boil, cover, and reduce heat to low. Cook until split peas soften to a puree, 50 minutes to 1 hour.

3. Discard bay leaves and stir in liquid smoke. Serve hot, with a dollop of sour cream.

89   LENTIL DAL

Prep: 10 minutes   Cook: 44 to 51 minutes   Serves: 6

Dal is a souplike concoction of spicy lentils, which is commonly served as part of an Indian meal. Dal can be eaten hot or at room temperature. It can also serve as a topping for rice dishes and curries.

1½ cups red lentils
1 bay leaf
2 tablespoons vegetable oil
1 medium onion, diced
1 (14-ounce) can stewed tomatoes
1 tablespoon minced ginger
4 garlic cloves, minced

2 teaspoons garam masala (see Note)
1 teaspoon ground cumin
2 tablespoons chopped cilantro or parsley
1 green chile, finely diced
1½ teaspoons salt
⅛ teaspoon cayenne

1. In a large bowl, soak lentils for 10 minutes in water to cover. Discard any impurities; drain. In a large pot, combine 6 cups water, lentils, and bay leaf. Cook, covered, over medium heat until lentils are tender, 30 to 35 minutes. Drain and return to pan. Discard bay leaf.

2. Meanwhile, in a medium frying pan, heat oil over medium-high heat. Add onion, stirring occasionally until golden, 4 to 5 minutes. Add tomatoes and cook, stirring occasionally, until most of the liquid evaporates, 5 to 6 minutes. Add ginger, minced garlic, garam masala, cumin, cilantro, diced chile, salt, and cayenne. Cover and simmer 5 minutes. Add to cooked lentils and heat through.

NOTE: *Garam masala is an Indian spice blend available in Indian markets, in the ethnic section of specialty food shops, and in the spice section of some supermarkets.*

90 MINIATURE PUMPKINS STUFFED WITH SPICED LENTILS
Prep: 15 minutes   Cook: 1 hour 33 minutes to 1¾ hours
Serves: 6

Plan on one "Jack Be Little" or other miniature pumpkin per person. The lentils are also delicious when served by themselves as a side dish.

6 **miniature pumpkins**	2 **cups brown lentils, rinsed**
2 **tablespoons olive oil**	**and picked over**
1 **medium onion, sliced**	3½ **cups vegetable broth or**
1 **(8-ounce) can tomato sauce**	**reduced-sodium**
1 **teaspoon sugar**	**chicken broth**
1 **tablespoon ground cumin**	1 **teaspoon salt**
1 **teaspoon sweet paprika**	⅛ **teaspoon cayenne**
½ **teaspoon cinnamon**	

1. Preheat oven to 325°F. Fill a 9 x 13-inch baking pan with 1 inch of water. Set whole pumpkins in pan and bake 40 to 45 minutes, until blade of a knife penetrates flesh easily. (Or microwave: With tip of a sharp knife, poke holes in each pumpkin. Set pumpkins in a microwave-proof dish filled with 1 inch of water, cover with microwave-safe plastic wrap, and microwave on High for 7 minutes. Rotate pumpkins and microwave 4 to 5 minutes longer.) Let cool, then carefully remove tops to make a lid. Scoop out seeds.

2. While pumpkins are baking, in a large saucepan, heat oil over medium-high heat. Add onion and cook, stirring occasionally, until golden, 2 to 3 minutes. Stir in tomato sauce, sugar, cumin, paprika, and cinnamon. Add lentils and broth. Cover and cook until lentils are tender, 40 to 45 minutes. Drain into a colander. Season lentils with salt and cayenne.

3. Fill hollowed pumpkins with equal amounts of hot lentil mixture. Cover each pumpkin with its lid and serve at once.

91   YELLOW SPLIT PEAS WITH CASHEWS

Prep: 10 minutes   Cook: 58 minutes to 1 hour 10 minutes   Serves: 6

This dynamite stew stands heartily on its own or can be served over cooked white rice.

2 tablespoons vegetable oil
2 medium onions, diced
2 medium carrots, peeled and thinly sliced
4 garlic cloves, sliced
2 cups dried yellow split peas, rinsed and drained
⅓ cup dry white wine
3 medium tomatoes, cut into 1-inch dice

2 (14½-ounce) cans vegetable or reduced-sodium chicken broth
2 teaspoons powdered mustard
2 teaspoons sweet paprika
½ teaspoon garlic salt
2 tablespoons white wine Worcestershire sauce
1 cup whole roasted cashews
Hot pepper sauce

1. In a large saucepan or soup pot, heat oil over medium-high heat. Add onions, carrots, and garlic and cook, stirring often, until onions are golden brown, 8 to 10 minutes.

2. Stir in split peas, wine, tomatoes, and broth. Bring to a boil, cover, and reduce heat to low. Cook until peas turn soft, 50 to 60 minutes. Stir in mustard, paprika, garlic salt, and Worcestershire.

3. Add cashews and cook 5 minutes. Serve hot, with hot sauce on the side.

Chapter 4

Meatless Main Courses

Mention a one-dish meal and chances are visions of an oven-baked casserole or a mouth-watering stew simmered at length over a low flame come to mind. In this busy world of two-career families, one-dish meals are the ultimate time-saving device. Choosing a pot or baking dish that can go directly from oven to table will cut down even further on dishwashing chores. Ovenproof glass casseroles are a good choice. Heavier enameled cast-iron cooking pots work well, too, for they retain heat better and they do not react with tomatoes, wine, or other acidic foods. At home, I always seem to gravitate to my grandmother's old-fashioned black cast-iron pot, which holds a privileged spot on top of my stove. Using nonstick pans or skillets to start up a dish will allow you to cut down on the amount of oils or fat used for sautéing and browning.

These days, one-dish meals have taken on a new dimension, for they can just as well refer to an elegant platter lined with an assortment of vegetables, like Roasted Vegetables with Teriyaki Vinaigrette. Other variations include Grandmother's Gnocchi, plump dumplings smothered in a fragrant cheese sauce, or the easy-to-assemble Corn Fritters with Creamed Spinach. Add a bowl of rice to East-West Meatless Stroganoff, and dinner is ready.

Other easy choices include Baked Kefta with Eggs in Cumin Tomato Sauce, which was adapted from a traditional one-dish meal often served in Moroccan households, and Pan-Fried Cheese Cutlets, which offer a substantial alternative to meat. Mushroom Ravioli Divan is a cinch to make with any of the ready-made fresh ravioli available in the refrigerated or frozen section of supermarkets. Most dishes will need only a salad and a loaf of fresh bread as accompaniments.

92 CHILIED CORN AND BROCCOLI BAKE
Prep: 10 minutes   Cook: 30 to 35 minutes   Serves: 4

1 (15¾-ounce) can cream-style corn
1 (10-ounce) box frozen chopped broccoli, thawed
½ medium onion, finely chopped
1 egg, lightly beaten
¼ cup milk

4 tablespoons butter, melted
1¼ cups onion-flavored cracker crumbs (see Note)
2 tablespoons diced green chiles
1 teaspoon chili powder
1 teaspoon salt

1. Preheat oven to 350°F. In a large bowl, mix together corn, broccoli, onion, egg, milk, melted butter, 1 cup cracker crumbs, green chiles, chili powder, and salt.

2. Pour mixture into a generously greased shallow 2-quart casserole. Sprinkle with remaining cracker crumbs.

3. Bake 30 to 35 minutes, until bubbly and golden brown on top.

   NOTE: *To make crumbs, grind about 30 onion-flavored crackers, such as Keebler or Sunshine, in a blender or food processor.*

93 CHILE AND ROASTED RED PEPPER PIE
Prep: 15 minutes   Cook: 31 to 38 minutes   Serves: 4

2 large red bell peppers
1 tablespoon olive oil
2 teaspoons ground cumin
1 garlic clove, minced
1 (7-ounce) can whole roasted green chiles, drained
1 cup cooked rice

2 tablespoons minced onion
⅛ teaspoon cayenne
4 eggs, lightly beaten
1 cup shredded hot pepper Jack cheese
1 teaspoon salt

1. Preheat broiler. Set peppers on a baking sheet. Broil as close to heat as possible, turning, until skins blister evenly, 6 to 8 minutes. Transfer peppers to a bag and seal. Let steam 10 minutes. When cool enough to handle, peel and seed peppers under running water. Dice half a pepper and set aside. Cut remaining peppers into ½-inch strips.

2. In a medium bowl, mix pepper strips with olive oil, 1 teaspoon cumin, and minced garlic. Set aside.

3. Cut whole green chiles in half to flatten. Rinse under running water and drain on paper towels.

4. Line bottom and sides of a 9-inch pie plate with green chiles. Set aside.

5. In a medium bowl, combine rice, onion, cayenne, eggs, Jack cheese, salt, remaining cumin, and diced pepper. Fill pie plate with rice mixture. Set marinated red pepper strips in lattice pattern over the top. Bake until pie is firm, 25 to 30 minutes.

94 CORN AND CHILI PIE

Prep: 10 minutes   Cook: 50 minutes to 1 hour   Serves: 6 to 8

This is perfect for a brunch. It can be cooked and frozen for up to 3 months.

3 eggs
1 (8-ounce) can cream-style corn
1 (10-ounce) package frozen whole-kernel corn, thawed
½ cup yellow cornmeal
1 cup sour cream or plain yogurt
4 ounces Cheddar cheese, diced

4 ounces hot pepper Jack cheese, diced
1 (4-ounce) can diced green chiles, drained
2 teaspoons chili powder
2 teaspoons Worcestershire sauce
½ teaspoon salt

1. Preheat oven to 350°F. In a large bowl, mix eggs with cream-style corn, corn kernels, cornmeal, sour cream, Cheddar and pepper Jack cheeses, green chiles, chili powder, Worcestershire, and salt. Blend well. Pour mixture into a generously oiled 9-inch pie pan.

2. Bake 50 minutes to 1 hour, until firm and golden brown. Let stand 10 minutes. Cut into wedges and serve.

95 CHEESY CHILES

Prep: 15 minutes   Cook: 25 to 30 minutes   Serves: 6 to 8

This recipe is from my friend Margie Oakes, who not only grows her own chiles but also knows the best way to cook them.

1½ pounds Monterey Jack cheese
1 (27-ounce) can whole green chiles, drained
1 (16-ounce) container black bean dip

8 ounces whipped cream cheese
2 tablespoons milk

1. Preheat oven to 350°F. Shred ½ pound of Monterey Jack cheese. Set aside. Cut remaining cheese into ½ x 3-inch sticks.

2. Stuff each chile with 1 or 2 sticks of cheese. Set chiles snugly in a 7 x 11-inch baking dish.

3. In a medium bowl, mix bean dip with whipped cream cheese and milk until well blended. Cover chiles evenly with bean mixture. Sprinkle shredded cheese on top. Cover with aluminum foil.

4. Bake 25 to 30 minutes, until casserole is bubbly.

96   EGGPLANT ENCHILADAS

Prep: 20 minutes   Cook: 39 to 51 minutes   Serves: 6

Regular eggplant will do fine for this dish, but I favor the slender, bright purple Japanese eggplant when it is in season.

4 medium Japanese eggplants or 1 medium eggplant Vegetable oil cooking spray	2 garlic cloves, minced 1 tablespoon tomato paste
5 large tomatoes, peeled, seeded, and cut into ½-inch dice, or 1 (28-ounce) can Italian peeled tomatoes, drained and coarsely chopped	1 teaspoon salt ½ teaspoon pepper ½ teaspoon sugar 1 (10-ounce) container prepared Alfredo sauce ½ cup dry white wine
2 teaspoons dried basil	1 (16-ounce) package 6- to 7-inch flour or corn tortillas

1. Preheat broiler. Peel eggplant and cut lengthwise into ¼-inch-thick slices. Set on a kitchen towel to drain 5 minutes on each side. Pat dry.

2. Set eggplant slices in a single layer on a lightly oiled baking sheet. Spray lightly with vegetable oil. Broil slices as close to heat as possible until light brown, turning over with tongs and watching carefully to prevent scorching, 2 to 3 minutes on each side. Transfer slices to a platter to cool. Cut each slice lengthwise into ¼-inch strips. Reduce oven temperature to 375°F.

3. In a large nonreactive flameproof casserole, combine tomatoes, basil, garlic, tomato paste, salt, pepper, and sugar. Partially cover and cook over medium heat until mixture thickens, 10 to 15 minutes. Add cooked eggplant to tomato mixture. Remove from heat.

4. To assemble enchiladas, in a medium bowl, mix Alfredo sauce with wine. Spoon a little sauce on bottom of a 7 x 11-inch baking dish. Fill tortillas with equal amounts of eggplant and tomato filling. Roll tortillas up, jelly-roll style, and set snugly in baking dish. Top with remaining Alfredo sauce.

5. Bake until bubbly, 25 to 30 minutes. Serve hot.

97 EGGPLANT RISOTTO TORTA

Prep: 10 minutes   Cook: 1 hour 8 minutes to 1 hour 25 minutes
Serves: 6 to 8

This thick pie is a good way to use up leftover rice or rice stuffing. I have chosen here to make a simple risotto, using Spanish saffron as the classic flavoring. Your own creativity can dictate the ingredients to add to the rice. Serve the torta hot with a bowl of tomato sauce on the side. It is also good the next day, at room temperature.

4 tablespoons butter
½ medium onion, chopped
½ red bell pepper, seeded and finely diced
2 garlic cloves, minced
1 cup long-grain white rice
½ cup dry white wine
1 (14½-ounce) can reduced-sodium chicken broth
6 saffron threads, crushed

½ teaspoon pepper
½ cup grated Parmesan or Romano cheese
2 large eggplants
¼ cup olive oil
2 tablespoons sun-dried tomatoes, diced
2 cups shredded mozzarella cheese

1. In a heavy medium saucepan, melt 2 tablespoons butter over medium-high heat. Add onion, pepper, and garlic and cook, stirring occasionally, until onion is golden, 4 to 5 minutes. Add rice and cook, stirring, until it turns light golden, 6 to 8 minutes. Pour in wine and cook, stirring, until liquid is absorbed, 2 to 3 minutes.

2. Add 1 cup broth, saffron, and pepper. Reduce heat to medium-low. Cook, stirring, until broth is absorbed, 7 to 10 minutes. Slowly add remaining broth, stirring continuously. Cover and cook without disturbing rice until tender but not mushy, 25 to 30 minutes in all.

3. Stir in grated cheese and remaining 2 tablespoons butter. Set aside.

4. Preheat broiler. While rice is cooking, peel eggplants and cut crosswise into ¼-inch-thick slices. Pat dry. Set on a baking sheet and paint lightly with olive oil. Broil 2 minutes, or until lightly browned. Turn over with tongs, paint other side with olive oil, and broil until browned on second side, about 2 minutes longer. Set aside. Reduce oven temperature to 375°F.

5. Line bottom and sides of a generously oiled 10-inch pie pan with eggplant slices, trimming to fit. Spoon half of cooked rice mixture over eggplant. Sprinkle with sun-dried tomatoes and half of mozzarella. Top with remaining rice. Arrange remaining eggplant slices decoratively on top to cover rice. Sprinkle with remaining mozzarella.

6. Bake until pie is hot, 20 to 25 minutes. Let stand 10 minutes before cutting into wedges to serve.

98   LIGHT RICOTTA MOUSSAKA

Prep: 20 minutes   Cook: 36 to 46 minutes   Stand: 10 minutes
Serves: 8

You can prepare this lighter version of the traditional Greek dish a day ahead and keep it refrigerated until cooking time. It tastes as good the next day as it does right out of the oven.

2 **large eggplants, peeled**	1 **pound mushrooms, sliced**
½ **cup olive oil**	1 **garlic clove, minced**
1 **(15-ounce) container ricotta**	½ **cup seasoned bread crumbs**
cheese	½ **teaspoon salt**
1 **large egg**	¼ **teaspoon pepper**
¼ **cup grated Parmesan cheese**	½ **cup dry white wine**
¼ **cup flour**	1 **cup milk**
½ **teaspoon curry powder**	2 **large tomatoes, thinly sliced**
4 **tablespoons butter**	

1. Preheat broiler. Slice whole eggplant lengthwise in ¼-inch slices. Lightly paint slices with olive oil. Set in a single layer on a large baking sheet. Broil slices until brown, turning over carefully with tongs, 2 to 3 minutes on each side. Transfer grilled slices to a platter. Reduce oven temperature to 375°F.

2. In a medium bowl, mix ricotta, egg, 2 tablespoons Parmesan cheese, 3 tablespoons flour, and curry powder. Stir until well blended.

3. In a large skillet, melt 2½ tablespoons butter over medium heat. Add mushrooms and cook, stirring occasionally, until limp, 3 to 4 minutes. Transfer to a medium bowl. Stir in garlic and bread crumbs. Season with salt and pepper.

4. In a medium saucepan, melt remaining 1½ tablespoons butter over medium heat. Whisk in remaining 1 tablespoon flour, and cook, stirring, 1 minute. Whisk in wine and boil 1 to 2 minutes. Add milk all at once and bring to a boil, whisking, until sauce is thick and smooth, 2 to 3 minutes. Stir in remaining Parmesan cheese. Set sauce aside.

5. Arrange half of sliced tomatoes in bottom of a lightly oiled 9 x 13-inch baking dish. Top with a layer of one-third of grilled eggplant, then with mushroom mixture. Add remaining tomato slices and half of remaining grilled eggplant. Spread ricotta mixture evenly over eggplant. Top with final layer of eggplant slices. Cover evenly with sauce. Cover tightly with foil.

6. Bake 15 minutes. Remove foil and bake 10 to 15 minutes longer, until bubbly and golden brown. Let stand 5 to 10 minutes before serving.

99   MACARONI MOUSSAKA

Prep: 35 minutes   Cook: 1 hour 5 minutes to 1 hour 17 minutes
Serves: 4

1 (5-ounce) package Cheddar
  macaroni and cheese
2 medium eggplants, peeled
⅓ cup olive oil
½ pound mushrooms, sliced

2 (14½-ounce) cans Italian-
  style stewed tomatoes
½ cup dry red wine
1 cup shredded Cheddar
  cheese

1. Preheat broiler. In a large saucepan filled with lightly salted boiling water, cook macaroni according to package directions, about 9 minutes. Mix with sauce and seasonings and set aside.

2. Meanwhile, peel eggplants and cut in ¼-inch slices horizontally. Pat dry. Set slices in single layer on a baking sheet. With a pastry brush, paint each slice with olive oil. Broil as close to heat as possible until lightly browned, 2 to 3 minutes. Turn slices over, paint with oil, and broil until browned on second side, about 2 minutes. Set aside. Reduce oven temperature to 350°F.

3. In a large frying pan, heat 1 tablespoon olive oil over medium-high heat. Add mushrooms and cook until barely tender, 2 to 3 minutes. Mix mushrooms with cooked macaroni.

4. In a small bowl, mix 1 cup stewed tomatoes with red wine; set aside. Spoon ⅔ cup stewed tomatoes over bottom of a 10-inch square baking dish. Mix remaining tomatoes with cooked macaroni and mushrooms.

5. Place one-third of eggplant slices on bottom of baking dish. Cover with half of cooked macaroni mixture. Layer on half of remaining eggplant. Top with remaining macaroni. Cover with last layer of eggplant. Spoon reserved stewed tomatoes and wine over top. Sprinkle with grated Cheddar cheese. Cover tightly with foil.

6. Bake 50 minutes to 1 hour, until moussaka is bubbly.

100 GRANDMOTHER'S GNOCCHI

Prep: 20 minutes   Cook: 26 to 35 minutes   Serves: 2

My grandmother was born in the Champagne region of France, and these feathery gnocchi were one of her specialties. This light dumpling is made with cream puff dough rather than cornmeal. Serve as a first course or for a light dinner, with a green salad.

1½ sticks (6 ounces) butter	1½ cups milk
½ teaspoon salt	½ cup half-and-half
¾ cup flour	½ teaspoon grated nutmeg
2 teaspoons Dijon mustard	¼ teaspoon pepper
¼ cup grated Parmesan cheese	1¼ cups shredded Gruyère
2 eggs	cheese

1. Preheat oven to 400°F. In a medium saucepan with a heavy bottom, melt 1 stick butter over medium heat. Add ½ cup water and salt and bring to a boil. Remove pan from heat and stir in ½ cup flour all at once, stirring with a wooden spoon until smooth. Stir in mustard and Parmesan cheese. Add eggs, one at a time, stirring briskly until dough separates from sides of pan in one lump, 2 to 3 minutes.

2. In a large saucepan, bring 2 quarts lightly salted water to a boil. Drop balls of dough by tablespoons into boiling water. Poach until gnocchi float to surface, 3 to 4 minutes. Inside should be soft but not runny. With a slotted spoon, transfer gnocchi to a colander to drain.

3. In a medium saucepan, melt remaining 4 tablespoons butter over medium heat. Whisk in remaining ¼ cup flour and cook, stirring, 1 to 2 minutes without allowing flour to color. Whisk in milk and half-and-half. Bring to a boil, whisking, until sauce thickens, 2 to 3 minutes. Add nutmeg and pepper, reduce heat to medium-low, and simmer 3 minutes. Stir in 1 cup cheese until melted.

4. Spoon a thin layer of sauce on bottom of a medium oval baking dish. Set gnocchi in a single layer in sauce. Cover with remaining sauce. Sprinkle remaining ¼ cup Gruyère cheese on top. Bake 15 to 20 minutes, until bubbly and golden brown.

101 KITTY'S EGGPLANT AND SPINACH LASAGNE

Prep: 30 minutes   Cook: 47 to 61 minutes   Serves: 6

½ cup bulgur wheat
1 large eggplant
1 teaspoon salt
¼ cup olive oil
2 garlic cloves, minced
1 teaspoon oregano
1 (10-ounce) package frozen chopped spinach, thawed
1 tablespoon butter

¼ pound mushrooms, sliced
2 tablespoons flour
1½ cups milk
½ teaspoon pepper
2 tablespoons grated Parmesan cheese
2 tablespoons prepared pesto
½ cup bread crumbs

1. In a medium saucepan, bring 1½ cups water to a boil. Add bulgur and reduce heat to medium-low. Cover and cook until bulgur is tender, 15 to 18 minutes. Remove from heat and fluff with a fork.

2. Preheat broiler. Slice unpeeled eggplant lengthwise into ¼-inch slices. Lay slices on a clean towel and sprinkle with salt. Let eggplant "sweat" for 5 minutes on each side. Pat dry and set in a single layer on a large ungreased baking sheet.

3. In a small bowl, mix olive oil, garlic, and oregano. Brush each eggplant slice on both sides with garlic oil. Broil until lightly browned, turning with tongs and watching carefully to avoid burning, 2 to 3 minutes on each side. Remove eggplant from oven. Reduce oven temperature to 350°F.

4. With your hands, press out all liquid from thawed spinach. Set in a colander.

5. In a medium saucepan, melt butter over medium heat. Add mushrooms and cook, stirring occasionally, until they turn limp, 2 to 3 minutes. Sprinkle with flour and cook, stirring, 1 to 2 minutes. Add milk and continue stirring until mixture boils and thickens somewhat, 3 to 4 minutes. Add spinach and cook until heated through, 2 to 3 minutes. Stir in pepper and Parmesan cheese.

6. To assemble lasagne, lightly oil a 9 x 13-inch baking dish. Arrange half of eggplant slices in one layer on bottom of dish. Spread cooked bulgur over eggplant. Cover with spinach and mushroom mixture. Top with remaining eggplant slices.

7. In a small bowl, mix pesto with bread crumbs. Sprinkle evenly over top of lasagne. Bake 20 to 25 minutes, until piping hot.

102   MUSHROOM GOUGÈRE RING

Prep: 20 minutes   Cook: 45 to 50 minutes
Stand: 15 minutes   Serves: 6

This festive puffed pastry ring is known in France as a *gougère*. Gougère fillings can vary from creamed mushrooms to scrambled eggs or steamed vegetables. This is a great brunch entree.

1½ sticks (6 ounces) butter	1½ teaspoons dried tarragon
1¾ cups plus 2 tablespoons flour	½ teaspoon grated nutmeg
3 eggs, lightly beaten	¾ teaspoon salt
1 pound mushrooms, sliced	¼ teaspoon pepper
1 cup heavy cream	2 cups shredded Swiss cheese

1. Preheat oven to 400°F. In a medium saucepan, bring 1 stick butter and 1 cup water to a boil. When butter is melted, remove from heat and, with a wooden spoon, stir in 1¾ cups flour all at once. Mix dough vigorously until it separates from sides of pan in a mass. Add eggs, one at a time, mixing dough until smooth and fairly stiff in between each addition.

2. Spoon batter evenly into a generously greased 6-cup ring mold. Bake 35 to 40 minutes, until gougère is golden and crusty. Let cool 15 minutes. Unmold carefully onto a serving platter. With a sharp knife, split ring horizontally into 2 halves.

3. Meanwhile, in a medium saucepan over medium heat, melt remaining 4 tablespoons butter. Add mushrooms and cook, stirring occasionally, until limp, 3 to 4 minutes. Add remaining 2 tablespoons flour and cook, stirring, 1 minute. Add cream all at once and cook, stirring continuously, until flour is absorbed, 3 to 4 minutes. Add tarragon, nutmeg, salt, pepper, and cheese. Continue cooking until cheese melts and mixture thickens, 2 to 3 minutes.

4. Spoon mushroom filling onto bottom half of gougère ring. Cover with top half. If cool, carefully return to baking sheet and heat through in oven for about 10 minutes. Serve hot.

103 TERIYAKI MUSHROOM-WALNUT LOAF
Prep: 10 minutes   Cook: 35 to 40 minutes   Serves: 4 to 6

4 eggs
1 cup small-curd
   cottage cheese
1¼ cups walnut pieces,
   coarsely ground
¼ pound mushrooms,
   chopped

1 cup cracker crumbs
1 medium onion, diced
2 tablespoons vegetable broth
   or reduced-sodium
   chicken broth
2 tablespoons teriyaki sauce
½ teaspoon salt

1. Preheat oven to 375°F. In a large bowl, beat eggs lightly. Add cottage cheese, ground walnuts, mushrooms, cracker crumbs, onion, broth, teriyaki sauce, and salt. Blend well.

2. Pack mixture into a nonstick 9 x 5 x 3-inch meatloaf pan. Bake 35 to 40 minutes, until a knife inserted in center of loaf comes out clean.

104 CORN FRITTERS WITH CREAMED SPINACH
Prep: 10 minutes   Cook: 8 to 11 minutes per batch   Serves: 4 to 6

2 cups packaged biscuit mix
2 cups buttermilk
1 egg, lightly beaten
1 teaspoon salt
½ teaspoon pepper
2 teaspoons dried basil
¼ cup grated Parmesan cheese
1 (15-ounce) can whole-kernel
   corn, drained

1 (10-ounce) package frozen
   spinach
3 tablespoons butter
2 tablespoons flour
½ cup milk
½ teaspoon grated nutmeg
2 tablespoons vegetable oil

1. Preheat oven to 200°F. Line a baking sheet with a double layer of paper towels. In a large bowl, combine biscuit mix, buttermilk, egg, ½ teaspoon salt, ¼ teaspoon pepper, basil, and Parmesan cheese. Beat until smooth. Stir in corn.

2. Cook spinach according to package directions; drain, rinse, and squeeze dry. In a medium saucepan, melt butter over medium heat. Sprinkle in flour and cook, stirring, 1 minute. Add milk. Bring to a boil, whisking, until sauce is thick, 1 to 2 minutes. Add spinach, nutmeg, and remaining salt and pepper. Simmer 2 minutes. Remove from heat and set aside.

3. On a griddle or in a large nonstick frying pan, heat 1 tablespoon oil over medium-high heat. Drop batter by ¼ cupfuls onto hot griddle. With a spatula, flatten to form fritters 3 inches in diameter. Cook in batches, turning once, until golden brown, 2 to 3 minutes on each side. Transfer fritters to baking sheet and keep warm in oven while cooking remaining batter. Add more oil when pan is dry.

4. Reheat spinach, if necessary. Serve fritters topped with creamed spinach.

105 MUSHROOM RAVIOLI DIVAN

Prep: 10 minutes   Cook: 25 to 27 minutes   Serves: 6

3 cups fresh broccoli florets
2 tablespoons olive oil
1 pound mushrooms, sliced
2 garlic cloves, minced
½ teaspoon salt
¼ teaspoon pepper

2 (9-ounce) packages fresh
  cheese-filled ravioli
1 cup milk
1 (12-ounce) container
  prepared Alfredo sauce
½ cup grated Romano cheese

1. Preheat oven to 375°F. In a large saucepan of boiling water, cook broccoli florets until just tender, 2 to 3 minutes. Drain and rinse under cold running water; drain well and coarsely chop. Place in a large bowl.

2. In a large frying pan, heat oil over medium-high heat. Add mushrooms and garlic and cook, stirring occasionally, until limp, 3 to 4 minutes. Season with salt and pepper. Add mushrooms and any liquid in pan to broccoli.

3. In a large pot of boiling salted water, cook ravioli according to package directions. Drain into a colander.

4. Place half of cooked ravioli on bottom of a lightly greased 7 x 11-inch baking dish. Top with all of broccoli-mushroom mixture. Cover with second layer of ravioli. Pour in milk. Spoon Alfredo sauce evenly over top. Sprinkle with grated cheese. Cover dish with aluminum foil.

5. Bake 15 minutes. Remove foil and bake until sauce is bubbly and top is brown, about 5 minutes longer.

106 FANCY POTATO MUSHROOM LOAF

*Prep: 10 minutes   Cook: 32 to 38 minutes   Chill: 2 hours
Serves: 6 to 8*

This garlic-scented potato loaf is deliciously simple and also very pretty to look at. Serve it at room temperature, as a first course or as an entree.

2½ pounds russet potatoes,
   quartered
¼ cup olive oil
¾ cup plain yogurt
½ teaspoon salt
½ teaspoon pepper
½ cup frozen green peas,
   thawed
1 cup sour cream

½ cup mayonnaise
1 (1.4-ounce) envelope
  fines herbes soup mix
2 tablespoons butter
¼ pound mushrooms,
  chopped
2 teaspoons dried tarragon
¼ cup sliced olives

1. In a large saucepan of lightly salted boiling water, cook potatoes until tender, 30 to 35 minutes. Let potatoes cool. Peel and transfer to a large bowl. Mash potatoes, adding olive oil, ¼ cup yogurt, salt, and pepper. Stir in peas.

2. Meanwhile, in a medium bowl, mix sour cream, remaining ½ cup of yogurt, mayonnaise, and soup mix. Cover and refrigerate.

3. In a medium frying pan, melt butter over medium heat. Add mushrooms and cook, stirring, until barely tender, 2 to 3 minutes. Stir in tarragon. Remove from heat.

4. Set a 12 x 8-inch layer of plastic wrap on a flat surface. With a spatula, spread mashed potato mixture evenly over wrap. Spread mushrooms in center. Roll up potato loaf from a long side, jelly-roll style, squaring off edges. Gently lift potato roll onto serving platter. Discard plastic wrap.

5. Frost loaf with sour cream mixture. Decorate with sliced olives. Refrigerate until chilled, 2 hours or overnight.

---

107 POTATO PANCAKES
Prep: 10 minutes   Cook: 9 to 11 minutes per batch   Serves: 4

I prefer to use the large hole of a hand grater rather than a food processor to shred the potatoes and grate the onion. This gives the potato pancakes, or *latkes*, a slightly firmer texture. Potato pancakes are wonderful for brunch, lunch, or a light supper.

4 medium russet potatoes	**2 tablespoons chopped**
(about 2½ pounds)	**parsley**
2 eggs	**1 medium onion, grated**
2 tablespoons flour	**⅓ cup vegetable oil**
½ teaspoon baking powder	**2 cups applesauce**
½ teaspoon salt	**1 teaspoon cinnamon**
¼ teaspoon pepper	**1 cup sour cream or yogurt**

1. Preheat oven to 200°F. Peel potatoes and grate on large holes of a hand grater or with shredding disk of a food processor. Place shredded potatoes in a colander to drain.

2. In a large bowl, beat eggs and whisk in flour, baking powder, salt, pepper, and parsley. Stir in potatoes and onion.

3. In a large frying pan, heat half of oil until hot but not smoking. Drop potato mixture into pan 2 tablespoonfuls at a time. With a spatula, flatten each pancake to 3 inches in diameter. Fry, turning once, until golden, 3 to 4 minutes on each side. With spatula, transfer latkes to a baking sheet lined with a double layer of paper towels to drain. Keep warm in oven. Fry remaining pancakes in batches, adding more oil as needed.

4. Meanwhile, in a medium saucepan, heat applesauce with cinnamon over medium heat until warm, about 3 minutes. Serve latkes hot, with applesauce and sour cream on the side.

108   HASH-BROWN CASSEROLE
Prep: 10 minutes   Cook: 40 to 45 minutes   Serves: 4 to 6

This hearty casserole tastes even better the next day—assuming you have any leftovers.

2 (16-ounce) packages frozen
   hash-brown potatoes,
   slightly thawed
1 small onion, chopped
6 tablespoons butter, melted
½ teaspoon pepper
1 (10¾-ounce) can cream of
   mushroom soup
2 tablespoons soy sauce or
   tamari

1 (2-ounce) jar diced red
   pimientos, drained
1 cup shredded Cheddar
   cheese
1 cup sour cream
1 cup plain yogurt
2 cups crushed cornflakes

1. Preheat oven to 350°F. In a lightly oiled 2-quart baking pan, combine potatoes, onion, 4 tablespoons butter, pepper, mushroom soup, soy sauce, pimientos, cheese, sour cream, and yogurt. Mix well.

2. In a bowl, mix cornflakes with remaining 2 tablespoons butter. Spread evenly over potatoes.

3. Bake 40 to 45 minutes, until top is nicely browned.

109   MEATLESS SHEPHERD'S PIE
*Prep: 30 minutes   Cook: 1 hour 5 minutes to 1 hour 17 minutes
Serves: 6 to 8*

2 pounds boiling potatoes,
   peeled and cut into
   1-inch chunks
4 tablespoons butter
1 cup plain yogurt
1 teaspoon paprika
½ teaspoon salt
2 tablespoons olive oil
1 small onion, chopped
1 cup cut-up fresh green beans
2 medium carrots, peeled
   and sliced

1 cup vegetable broth or
   reduced-sodium
   chicken broth
1 cup frozen peas, thawed
1 cup corn kernels
1 garlic clove, minced
1 (1.4-ounce) envelope
   vegetable soup mix
1 cup bread crumbs

1. Preheat oven to 375°F. In a large saucepan filled with boiling water, cook potatoes until tender, 20 to 25 minutes. Drain well. In a medium bowl, mash potatoes with butter, yogurt, paprika, and salt.

2. In a large frying pan, heat oil over medium heat. Add onion and cook, stirring occasionally, until golden, 4 to 5 minutes. Add beans, carrots, and broth. Cover and cook until carrots are tender, 6 to 7 minutes. Add peas, corn, garlic, and dry soup mix. Stir to blend and remove from heat.

3. Pour vegetable mixture into a 7 x 11-inch baking dish. With a spatula, spread mashed potatoes evenly over top. Sprinkle bread crumbs over potatoes.

4. Bake 35 to 40 minutes, until casserole is bubbling and crumbs turn nice and brown. Serve hot.

110 LAYERED TWO-POTATO CAKE

Prep: 10 minutes   Cook: 33 to 43 minutes   Serves: 4

2 medium sweet potatoes, peeled and shredded
2 large baking potatoes, peeled and shredded
2 tablespoons flour
2 eggs
1 teaspoon salt

½ teaspoon pepper
3 tablespoons olive oil
¼ cup chopped onion
2 crookneck or zucchini squash, thinly sliced
¼ teaspoon dried basil
1 cup prepared Mexican salsa

1. Preheat oven to 350°F. Place sweet potato and baking potato in separate bowls. To each bowl add 1 tablespoon flour, 1 egg, ½ teaspoon salt, and ¼ teaspoon pepper. Stir both mixtures well and set aside.

2. In a large nonstick frying pan, heat 1 tablespoon olive oil. Add onion and cook over medium heat, stirring occasionally, until golden, 4 to 5 minutes. Add sliced squash, cover, and cook until tender, 5 to 6 minutes. Season with basil. Transfer to a bowl and set aside.

3. In same pan, heat 1 tablespoon olive oil. With a spatula, spread sweet potato mixture evenly in pan. Cook over medium heat until bottom turns crisp and brown, 7 to 10 minutes. Remove pan from heat and slide potato cake, raw side up, onto a large plate. Cover with inverted frying pan and carefully flip cake back into pan. Cook until bottom turns brown, 7 to 10 minutes. Slide onto a large cookie sheet. Repeat process with baking potato mixture to make a second cake.

4. Spread sweet potato cake evenly with cooked squash. Top with baking potato cake.

5. Bake 10 to 12 minutes, until hot. Let stand 10 minutes before cutting. Serve with Mexican salsa on the side.

111　POTATOES ITALIANO BAKE

Prep: 15 minutes　Cook: 30 to 38 minutes　Serves: 4 to 6

1 (6-ounce) jar marinated artichoke hearts	1 tablespoon diced sun-dried tomatoes
1 medium onion, coarsely chopped	½ teaspoon salt
1 (24-ounce) package frozen potatoes O'Brien with onion and peppers, thawed	⅛ teaspoon cayenne
	2 cups shredded mozzarella cheese
	1 egg, lightly beaten

1. Preheat oven to 350°F. Drain artichoke hearts, reserving marinade. Coarsely dice artichokes.

2. In a large frying pan, heat artichoke marinade over medium heat. Add onion and cook, stirring occasionally, until softened, 2 to 3 minutes. Stir in potatoes, sun-dried tomatoes, and diced artichoke hearts. Remove from heat and let cool 5 minutes. Stir in salt, cayenne, mozzarella, and egg. Scrape potato mixture into a generously greased shallow 2-quart baking dish. Cover tightly with foil.

3. Bake 20 to 25 minutes, until potatoes are tender and casserole is piping hot. Remove foil and bake until lightly browned on top, 8 to 10 minutes. Let stand 5 minutes before serving.

112　PAN-FRIED CHEESE CUTLETS

Prep: 10 minutes　Cook: 4 to 6 minutes　Serves: 4

These crusty cheese "scaloppini" need be accompanied by only a green salad or a bowl of soup for a complete meal. This amount of cheese yields about 2 slices per person.

½ pound Gruyère or Swiss cheese, chilled	1 egg, lightly beaten
2 tablespoons Dijon mustard	½ cup bread crumbs
	4 tablespoons butter

1. Cut cheese into rectangular 4½ x 1 x ⅜-inch slices. With a knife, generously lather with mustard on both sides.

2. Dip each cheese slice in beaten egg. Pat each slice carefully in bread crumbs on both sides. Bread crumbs must cover whole slice or cheese will lose shape when cooked.

3. In a large frying pan, melt butter over medium-low heat. Add cutlets and cook, turning once, until bread crumb crust is golden, 30 to 45 seconds on each side. Serve immediately.

113   QUICK BROWN RICE PAELLA
Prep: 5 minutes   Cook: 31 to 39 minutes   Serves: 4

This quick and flavorful paella is as easy to make as 1-2-3. Cook it in a skillet handsome enough to go from stovetop to table, and you have a lovely party dish. To dress up the paella, substitute robust-flavored shiitake mushrooms for the button mushrooms. Cook the vegetables in the same pan to allow all the juices to mingle.

⅓ cup olive oil
2 medium onions, finely diced
4 garlic cloves, minced
1 (10-ounce) package frozen peas and carrots, thawed
1½ cups instant brown rice
1 (14½-ounce) can vegetable broth or reduced-sodium chicken broth
4 saffron threads

2 teaspoons turmeric
1 large red bell pepper, cut into ¼-inch strips
½ pound mushrooms, sliced
2 medium zucchini, cleaned
1 pound asparagus spears, trimmed
1 (15-ounce) can artichoke quarters, drained
½ teaspoon pepper

1. In a large flameproof casserole, heat 2 tablespoons olive oil over medium-high heat. Add onions and cook, stirring occasionally, until golden, 4 to 5 minutes. Stir in 2 minced garlic cloves and peas and carrots. Cook 2 minutes. Stir in rice, 1¾ cups broth, saffron, and turmeric. Bring to a simmer, cover, and reduce heat to medium-low. Cook until rice is tender, 10 minutes. Remove from heat and set aside, covered, to keep warm.

2. Meanwhile, in a large frying pan, heat 2 tablespoons olive oil and 2 minced garlic cloves over medium heat. Add red pepper strips and cook, stirring occasionally, until softened, 3 to 5 minutes. With a slotted spoon, transfer pepper strips to a plate. In the same pan, cook mushrooms, stirring gently until they have given up their juices, 3 to 4 minutes. With a slotted spoon, transfer mushrooms to another plate.

3. Trim zucchini and cut in half crosswise. Then cut lengthwise into slices ¼ inch thick. Add remaining olive oil to pan and heat over medium-high heat. Cook zucchini, stirring occasionally, until lightly browned, 4 to 5 minutes. With a slotted spoon transfer cooked zucchini to a plate. In same pan, add remaining ¼ cup broth and steam asparagus, covered, until crisp-tender, 3 to 5 minutes. Transfer to a small plate. In the same pan, cook artichoke hearts, stirring occasionally, until heated through, 2 to 3 minutes. Set aside.

4. Keep rice in cooking vessel. Arrange cooked vegetables attractively on top. Spoon any vegetable juices over. Sprinkle with pepper. Serve immediately.

114 ROASTED VEGETABLES WITH TERIYAKI VINAIGRETTE

Prep: 20 minutes   Stand: 20 minutes   Cook: 40 to 45 minutes
Serves: 4

This is a stunning presentation for vegetable lovers. If you are serving it as a main course, be sure you add some protein from another source.

8 small new potatoes, scrubbed and halved	4 medium zucchini, scrubbed and halved
1 pound baby carrots, scrubbed	8 medium button mushroom caps, wiped clean
1 medium eggplant, peeled and cut into chunks	4 medium tomatoes, quartered
1 red bell pepper, seeded and quartered	½ cup extra-virgin olive oil
1 green bell pepper, seeded and quartered	1½ teaspoons dried tarragon, rosemary, or oregano
2 medium onions, peeled and quartered	Teriyaki Vinaigrette (recipe follows)

1. In a large bowl, mix potatoes, carrots, eggplant, peppers, onions, zucchini, mushrooms, and tomatoes. Add olive oil and tarragon. Set aside to marinate 20 minutes, tossing once or twice. Meanwhile, preheat oven to 425°F.

2. Remove marinated vegetables from oil and place in single layer on a foil-lined baking sheet. Bake until potatoes and carrots are tender, 40 to 45 minutes. Check vegetables several times during cooking. With tongs, remove faster-cooking vegetables such as tomatoes, mushrooms, zucchini, and eggplant. Keep warm.

3. To serve, arrange roasted vegetables on a serving platter. Pass vinaigrette on the side.

TERIYAKI VINAIGRETTE

Prep: 5 minutes   Cook: none   Makes: ½ cup

Bottled teriyaki sauce, available in the sauces and dressings section of supermarkets, is the surprise ingredient in this flavor-packed vinaigrette. It is my family's favorite salad dressing, and it makes a great dipping sauce.

1 teaspoon Dijon mustard	¼ cup olive oil
2 tablespoons rice vinegar	2 tablespoons teriyaki sauce
⅛ teaspoon freshly ground pepper	1 garlic clove, minced
	1 tablespoon chopped parsley

In a small bowl, whisk together mustard, vinegar, and pepper until smooth. Add 1 tablespoon water, whisking continuously until blended. Gradually beat in olive oil, whisking until dressing is almost consistency of mayonnaise, 1 to 2 minutes. Whisk in teriyaki sauce until well blended. Stir in garlic and parsley. Cover and refrigerate until ready to use.

115 VEGETABLE TEMPURA
Prep: 30 minutes   Cook: 2 to 3 minutes per batch   Serves: 4

You can adjust the quantities of this classic Japanese specialty to suit any number of people. Tempura batter mix is also found in the Asian food section of most supermarkets. If you prefer to use it for convenience, follow package directions. This is traditionally accompanied by a bowl of cooked white rice.

1 egg
½ cup ice water
½ cup flour
1 teaspoon baking soda
2 teaspoons minced parsley
½ teaspoon salt
12 small button mushroom caps, wiped clean
1 green bell pepper, cut into ½-inch strips
12 asparagus spears, trimmed and cut into 3-inch pieces
1 sweet potato, peeled and sliced ¼ inch thick
2 medium carrots, halved and quartered lengthwise

1 medium zucchini, halved crosswise and quartered lengthwise
1 square of firm tofu, cut into ½ x ¼ x 2-inch slices
Vegetable oil, for deep-frying
3 tablespoons soy sauce or tamari
2 tablespoons sake or rice wine
2 teaspoons rice vinegar
2 garlic cloves, minced
½ teaspoon minced ginger
2 teaspoons brown sugar

1. Preheat oven to 200°F. Line a baking sheet with a double layer of paper towels. In a medium bowl, whisk together egg, ice water, flour, baking soda, parsley, and salt. Let stand 10 minutes.

2. In a deep-fat fryer or a deep saucepan, heat 3 inches of vegetable oil until it registers 375°F on a deep-fat thermometer. In batches, with a fork or chopsticks, dip each vegetable and tofu in batter. Deep-fry until golden, 2 to 3 minutes. Don't fry more than 6 pieces at a time, or the temperature will drop. With a slotted spoon, transfer cooked vegetables to baking sheet to drain. Keep warm in oven while cooking remaining batches.

3. In a small bowl, mix soy sauce, sake, vinegar, garlic, ginger, and brown sugar. Serve tempura vegetables with dipping sauce on the side.

116 ITALIAN TOMATO PIE WITH POTATO CRUST

Prep: 10 minutes   Cook: 43 to 51 minutes   Serves: 4 to 6

¼ cup olive oil
3 medium russet potatoes, peeled and thinly sliced
½ teaspoon salt
¼ teaspoon pepper
1 small onion, chopped
2 garlic cloves, minced

½ green bell pepper, finely diced
3 small tomatoes, diced
1 cup prepared spaghetti sauce
3 eggs, lightly beaten
1 cup frozen peas

1. Preheat oven to 375°F. In a large frying pan, heat 2½ tablespoons olive oil over medium-high heat. Cook potatoes, stirring often, until potatoes turn golden, 8 to 10 minutes. Line bottom and sides of a 10-inch pie plate with potato slices. Season with salt and pepper.

2. In same frying pan, heat remaining 1½ tablespoons oil. Add onion, garlic, and bell pepper and cook over medium heat until onion is softened, 2 to 3 minutes. Add diced tomatoes and cook until mixture thickens slightly, about 3 minutes. Stir in spaghetti sauce and remove from heat.

3. Whisk beaten eggs into tomato sauce. Stir in peas. Pour mixture into prepared potato crust.

4. Bake 30 to 35 minutes, until filling is set. Let stand 10 minutes before cutting into wedges. Serve hot or at room temperature.

117 EAST-WEST MEATLESS STROGANOFF

Prep: 15 minutes   Cook: 17 to 18 minutes   Makes: about 24

Larger-sized nut balls are well suited to dinner fare, served over rice or egg noodles. Smaller ones can be passed with toothpicks as an appetizer.

2 tablespoons vegetable oil
½ pound mushrooms, sliced
2 garlic cloves, minced
½ cup dry sherry
1 cup vegetable broth or reduced-sodium chicken broth
1 (10-ounce) can cream of mushroom soup
4 ounces commercial stuffing mix

1¼ cups walnut pieces
2 eggs
2 tablespoons mayonnaise
1 tablespoon soy sauce or tamari
1 tablespoon chopped parsley
1 cup sour cream
1 teaspoon prepared white horseradish

1. In a large saucepan, heat oil over medium heat. Add mushrooms and garlic and cook, stirring occasionally, until mushrooms turn limp, 2 to 3 minutes. Reduce heat to medium-low and add sherry, broth, and mushroom soup. Cover and simmer 5 minutes.

2. Meanwhile, in a food processor, combine stuffing mix and walnuts. Process, pulsing machine quickly on and off, until nuts are ground. Do not overprocess.

3. In a medium bowl, beat eggs lightly. Add ground walnut mixture, mayonnaise, soy sauce, and parsley and blend well. With your hands, fashion nut balls about 1 inch in diameter and drop into simmering mushroom sauce until all mix is used. Cover and simmer 10 minutes.

4. Before serving, stir sour cream and horseradish into sauce. Heat through but do not boil.

---

118   WALNUT DUMPLINGS IN LEMON SAUCE
Prep: 20 minutes   Cook: 15 to 19 minutes   Serves: 4

These dumplings in their lemony sauce can be used as a topping for cooked rice or couscous.

1 medium onion, coarsely chopped	2 teaspoons ground cumin
12 sprigs of parsley plus 2 tablespoons chopped	½ teaspoon salt
4 eggs	3 cups vegetable broth or reduced-sodium chicken broth
1 cup walnut pieces	1 teaspoon grated lemon zest
1 cup matzoh meal or crushed reduced-sodium saltine crackers	¼ cup lemon juice
2 tablespoons butter, melted	2 cups frozen petite peas, thawed

1. Preheat oven to 250°F. In a blender or food processor, place onion, parsley sprigs, 2 eggs, and walnut pieces. Process until fairly smooth. Transfer to a bowl and mix in matzoh meal and melted butter. Season with cumin and salt.

2. In a medium saucepan, bring broth and lemon zest to a simmer. Reduce heat to medium-low. Drop walnut mixture by tablespoons into simmering broth. Cook until dumplings float to top, 8 to 10 minutes. With a slotted spoon, transfer to a 2-quart ovenproof serving dish and keep warm in oven.

3. Strain broth through a fine sieve into a medium bowl and return to pan. In a small bowl, beat remaining 2 eggs with lemon juice until frothy. Gradually whisk ½ cup hot broth into beaten eggs.

4. Stir lemon mixture into broth in pan and cook over low heat, whisking, until sauce turns consistency of a light custard, 5 to 6 minutes. Do not boil or mixture will curdle. Stir in peas and heat through, 2 to 3 minutes. Pour lemon sauce over walnut dumplings. Sprinkle with chopped parsley and serve.

119   NO-MEAT LOAF

Prep: 15 minutes   Cook: 45 to 50 minutes
Stand: 5 minutes   Serves: 4 to 6

1 tablespoon cornmeal	¾ cup seasoned bread crumbs
2 medium onions, finely diced	2 eggs, lightly beaten
2 celery ribs, chopped	2 tablespoons mustard
2 medium carrots, shredded	¼ teaspoon pepper
½ green bell pepper, finely diced	½ cup plain yogurt
1 cup walnut pieces, chopped	2 garlic cloves, minced
	¼ cup chopped parsley

1. Preheat oven to 350°F. Lightly oil a 9 x 5 x 3-inch loaf pan. Sprinkle with cornmeal to coat lightly.

2. In a large bowl, combine onions, celery, carrots, bell pepper, walnuts, bread crumbs, eggs, mustard, pepper, yogurt, garlic, and parsley. Mix well. Fill loaf pan with mixture.

3. Bake 45 to 50 minutes, until top is golden brown. Let cool in pan for 5 minutes. Invert onto a platter and serve hot or cold.

120   VEGETABLE TOSTADAS

Prep: 15 minutes   Cook: 9 to 13 minutes   Serves: 6

2 tablespoons olive oil	2 tablespoons vegetable oil
1 large onion, finely sliced	6 (7-inch) corn tortillas
1 large zucchini, shredded	2 cups shredded iceberg lettuce
1 large carrot, shredded	1 large tomato, diced
1 green bell pepper, seeded and finely diced	1 avocado, diced
1 red bell pepper, seeded and finely diced	Sour cream, shredded Monterey Jack cheese, and salsa
1 envelope taco seasoning mix	
1 (16-ounce) can refried beans	

1. In a large pan, heat olive oil over medium heat. Add onion and cook, stirring occasionally, until softened, 2 to 3 minutes. Add zucchini, carrot, green and red peppers, and taco seasonings. Stir to blend. Cover and cook until vegetables are just tender, 3 minutes.

2. In a small saucepan, heat refried beans over low heat, stirring until hot, 2 to 3 minutes.

3. In a medium pan, heat vegetable oil. Quickly fry tortillas one at a time, turning, until crisp, 10 to 20 seconds on each side. With tongs, transfer tortillas to paper towels to drain.

4. To assemble tostadas, spread refried beans over each tortilla. Cover with cooked zucchini mixture. Top with shredded lettuce, diced tomato, and diced avocado. Serve with sour cream, shredded cheese, and salsa on the side.

---

121 BAKED KEFTA WITH EGGS IN CUMIN TOMATO SAUCE

Prep: 20 minutes   Cook: 26 to 30 minutes   Serves: 4 to 6

This traditional Moroccan recipe has been adapted to use "no-meat" balls made of ground walnuts. You can serve this dish with lots of crusty bread to mop up the sauce, or else use it as a topping for cooked rice.

1 **(28-ounce) can tomato sauce**	¼ **teaspoon pepper**
1 **cup chopped cilantro**	¼ **cup chopped parsley**
2 **medium onions, chopped**	6 **to 8 eggs**
1 **tablespoon tomato paste**	1 **cup walnut pieces**
1 **teaspoon cinnamon**	1 **cup bread crumbs**
1 **teaspoon sugar**	2 **tablespoons olive oil**
½ **teaspoon salt**	2 **teaspoons ground cumin**

1. Preheat oven to 375°F. In a large nonreactive saucepan, combine tomato sauce, cilantro, half of onion, tomato paste, cinnamon, sugar, ¼ teaspoon salt, and pepper. Cover and cook over medium heat 10 minutes.

2. Meanwhile, in a blender or food processor, place remaining onion, parsley, 2 eggs, and walnut pieces. Process until smooth. Transfer to a bowl and stir in bread crumbs, olive oil, cumin, and remaining ¼ teaspoon salt.

3. Uncover tomato sauce and adjust heat to a simmer. Drop walnut mixture by tablespoons into sauce. Simmer until fairly firm, 8 to 10 minutes. Remove from heat and transfer sauce and nut balls to a shallow 2-quart baking dish. Carefully break remaining eggs atop nut balls.

4. Bake until eggs reach desired doneness, 8 to 10 minutes. Serve immediately.

122 LAYERED ENCHILADAS WITH GREEN CHILE SAUCE

Prep: 30 minutes   Cook: 12 to 18 minutes   Serves: 4

1 (15-ounce) can black beans,
    liquid reserved
2 medium onions, chopped
½ cup chopped parsley
¼ cup chopped cilantro
1 tablespoon chili powder
2 garlic cloves, minced
1 (28-ounce) can green
    enchilada sauce

12 (7-inch) corn tortillas
⅔ cup sliced black olives
2 cups shredded Monterey
    Jack cheese
2 cups shredded iceberg
    lettuce
1 cup sour cream

1. Preheat oven to 375°F. In a medium bowl, coarsely mash beans and their liquid with a fork. Stir in onions, parsley, cilantro, chili powder, and garlic.

2. In a large frying pan, heat 1 cup enchilada sauce over medium heat until very hot but not boiling, 2 to 3 minutes. Remove from heat.

3. With tongs, dip each tortilla in hot sauce. Let excess drip back into pan. Set 4 tortillas in a single layer on a large foil-lined baking sheet. Spread equal amounts of bean mixture over tortillas. Top with a second layer of dipped tortillas. Spread remaining beans over second stack. Cover with olives. Dip last 4 tortillas and use as final layer. Spoon some enchilada sauce over each stack. Sprinkle cheese on top.

4. Bake 10 to 15 minutes, until cheese melts. Line 4 large dinner plates with shredded iceberg lettuce. With 2 spatulas, carefully transfer each stack to an individual plate. Serve with remaining enchilada sauce and sour cream on the side.

Chapter 5

Pasta Perfect

At times it seems Italian has become America's second language in culinary matters. Once upon a time, the words *spaghetti* or *noodles* filled the bill. These days, *pasta* is the byword. Variations on the theme are seemingly endless. We have ravioli with a variety of stuffings, dainty little tortellini, delicate cannelloni, farfalle (bow ties), fettuccine, and linguine in a rainbow of colors, to name just a few. To those, add a new vocabulary of Asian-style noodles, from mung bean noodles and Chinese vermicelli to Japanese soba noodles. Whatever their shape or ethnic origins, all those noodles are firmly entrenched in America's diet.

Italian pasta requires a pot large enough to cook in so it doesn't get overcrowded and stick together. Each pound of dry pasta requires 4 to 6 quarts of lightly salted boiling water. Add the pasta, stir until it separates, and let the water return to a rolling boil. (When purchasing fresh pasta, however, follow package directions, for the cooking time will be reduced.) Then let it cook until it reaches the *al dente* stage, when it is tender but still feels slightly firm to the bite. There is no need to rinse cooked pasta under cold running water unless you are preparing a cold pasta salad. Toss the drained pasta with butter, pesto, or olive oil. Add your favorite topping, and presto—dinner is served.

Many pasta specialties qualify as meals-in-a-dish, and for that reason they are easily taken to picnics or potlucks. Such is the case with Butterfly Noodle Pie, Mushroom Tetrazzola with its pungent cheese sauce, as well as Cool California Fettuccine Toss. Easy Overnight Lasagne, chock-full of fresh vegetables, is conveniently assembled the night before. Among other Italian-influenced pasta dishes, this chapter features Pasta e Fagioli with Fresh Sorrel, my neighbor Ed's Spinach Fettuccine with its dynamite Cream Cheese Pesto, and my friend Brenda's Asparagus and Olive Linguine. For an elegant twist, try Egg Noodles with Artichoke Hearts in Whiskey Saffron Sauce.

Unlike their Italian cousins, translucent mung bean noodles (sometimes called Chinese vermicelli or bean threads) simply require soaking in warm water for 30 minutes and then draining before proceeding with the recipe. My friend Jan hails from Singapore, and her Chinese Vermicelli is one of her favorite family meals. One of the most popular appetizers at our local Chinese restaurant is a dish of cold sesame noodles. Here, I offer you an adaptation of Cold Szechuan Sesame Noodles, made with Japanese soba (buckwheat) noodles. The chapter also includes Noodle Kugel Hawaiian and Spaghetti and No-Meat Balls—just for old time's sake.

---

123   CANNELLONI CHINOISE
Prep: 20 minutes   Cook: 34 to 44 minutes   Serves: 6

Using Chinese egg roll wrappers instead of the traditional pasta squares makes it a cinch to prepare this Italian delicacy.

1 **stick (4 ounces) butter**	¼ **teaspoon pepper**
2 **pounds mushrooms, sliced**	½ **teaspoon grated nutmeg**
1 **small onion, chopped**	1½ **cups shredded Monterey**
2 **tablespoons flour**	**Jack cheese**
1 **cup milk**	1 **(16-ounce) package Chinese**
1 **teaspoon dried dill**	**egg roll wrappers**
½ **teaspoon salt**	¼ **cup grated Parmesan cheese**

1. Preheat oven to 375°F. In a large frying pan, melt 2 tablespoons butter over medium heat. Add mushrooms and onion and cook, stirring occasionally, until mushrooms give up some of their liquid, 4 to 5 minutes. Drain, reserving cooking liquid. Set aside.

2. In a large saucepan, melt remaining butter over medium heat. Whisk in flour and cook until flour turns golden, 1 minute. Whisk in reserved mushroom cooking liquid. Cook, stirring, until liquid is absorbed, 1 to 2 minutes. Whisk in milk all at once and continue stirring until thick and smooth, 4 to 5 minutes. Add dill, salt, pepper, nutmeg, and Monterey Jack cheese. Cook, stirring, until cheese melts, 2 to 3 minutes. Stir in cooked mushrooms. Set aside.

3. Unwrap egg roll skins. Spread a thin layer of mushroom filling in bottom of a lightly oiled 9 × 13-inch baking dish.

4. Place 3 tablespoons mushroom filling down center of an egg roll skin. Roll up and transfer to baking dish. Repeat procedure with remaining wrappers. This amount should yield enough filling for 14 cannelloni.

5. Top dish with any remaining filling. Sprinkle with Parmesan cheese.

6. Bake until bubbly, 20 to 25 minutes. Turn oven on to broil. Brown top, watching carefully to avoid burning, 2 to 3 minutes. Serve hot.

124 BOW TIES WITH CHEESY PATTYPANS
Prep: 10 minutes   Cook: 26 to 35 minutes   Serves: 4

I am partial to the sweet-tasting flesh of the delicate pattypan squash, known in some parts as "scaloppini." This is a delicious, simple topping for pasta or rice.

2 tablespoons olive oil	1 teaspoon sugar
1 pound small pattypan squash, cleaned and sliced	½ teaspoon salt
	12 ounces bow tie pasta
	2 tablespoons butter
1 cup stewed tomatoes	½ teaspoon dried oregano
2 garlic cloves, minced	1 cup shredded provolone cheese
1 teaspoon dried rosemary	

1. In a large frying pan, heat oil. Add squash and cook over medium heat, stirring occasionally, until nicely browned, 8 to 10 minutes. Add tomatoes, garlic, rosemary, sugar, and salt. Cover and cook over medium-low heat until sauce thickens somewhat, 10 to 15 minutes.

2. Meanwhile, in a large pan filled with lightly salted boiling water, cook pasta until tender but still firm, 8 to 10 minutes; drain. Transfer to a serving bowl and toss with butter.

3. Toss squash with hot pasta, oregano, and cheese. Serve hot.

125 EGG NOODLES WITH ARTICHOKE HEARTS IN WHISKEY SAFFRON SAUCE
Prep: 5 minutes   Cook: 19 to 24 minutes   Serves: 4

6 tablespoons butter	6 saffron threads
1 garlic clove, minced	½ teaspoon salt
1 (14-ounce) can artichoke quarters, drained	⅛ teaspoon pepper
	⅛ teaspoon grated nutmeg
1 tablespoon flour	12 ounces wide egg noodles
¼ cup whiskey	1 cup grated Romano cheese
1½ cups half-and-half	

1. In a medium frying pan, melt 4 tablespoons of butter over medium heat. Add garlic and artichoke pieces and cook, stirring occasionally, until garlic is soft, 2 to 3 minutes. Stir in flour and add whiskey. Cook, stirring, until steam evaporates, 2 to 3 minutes. Whisk in half-and-half. Add saffron, salt, pepper, and nutmeg. Bring to a boil, whisking, until thick and smooth, 2 to 3 minutes. Reduce heat to low and simmer 5 minutes longer.

2. Meanwhile, in a large saucepan filled with lightly salted boiling water, cook egg noodles until tender but still firm, 8 to 10 minutes. Drain well. Toss with 2 tablespoons butter and transfer to a serving platter.

3. Spoon sauce over cooked noodles. Serve with Romano cheese on the side.

126   BROCCOLI RABE WITH BOW TIES

Prep: 5 minutes   Cook: 15 to 20 minutes   Serves: 4

Broccoli rabe, also called rapini, is a variety of flowering broccoli available in Italian markets and many supermarkets. Its unusual mustardy taste is ideally suited to pasta dishes.

1 **pound bow tie pasta**	⅓ **cup dry white wine**
1 **tablespoon butter**	½ **cup heavy cream**
2 **tablespoons olive oil**	½ **teaspoon salt**
2 **garlic cloves, thinly sliced**	¼ **teaspoon pepper**
1 **pound broccoli rabe, cut**	¼ **cup grated Parmesan cheese**
into 2-inch pieces	

1. In a large saucepan filled with lightly salted boiling water, cook bow ties until tender but still firm, 8 to 10 minutes. Drain. Transfer to a serving bowl and toss with butter.

2. Meanwhile, in a large frying pan, heat oil and cook garlic slices over medium heat until just golden, 2 minutes; do not burn, or sauce will be bitter.

3. Add broccoli rabe and cook, stirring often, until wilted, 2 to 3 minutes. Add wine and cook, stirring, until liquid evaporates, 1 to 2 minutes. Add cream and season with salt and pepper. Cook until heated through, 2 to 3 minutes.

4. In a large bowl, toss the sauce with cooked bow ties and Parmesan cheese. Serve hot.

127   BUTTERFLY NOODLE PIE

Prep: 25 minutes   Cook: 59 minutes to 1 hour 10 minutes
Stand: 15 minutes   Serves: 8 to 10

This elegant farfalle ("butterfly" in Italian) pie uses the pretty noodles we know as bow ties. It is easier to cut and unmold if made a day ahead.

1 **pound bow tie pasta**	½ **cup grated Parmesan cheese**
3 **tablespoons pesto**	1 **teaspoon salt**
1 **stick (4 ounces) butter**	½ **teaspoon pepper**
½ **cup flour**	1 **cup frozen baby peas,**
¾ **cup dry white wine**	**thawed**
2 **cups milk**	2 **tablespoons imitation**
1 **cup half-and-half**	**bacon bits**
2 **tablespoons minced onion**	
3 **cups shredded Jarlsberg**	
cheese	

1. Preheat oven to 350°F. In a large pot filled with lightly salted boiling water, cook bow ties 10 to 12 minutes; drain. Rinse under cold running water and drain again. Transfer to a large bowl and toss with pesto.

2. In a large saucepan, melt butter over medium heat. Add flour and cook, stirring, 1 to 2 minutes. Whisk in wine and cook, stirring, until wine is absorbed, 2 to 3 minutes. Whisk in milk all at once and continue whisking until sauce is thick and smooth, 4 to 5 minutes. Add half-and-half, onion, grated cheeses, salt, pepper, and peas. Cook, stirring, until cheeses melt, 2 to 3 minutes. Remove from heat.

3. Spoon half of pasta over bottom of a lightly greased 9-inch springform pan. Cover with half of cheese sauce. Sprinkle 1 tablespoon bacon bits over sauce. Top with remaining pasta. Spread on remaining sauce and sprinkle remaining bacon bits over all.

4. Bake 40 to 45 minutes, until top is nicely browned. Let stand at least 15 minutes before unmolding or cutting. Serve warm or at room temperature.

---

128 NOODLE KUGEL HAWAIIAN
Prep: 5 minutes   Cook: 53 to 55 minutes
Stand: 20 minutes   Serves: 8 to 10

A touch of pineapple juice and the last-minute addition of crushed pineapple make this noodle pudding lighter than most.

8 ounces wide egg noodles	**1½ cups milk**
3 tablespoons butter	**1 (15¾-ounce) can crushed**
3 eggs	**unsweetened pineapple,**
⅓ cup sugar	**drained, juice reserved**
Grated zest of 2 limes	**1 cup raisins**
¼ teaspoon salt	

1. Preheat oven to 350°F. In a large saucepan of lightly salted boiling water, cook egg noodles until just tender, 8 to 10 minutes; drain. Rinse briefly under cold running water and drain again. Transfer to a large bowl and toss with butter.

2. In a medium bowl, whisk eggs with sugar, lime zest, salt, milk, and ½ cup reserved pineapple juice. Stir in raisins. Add mixture to noodles.

3. Pour mixture into a lightly greased 9 × 13-inch baking dish. Bake, uncovered, 30 minutes.

4. Remove kugel from oven and spread reserved pineapple evenly over noodles. Bake until heated through, about 15 minutes longer. Let stand 20 minutes before cutting.

129   MUSHROOMS PAPRIKASH WITH EGG NOODLES

Prep: 10 minutes   Cook: 18 to 23 minutes   Serves: 4

6 tablespoons butter	1 tablespoon paprika
1 medium onion, sliced	¼ teaspoon salt
1 garlic clove, minced	1 cup sour cream
1 pound mushrooms, sliced	12 ounces egg noodles
1 tablespoon tomato paste	

1. In a large frying pan, melt 4 tablespoons butter over medium heat. Add onion and cook, stirring occasionally, until golden, 4 to 5 minutes. Add garlic and mushrooms. Cook over medium heat until most liquid evaporates, 4 to 5 minutes. Add tomato paste, paprika, and salt. Simmer, stirring, until well blended and heated through, 2 to 3 minutes. Remove from heat and stir in sour cream.

2. Meanwhile, in a large saucepan filled with lightly salted boiling water, cook egg noodles until tender but still firm, 8 to 10 minutes. Drain noodles and transfer to a serving bowl. Toss with remaining 2 tablespoons butter.

3. Pour sauce over noodles and toss. Serve at once.

130   COOL CALIFORNIA FETTUCCINE TOSS

Prep: 15 minutes   Cook: 10 to 12 minutes   Serves: 6 to 8

To prevent avocados from turning brown, sprinkle them with a little lemon juice before adding to the dish.

4 ounces spinach fettuccine	½ pound asparagus, trimmed and cut into 2-inch pieces
4 ounces regular fettuccine	2 medium carrots, shredded
1 (6-ounce) jar marinated artichoke bits	1 large sweet onion, very thinly sliced
2 tablespoons balsamic vinegar	1 (8-ounce) bottle zesty Italian dressing
1 tablespoon chopped sun-dried tomatoes	½ cup shelled pistachio nuts
4 ounces feta cheese, crumbled (about 1 cup)	1 ripe medium avocado, cut into ¼-inch dice

1. In a large saucepan filled with lightly salted boiling water, cook fettuccine until tender but still firm, 8 to 9 minutes. Drain well. Transfer to a serving bowl and toss with artichoke bits, balsamic vinegar, sun-dried tomatoes, and feta cheese.

2. In a medium saucepan filled with water, cook asparagus until barely tender, 2 to 3 minutes; drain. Toss with fettuccine.

3. Add carrots, onion slices, and dressing to fettuccine. Toss to mix. Place salad in a serving bowl or on a platter. Sprinkle with pistachios and cubed avocado. Serve immediately.

131   SPINACH FETTUCCINE WITH CREAM CHEESE PESTO

Prep: 10 minutes   Cook: 8 to 10 minutes   Serves: 4

My neighbor Ed Castagna, who is of Italian descent, calls this his Irish pesto because of its lovely emerald green color. Ed uses cream cheese as a base rather than olive oil. This pesto makes a terrific, garlic-packed spread for sandwiches. You can freeze the leftover pesto in ice cube trays and use it as needed.

3 cups Italian flat-leaf parsley	1 (8-ounce) package cream cheese, softened
1 tablespoon chopped basil	
5 garlic cloves, minced	½ cup grated Parmesan cheese
¼ cup extra-virgin olive oil	12 ounces spinach fettuccine

1. Remove all stems from parsley. In a blender or food processor, process parsley, basil leaves, garlic, and olive oil until fairly smooth.

2. In a medium bowl, with a fork, mix cream cheese with herb mixture until smooth. Blend in Parmesan cheese. To store pesto, place in airtight container and refrigerate or freeze until ready to use.

3. In a large pot filled with lightly salted boiling water, cook fettuccine until tender but still firm, 8 to 10 minutes. Drain well. Transfer to a serving bowl and toss with enough pesto to coat fettuccine, ½ to ¾ cup. Reserve remaining pesto for future use.

132   MINTED PASTA

Prep: 5 minutes   Cook: 17 to 20 minutes   Serves: 2

1 tablespoon olive oil	1 (4-ounce) can whole corn kernels, drained
1 large onion, chopped	
1 (14½-ounce) can Italian-style stewed tomatoes	8 ounces fettuccine
	2 tablespoons butter
1 tablespoon tomato paste	2 tablespoons chopped fresh mint
½ cup sliced mushrooms	

1. In a medium saucepan, heat olive oil over medium-high heat. Add onion and cook, stirring occasionally, until golden, 4 to 5 minutes. Add tomatoes, tomato paste, and mushrooms. Reduce heat to medium-low. Partially cover and cook until slightly thickened, 4 to 5 minutes. Stir in corn and heat through, 1 minute. Set aside.

2. Meanwhile, in a large pot filled with lightly salted boiling water, cook fettuccine until tender but still firm, 8 to 9 minutes. Drain well. Transfer to a serving bowl. Toss with butter.

3. Spoon hot sauce over pasta. Sprinkle with chopped mint and serve.

133 FILIPINO STIR-FRIED NOODLES WITH EGGPLANT

Prep: 15 minutes   Cook: 14 to 18 minutes   Serves: 4

In the Philippines, fried noodles, or *pancit*, is a popular dish. You can find fresh Filipino-type noodles in Asian markets. Ramen or soba-type Japanese noodles are a good alternative. This stir-fry is best made with small Japanese eggplants. The little sprinkle of lime juice brings out the flavors at the end.

2 (3-ounce) packages dry
    ramen-type noodle soup
¼ cup vegetable oil
8 small Japanese eggplants,
    peeled and halved
    horizontally
1 large onion, thinly sliced
2 teaspoons minced garlic

1 tablespoon soy sauce or
    tamari
1 pound spinach leaves torn
    into large pieces
1 teaspoon Asian sesame oil
2 teaspoons sesame seeds
    Wedges of lime

1. In a large saucepan filled with boiling water, cook ramen noodles according to package directions, about 3 minutes. Do not add seasoning packet. Drain, reserving 1 cup cooking liquid. Set aside.

2. In a large frying pan, heat oil over medium heat. Add eggplants and cook, stirring, until softened, 3 to 4 minutes. Add onion. Cook, stirring occasionally, until onion is softened, 2 to 3 minutes. Add garlic, soy sauce, and spinach leaves. Cook until spinach wilts, 2 to 3 minutes. Add ½ cup water and seasonings from ramen noodles. Cook, stirring, until well blended, 1 to 2 minutes. Add cooked noodles and heat through, stirring occasionally, about 3 minutes.

3. Transfer to a serving bowl and sprinkle with sesame oil and sesame seeds. Serve immediately with wedges of lime.

134 ASPARAGUS AND OLIVE LINGUINE
Prep: 10 minutes   Cook: 20 to 25 minutes   Serves: 4

This recipe evolved after a conversation with Brenda Nelson, a friend and a terrific cook.

1 pound asparagus, trimmed and cut into 2-inch pieces	¼ pound Mediterranean-style black olives, pitted and coarsely chopped
3 tablespoons olive oil	
1 large Bermuda onion, very thinly sliced	12 ounces linguine
	1 cup grated Parmesan cheese

1. In a large saucepan filled with boiling water, cook asparagus until just tender, about 3 minutes. Drain and rinse under cold running water; drain well.

2. In a medium frying pan, heat 2 tablespoons olive oil over medium heat. Add onion and cook, stirring occasionally, until lightly browned, 8 to 10 minutes. Add olives and asparagus bits. Cook, stirring, to heat through, 1 to 2 minutes.

3. Meanwhile, in a large pot filled with lightly salted boiling water, cook pasta until tender but still firm, 8 to 10 minutes; drain. Transfer to a serving bowl and toss with 1 tablespoon olive oil. Keep warm.

4. To serve, place pasta on a large serving platter. Top with asparagus and olive mixture. Serve with grated cheese on the side.

135 CREAMY TOMATO AND FETA LINGUINE
Prep: 5 minutes   Cook: 17 to 20 minutes   Serves: 2

1 pound linguine	½ teaspoon salt
1 cup canned crushed tomatoes	2 teaspoons dried dill
	1 cup heavy cream
3 garlic cloves, minced	4 ounces feta cheese, crumbled
½ cup dry white wine	
2 tablespoons paprika	

1. In a large saucepan filled with lightly salted boiling water, cook linguine until tender but still firm, 9 to 10 minutes.

2. Meanwhile, in a medium nonreactive saucepan, combine tomatoes, garlic, and wine. Cook over medium-high heat until liquid evaporates by one third, 4 to 5 minutes. Reduce heat to medium. Simmer 3 minutes. Add paprika, salt, and dill. Add cream, stirring continuously until heated through, 1 to 2 minutes. Do not let mixture boil.

3. Drain pasta and place in a shallow serving bowl. Toss with feta cheese. Spoon hot sauce over pasta and serve immediately.

136   COLD LASAGNE SWIRLS

Prep: 25 minutes   Cook: 12 to 15 minutes   Chill: 1 hour
Serves: 4 to 6

8 lasagne noodles
1 (10-ounce) package frozen
   chopped spinach
2 tablespoons butter
1 medium sweet onion,
   minced
1 (2-ounce) jar diced red
   pimiento

6 ounces Gorgonzola cheese,
   crumbled
1 cup sour cream
2 teaspoons curry powder
   Lettuce leaves
2 tablespoons chopped
   parsley

1. In a large pot, bring lightly salted water to a boil. Cook lasagne until tender but still firm, 10 to 12 minutes; drain. Rinse noodles under cold water. Set in a single layer on a clean towel until ready to use.

2. Meanwhile, cook spinach according to package instructions. Drain into a colander and rinse under cold running water. With your hands, squeeze out all liquid from cooked spinach. In a large frying pan, melt butter over medium heat. Add onion and cook, stirring occasionally, until soft, 2 to 3 minutes. Add spinach and mix well. Transfer to a medium bowl and mix in pimiento. Set aside.

3. In a medium bowl, combine Gorgonzola, sour cream, and curry powder. Stir well and set curry sauce aside.

4. To assemble, spread a thin layer of curry sauce over entire length of a lasagne strip. Cover with about 2 tablespoons spinach mixture. Roll up strip to form a pinwheel. Secure with a toothpick, if necessary. Set wheel on its side in a medium baking dish. Proceed in similar fashion with remaining lasagne. Refrigerate until ready to serve.

5. To serve, discard toothpicks. Set swirls on a flat surface. With a sharp knife, carefully slice each swirl in half horizontally. Set swirls on serving platter lined with lettuce leaves. Spoon remaining curry sauce over swirls. Garnish with chopped parsley.

137   EASY OVERNIGHT LASAGNE

Prep: 35 minutes   Cook: 1 hour 48 minutes to 1 hour 54 minutes
Stand: 8 hours 15 minutes   Serves: 8 to 10

Margie Oakes, a farmer in San Diego County, introduced me to this unusual method of preparing lasagne. It is made with uncooked noodles and left to stand a minimum of 8 hours before baking. For best results, be sure to follow the order in which the vegetables are layered.

2 tablespoons olive oil	½ cup shredded Asiago cheese
1 large onion, chopped	½ cup chopped Italian flat-leaf
2 garlic cloves, minced	parsley
2½ cups prepared spaghetti	1 teaspoon salt
sauce	½ teaspoon pepper
½ cup dry red wine	9 ounces uncooked lasagne
1 (14½-ounce) can Italian-style	noodles
stewed tomatoes	4 medium zucchini, sliced
½ pound mushrooms, sliced	(about 4 cups)
2 eggs, lightly beaten	2 cups shredded provolone
3 cups small-curd cottage	cheese
cheese	

1. In a large nonreactive Dutch oven, heat olive oil. Add onion and garlic and cook over medium heat, stirring occasionally, until softened, 3 to 4 minutes. Add spaghetti sauce, wine, stewed tomatoes, and mushrooms. Cover and cook over medium heat 15 to 20 minutes. Remove from heat.

2. In a large bowl, combine eggs, cottage cheese, Asiago cheese, parsley, salt, and pepper. Mix until well blended.

3. Cover bottom of a lightly oiled 9 × 13-inch baking dish with a thin layer of sauce. Arrange half of uncooked lasagne noodles over sauce. Top noodles evenly with half of zucchini slices. Cover zucchini with half of cottage cheese mixture. Sprinkle with half of provolone. Repeat procedure in same order until all ingredients are used. Cover final layer of provolone with sauce. Cover tightly with aluminum foil and refrigerate 8 hours or overnight.

4. Preheat oven to 350°F. Bake lasagne, covered, 1 hour and 30 minutes. Let stand 15 minutes before cutting.

138   JIFFY SPINACH LASAGNE

Prep: 20 minutes   Cook: 46 to 49 minutes   Serves: 6

A jar of commercial spaghetti sauce and a couple of bunches of fresh spinach make this low-cal lasagne a snap to assemble, as my friend Andrea Peterson taught me.

12 lasagne noodles	¾ teaspoon salt
4 cups fresh spinach leaves, cleaned	½ teaspoon pepper
	1 cup pine nuts
1 (16-ounce) jar prepared spaghetti sauce	1 cup grated Parmesan cheese
1 (16-ounce) container ricotta cheese	

1. Preheat oven to 375°F. In a large pot filled with lightly salted boiling water, cook lasagne noodles until just tender, 9 to 11 minutes; drain. Rinse strips under cold water. Drain again. Set in a single layer on a clean towel until ready to use.

2. In a large saucepan, bring 3 cups lightly salted water to a boil. Add spinach and cook until wilted, 2 to 3 minutes. Drain spinach, reserving 1 cup cooking liquid.

3. To assemble, cover bottom of a 9 × 13-inch ovenproof dish with some spaghetti sauce. Arrange 4 or 5 slightly overlapping lasagne noodles in dish. Spread half of ricotta cheese over noodles. Season with half of salt and pepper. Top with half of spinach. Sprinkle with ½ cup pine nuts. Cover with 1 cup spaghetti sauce. Repeat layering process, beginning with a layer of lasagne, until all ingredients are used.

4. In a bowl, dilute any remaining spaghetti sauce with 1 cup reserved spinach cooking liquid and pour over layered lasagne. Sprinkle with Parmesan cheese. Cover with aluminum foil.

5. Bake 25 minutes. Remove foil and bake 10 minutes longer. Let stand 10 minutes before serving.

139 KOREAN CHAP CHAE

Prep: 30 minutes   Cook: 6 to 10 minutes   Serves: 2

To make this vegetable-studded Korean pasta dish, you will need bean threads, also known as saifun or mung bean noodles. They are commonly available in the Asian section of supermarkets.

4 ounces bean threads	2 tablespoons Asian sesame
⅓ cup dried Chinese	oil
mushrooms	4 scallions, cut into 2-inch
1 medium carrot, peeled	pieces
1 medium zucchini, peeled	2 cups fresh bean sprouts
2 tablespoons soy sauce or	(8 ounces)
tamari	2 cups spinach leaves, rinsed
3 garlic cloves, minced	and dried
1 teaspoon sugar	1 teaspoon sesame seeds

1. In a large bowl filled with warm tap water, soak bean threads for 30 minutes; drain. With a sharp knife or kitchen scissors, cut threads into 2-inch pieces.

2. Meanwhile, in a small bowl filled with hot tap water, soak dried mushrooms for 15 minutes; drain. Cut off woody stems and discard. Slice caps into thin strips.

3. While vegetables are soaking, cut carrot and zucchini into 2-inch matchsticks. Transfer to a medium bowl and toss with soy sauce, garlic, and sugar.

4. In a wok or large frying pan, heat sesame oil. Cook scallions over medium-high heat until barely tender, 1 to 2 minutes. Add carrot, zucchini, and mushrooms and stir-fry until barely tender, 2 to 3 minutes.

5. Stir in bean sprouts and spinach leaves and cook until heated through, 1 to 2 minutes. Add drained bean threads and cook, stirring, until heated through, 2 to 3 minutes. Sprinkle with sesame seeds. Serve at once.

140   FOUR-CHEESE MACARONI AU GRATIN

Prep: 10 minutes   Cook: 49 to 60 minutes   Serves: 4 to 6

1 pound elbow macaroni	⅛ teaspoon grated nutmeg
5 tablespoons butter	¼ teaspoon salt
¼ cup flour	¼ teaspoon pepper
2½ cups milk	1 egg, lightly beaten
4 ounces Gorgonzola cheese, crumbled (about 1 cup)	4 ounces mozzarella cheese, diced
4 ounces shredded sharp Cheddar cheese (about 1 cup)	4 ounces grated Parmesan cheese (about 1 cup)
	1 teaspoon paprika

1. Preheat oven to 350°F. In a large saucepan of lightly salted boiling water, cook pasta until tender but still firm, 8 to 10 minutes. Drain well and transfer to a large bowl. Toss with 1 tablespoon butter and set aside.

2. Meanwhile, in a medium saucepan, melt remaining 4 tablespoons butter over medium heat. Whisk in flour and cook, stirring, 1 or 2 minutes. Whisk in milk all at once. Bring to a boil, whisking, until sauce is thick and smooth, 3 to 5 minutes. Reduce heat to low. Stir in Gorgonzola and Cheddar and cook, stirring, until cheeses melt, 2 to 3 minutes. Season with nutmeg, salt, and pepper.

3. Add cheese sauce to cooked pasta. Stir in egg, mozzarella, and Parmesan cheese. Transfer to a lightly oiled 7 × 11-inch baking dish. Sprinkle with paprika.

4. Bake 35 to 40 minutes, until casserole is bubbling and top is nice and brown.

141   MACARONI FRITTERS

Prep: 5 minutes   Cook: 14 to 18 minutes   Serves: 2 to 3

This recipe yields about 10 fritters, 3 inches in diameter. Serve them with store-bought spaghetti or Alfredo sauce on the side, if you wish.

4 ounces uncooked small elbow macaroni	4 eggs
2 tablespoons butter	1 teaspoon Dijon mustard
1 cup grated Parmesan cheese	1 teaspoon dried basil
½ small onion, chopped	¼ teaspoon salt
2 garlic cloves, minced	⅛ teaspoon pepper
1 tablespoon bread crumbs	¼ cup vegetable oil

1. In a large saucepan filled with lightly salted boiling water, cook macaroni until tender but still firm, 8 to 9 minutes; drain. Transfer to a medium bowl and toss with 1 tablespoon butter and Parmesan cheese.

2. Meanwhile, in a small frying pan, melt remaining 1 tablespoon butter over medium heat. Cook onion, stirring occasionally, until softened, 2 to 3 minutes. Add to macaroni.

3. Add garlic, bread crumbs, and eggs. Stir to blend. Season with mustard, basil, salt, and pepper.

4. In a large frying pan, heat oil over medium-high heat. Drop batter by heaping tablespoons into hot oil. Fry each fritter, turning over carefully with spatula and flattening slightly, until golden brown, 2 to 3 minutes on each side. Transfer to paper towels to drain. Serve hot.

---

142   RED AND GREEN MACARONI AND CHEESE

Prep: 20 minutes   Cook: 36 to 45 minutes   Serves: 4 to 6

Tomatillo sauce lends this macaroni and cheese dish a south-of-the-border touch.

1 pound elbow macaroni	2 tablespoons minced onion
3 tablespoons butter	½ green bell pepper, chopped
2 tablespoons flour	2 cups shredded
1½ cups milk	Emmenthaler cheese
1 (7-ounce) can mild green	½ teaspoon salt
tomatillo sauce	1 teaspoon chili powder
1 (14½-ounce) can Mexican-style stewed tomatoes	

1. Preheat oven to 350°F. In a large saucepan filled with lightly salted boiling water, cook pasta until tender but still firm, 8 to 10 minutes; drain. Transfer to a large bowl and toss with 1 tablespoon butter.

2. In a medium saucepan, melt remaining 2 tablespoons butter over medium heat. Add flour and cook, stirring, 1 minute. Whisk in milk and bring to a boil, whisking until sauce is thick and smooth, 2 to 4 minutes. Stir in tomatillo sauce, stewed tomatoes, onion, and bell pepper. Bring to a boil, reduce heat to medium-low, and simmer 5 minutes. Remove from heat, add cheese and salt, and stir until cheese is melted. Mix with cooked macaroni.

3. Transfer mixture to a lightly buttered 9-inch square baking dish. Sprinkle with chili powder. Bake 20 to 25 minutes, until bubbly.

143 CHAMPAGNE ORZO RISOTTO WITH ARTICHOKE HEARTS

Prep: 10 minutes   Cook: 17 to 24 minutes   Serves: 4

Orzo is a tiny pasta shaped like rice. Cooked orzo will remain relatively moist. Don't let the finished product stand more than 15 minutes before serving or the resulting dish will turn into a solid mass.

2 tablespoons butter
½ medium onion, finely diced
4 medium mushrooms, wiped
   clean and sliced
1 cup orzo
½ cup champagne
1¼ cups vegetable broth or
   reduced-sodium
   chicken broth

2 canned artichoke hearts,
   drained and coarsely
   chopped
¼ teaspoon pepper
2 tablespoons shredded
   Asiago cheese

1. In a medium saucepan, melt butter over medium heat. Add onion and cook, stirring occasionally, until softened, 2 to 3 minutes. Add mushrooms and cook, stirring, until mushrooms start releasing their liquid, 1 to 2 minutes. Add orzo and continue stirring until orzo absorbs mushroom juices, 1 to 2 minutes.

2. Add champagne and cook, stirring, until all liquid is absorbed, 3 to 5 minutes.

3. Add broth, artichoke hearts, and pepper. Stir gently to blend. Cover and reduce heat to medium-low. Cook until orzo is tender, 10 to 12 minutes. Remove from heat and stir in shredded cheese. Serve hot.

144 PASTA E FAGIOLI WITH FRESH SORREL

Prep: 5 minutes   Cook: 19 to 25 minutes   Serves: 4

Seared cherry tomatoes and a few tangy sorrel leaves add a festive touch to this classic Italian dish. If cannellini beans are not available, use small navy beans instead.

10 ounces large shell noodles
3 tablespoons olive oil
8 cherry tomatoes, cut in half
1 medium onion, chopped
3 garlic cloves, minced
1 (16-ounce) can white
   cannellini beans

8 fresh sorrel leaves, cut into
   shreds
1 teaspoon dried basil
¼ cup dry white wine
⅛ teaspoon cayenne
1 tablespoon balsamic vinegar
1 cup shredded Asiago cheese

1. In a large pot filled with lightly salted boiling water, cook noodles until tender but still firm, 12 to 15 minutes; drain. Transfer to a serving bowl and toss with 1 tablespoon of olive oil.

2. Meanwhile, in a medium saucepan, heat remaining 2 tablespoons olive oil over medium-high heat. Sear cut sides of cherry tomatoes until lightly browned, 1 to 2 minutes. With a slotted spoon, transfer tomatoes to a bowl.

3. Add onion and garlic to same pan and cook, stirring occasionally, until onion is golden, 2 to 3 minutes. Add cannellini beans with liquid from can, sorrel, basil, and wine. Cover and reduce heat to medium. Cook until heated through, 4 to 5 minutes. Season with cayenne and balsamic vinegar.

4. To serve, toss beans with cooked shells. Gently blend in seared tomatoes. Mix with Asiago cheese and serve immediately.

---

145   PASTA WITH BUTTERNUT SQUASH
Prep: 15 minutes   Cook: 1 hour to 1 hour 12 minutes
Serves: 4

This delectable pasta topping may be made with pumpkin or any of the sweet yellow winter squashes.

1 butternut squash (about 1½ pounds)	½ cup shredded Monterey Jack cheese
2 tablespoons butter	½ teaspoon salt
1 medium onion, chopped	¼ teaspoon pepper
2 garlic cloves, minced	1 tablespoon chopped sun-dried tomatoes
½ cup vegetable broth or reduced-sodium chicken broth	12 ounces penne or ziti
½ cup milk	2 tablespoons chopped parsley

1. Preheat oven to 375°F. To cook squash, poke holes in flesh with tip of a knife. Bake until knife inserted in center comes out easily, 50 minutes to 1 hour. (To microwave squash, place in ovenproof dish filled with 1 inch water. Cover with plastic wrap and microwave on High for 6 minutes. Rotate squash and microwave until soft, another 5 or 6 minutes depending on size.) Let squash cool, then cut in half and scoop out seeds. Measure 2 cups squash into a bowl, mash with a fork, and set aside.

2. In a medium frying pan, melt 1 tablespoon butter over medium heat. Cook onion and garlic until golden, 2 to 3 minutes. Add cooked squash, broth, milk, and cheese. Stir until cheese melts and mixture thickens somewhat. Season with salt and pepper. Turn off heat and add sun-dried tomatoes. Set aside and keep warm.

3. Meanwhile, in a large saucepan filled with lightly salted boiling water, cook pasta until tender but still firm, 8 to 9 minutes. Drain and transfer to a serving bowl. Toss with remaining tablespoon of butter. Pour sauce over pasta. Sprinkle with parsley and serve immediately.

146 STUFFED PASTA SHELLS

Prep: 30 minutes   Cook: 31 to 40 minutes   Serves: 4

12 jumbo pasta shells
1 (16-ounce) container small-
    curd cottage cheese
1 egg
1 garlic clove, minced
3 tablespoons prepared
    pesto sauce
2 scallions, chopped
2 canned artichoke hearts,
    chopped

2 tablespoons butter
2 tablespoons flour
¼ cup dry white wine
1¾ cups milk
½ teaspoon pepper
½ teaspoon grated nutmeg
1 cup shredded Swiss cheese
½ cup Italian bread crumbs

1. Preheat oven to 350°F. In a large pan filled with lightly salted boiling water, cook pasta shells until soft, 10 to 12 minutes; drain. Place on a kitchen towel.

2. In a large bowl, combine cottage cheese, egg, garlic, pesto, scallions, and chopped artichoke hearts. Mix to blend well.

3. In a medium saucepan, melt butter over medium heat. Add flour and cook, stirring, 1 minute. Whisk in wine and cook, whisking, 1 minute. Whisk in milk all at once. Bring to a boil, whisking, until sauce is thick and smooth, 3 to 4 minutes. Stir in pepper, nutmeg, and ½ cup of Swiss cheese. Cook, stirring, until cheese is melted, 1 to 2 minutes. Remove sauce from heat.

4. Stuff each pasta shell with 1 heaping tablespoon cottage cheese mixture. Set shells snugly in a buttered 2-quart baking dish. Cover with sauce. Sprinkle cheese and bread crumbs on top. Bake 15 to 20 minutes, until bubbly.

147 PASTITSIO

Prep: 20 minutes   Cook: 55 minutes to 1 hour 13 minutes
Serves: 6 to 8

1 pound elbow macaroni
4 tablespoons butter
3 eggs, lightly beaten
2 cups shredded Asiago
    cheese
1 large onion, finely diced
2 garlic cloves, minced
¼ cup chopped parsley
¼ teaspoon cinnamon

⅛ teaspoon grated nutmeg
½ teaspoon salt
½ teaspoon pepper
½ cup dry red wine
1 (14½-ounce) can pizza-style
    chunky tomatoes
1 (23-ounce) jar prepared
    Alfredo sauce

1. Preheat oven to 350°F. In a large saucepan of lightly salted boiling water, cook macaroni until tender but still firm, 8 to 10 minutes; drain. Transfer to a large bowl and toss with 2 tablespoons of butter, eggs, and 1 cup Asiago cheese.

2. In a medium frying pan, melt remaining 2 tablespoons butter over medium heat. Add onion and garlic and cook, stirring occasionally, until soft, 2 to 3 minutes. Add to cooked macaroni. Stir in parsley, cinnamon, nutmeg, salt, and pepper.

3. In a small bowl, mix wine with tomatoes.

4. Spoon about ¾ cup Alfredo sauce over bottom of a 7 × 11-inch baking dish. Top with half of macaroni. Spread with all the tomatoes. Top with final layer of macaroni. Spoon remaining Alfredo sauce over all. Sprinkle with remaining cup of Asiago cheese.

5. Bake until dish is bubbly and brown, 45 minutes to 1 hour. Let stand 10 minutes before serving. Cut into squares.

148   RAVIOLI WITH SHERRIED CARROT PUREE

Prep: 10 minutes   Cook: 25 to 32 minutes   Serves: 2

4 tablespoons butter
2 medium onions, thinly
   sliced
4 medium carrots, peeled and
   sliced
½ cup dry sherry
½ teaspoon salt
¼ teaspoon pepper

½ cup vegetable broth or
   reduced-sodium
   chicken broth
1 (9-ounce) package fresh
   cheese ravioli
2 tablespoons chopped
   parsley

1. In a large frying pan, melt 2 tablespoons butter over medium heat. Add onions and cook, stirring occasionally, until just beginning to color, 2 to 3 minutes. Add carrots, sherry, salt, and pepper. Cover and cook until carrots are tender, 15 to 20 minutes. Let cool 5 minutes.

2. In a blender or food processor, puree carrot mixture with broth, in batches if necessary, until fairly smooth. Transfer to a small saucepan and cover to keep warm.

3. In a large saucepan of lightly salted boiling water, cook ravioli according to package directions 8 to 9 minutes; drain. Return to pan and toss with remaining 2 tablespoons of butter.

4. To serve, reheat carrot puree if necessary. Spoon over warm ravioli. Sprinkle with chopped parsley and serve at once.

149 COLD SZECHUAN SESAME NOODLES
Prep: 12 minutes   Cook: 9 to 10 minutes   Serves: 4 to 6

1 (6-ounce) package Japanese
   soba noodles
2 tablespoons Asian
   sesame oil
⅓ cup tahini (Middle Eastern
   sesame paste)
2 teaspoons minced fresh
   ginger
3 tablespoons dry sherry
3 tablespoons soy sauce
2 teaspoons sugar

2 garlic cloves, minced
¼ teaspoon Chinese chili paste
   or ¼ to ½ teaspoon
   Tabasco
2 tablespoons vegetable broth
   or reduced-sodium
   chicken broth or water
4 scallions, cut into 2-inch
   pieces
2 tablespoons sesame seeds

1. In a large pan filled with boiling salted water, cook soba noodles until tender, about 8 minutes. Drain under cold running water. Drain again. Transfer to a medium bowl and toss with sesame oil.

2. In a small bowl, whisk together sesame paste, ginger, sherry, soy sauce, sugar, garlic, chili paste, and broth.

3. In a small nonstick frying pan, toast sesame seeds over medium heat, tossing pan back and forth to prevent scorching, until lightly browned, 1 to 2 minutes.

4. Toss noodles with dressing. Decorate with scallions and toasted sesame seeds. Refrigerate until serving time.

150 SPAGHETTI AND NO-MEAT BALLS
Prep: 20 minutes   Cook: 18 to 20 minutes   Serves: 4

Make some of these nut balls ahead of time and freeze them for later use.

1 small onion
2 eggs
1 cup Italian seasoned bread
   crumbs
1 cup walnut pieces, finely
   ground
2 garlic cloves, minced
1 teaspoon salt
½ teaspoon pepper

2 tablespoons mayonnaise
1 tablespoon Worcestershire
   sauce
1 teaspoon dried basil
3 cups prepared spaghetti
   sauce
12 ounces spaghetti
1 tablespoon olive oil
½ cup grated Parmesan cheese

1. In a blender or food processor, chop onion with eggs until fairly smooth.

2. In a large bowl, mix bread crumbs, walnuts, garlic, salt, pepper, mayonnaise, Worcestershire, and basil. Stir in onion-egg mixture until moistened. With your hands, fashion into balls about 1 inch in diameter.

3. In a medium saucepan, bring spaghetti sauce to a simmer. Drop nut balls gently into simmering sauce. Simmer 10 minutes.

4. Meanwhile, in a large pan filled with lightly salted boiling water, cook spaghetti until tender but still firm, 8 to 10 minutes. Drain well. In a large bowl, toss spaghetti with olive oil. Serve immediately with spaghetti sauce and Parmesan cheese on the side.

---

151 SPAGHETTI QUICHE
Prep: 15 minutes   Cook: 50 to 55 minutes   Serves: 8 to 10

This unusual baked pasta can be prepared up to two days ahead and left in the refrigerator, uncooked, until baking time.

8 ounces spaghetti, broken up	1 tablespoon olive oil
4 scallions, chopped	1 cup grated Parmesan cheese
2 medium tomatoes, chopped	4 eggs, lightly beaten
1 cup cubed zucchini	2 cups milk
1 cup chopped mushrooms	½ teaspoon salt
1 cup prepared pesto sauce	¼ teaspoon pepper
1 (1½-ounce) envelope spaghetti sauce seasoning	

1. Preheat oven to 350°F. In a pan filled with lightly salted boiling water, cook spaghetti 5 minutes. (Spaghetti will continue cooking later.) Drain well and transfer to a large bowl. Immediately toss hot pasta with scallions, tomatoes, zucchini, mushrooms, pesto, and seasoning mix.

2. Generously grease a 9 × 13-inch baking dish with olive oil. Sprinkle bottom and sides liberally with 3 tablespoons of grated Parmesan cheese. Spoon spaghetti mixture into dish.

3. In a medium bowl, beat eggs with milk, remaining grated cheese, salt, and pepper. Pour mixture over prepared spaghetti.

4. Bake until quiche is set, 45 to 50 minutes. Let stand 10 minutes before serving. Cut into squares and serve.

152   MUSHROOM TETRAZZOLA

Prep: 10 minutes   Cook: 28 to 38 minutes   Serves: 6

8 ounces angel hair pasta
1 stick (4 ounces) butter
½ medium onion, chopped
½ pound mushrooms, sliced
1½ cups vegetable broth or
  reduced-sodium chicken
  broth

1 (.9-ounce) package dry
  mushroom soup mix
2 tablespoons crumbled
  Gorgonzola cheese
½ cup sour cream
½ cup bread crumbs

1. Preheat oven to 400°F. In a large pan filled with lightly salted boiling water, cook angel hair pasta until tender, 6 to 8 minutes; drain. Transfer to a bowl and toss with 2 tablespoons butter.

2. In a large frying pan, melt 4 tablespoons butter over medium heat. Add onion and cook, stirring occasionally, until golden, 2 to 3 minutes. Add mushrooms and cook, stirring occasionally, until most liquid evaporates, 3 to 4 minutes. Stir in broth and dry soup mix. Cook, stirring, until sauce thickens, 2 to 3 minutes. Remove from heat. Stir in Gorgonzola cheese and sour cream.

3. In a lightly oiled shallow 2-quart casserole, layer half the angel hair on bottom. Top with mushroom mixture. Cover with remaining pasta. Sprinkle with bread crumbs. Dot with remaining butter.

4. Bake 15 to 20 minutes, until casserole is hot and bubbly and bread crumbs are lightly browned.

153   RED, GREEN, AND WHITE TORTELLINI ALFREDO

Prep: 5 minutes   Cook: 10 to 13 minutes   Serves: 6

1 (9-ounce) package fresh
  cheese tortellini
1 (9-ounce) package fresh
  spinach tortellini
2 tablespoons butter
1 (14½-ounce) can Italian-style
  stewed tomatoes

1 cup heavy cream
1 cup shredded Swiss cheese
¼ cup chopped fresh basil or
  2 tablespoons chopped
  parsley

1. In a large saucepan of lightly salted boiling water, cook tortellini according to package directions 8 to 10 minutes; drain. Transfer to a serving bowl and toss with butter.

2. Meanwhile, in a medium saucepan over medium heat, heat tomatoes, crushing them lightly with a fork. Add cream and Swiss cheese. Cook, stirring, until cheese dissolves, 2 to 3 minutes.

3. To serve, divide cooked tortellini among 6 individual dinner plates. Top with sauce and garnish with chopped basil.

154 CHINESE VERMICELLI

Prep: 30 minutes   Cook: 4 to 7 minutes   Serves: 4

My friend Jan Chung, who was born in Singapore, often serves this light noodle dish to her family.

4 ounces bean threads	2 garlic cloves, minced
4 dried Chinese mushrooms	5 ounces green beans, cut in
3 tablespoons soy sauce or	2-inch pieces (1 cup)
tamari	1 cup shredded cabbage
2 teaspoons sugar	1 medium carrot, shredded
1 teaspoon Asian sesame oil	2 scallions, coarsely chopped
1 teaspoon pepper	1 tablespoon chopped cilantro
2 tablespoons vegetable oil	or parsley

1. In a large bowl filled with very hot tap water, soak bean threads for 30 minutes. Drain well and set aside.

2. In a small bowl filled with 1 cup warm water, soak mushrooms until softened, 10 to 15 minutes. Strain, reserving soaking liquid. Cut off and discard woody stems. Slice mushroom caps.

3. In another small bowl, mix mushroom liquid, soy sauce, sugar, sesame oil, and pepper. Add sliced mushroom caps to marinade and set aside.

4. In a large frying pan or wok, heat vegetable oil over medium-high heat. Add garlic and stir-fry until barely softened, 1 to 2 minutes. Add green beans and stir-fry until barely tender, 1 to 2 minutes. Add cabbage and carrot and stir-fry until cabbage wilts, 2 to 3 minutes. Add mushrooms and marinade and toss to mix. Add drained vermicelli and toss with vegetables. Transfer to a serving platter and top with scallions and cilantro. Serve hot.

155 VERMICELLI WITH CREAMED ZUCCHINI, CARROTS, AND WALNUTS

Prep: 5 minutes   Cook: 12 to 16 minutes   Serves: 5

1 **pound vermicelli**	1½ **cups half-and-half**
2 **tablespoons olive oil**	½ **teaspoon salt**
1 **large carrot, peeled and cut**	⅛ **teaspoon cayenne**
into matchsticks	⅓ **cup pesto sauce**
2 **garlic cloves, minced**	1 **cup walnut pieces**
2 **medium zucchini, peeled**	½ **cup grated Parmesan cheese**
and cut into matchsticks	

1. In a large saucepan filled with lightly salted boiling water, cook pasta until tender but still firm, 6 to 8 minutes.

2. Meanwhile, in a medium frying pan, heat olive oil over medium-high heat. Add carrot and garlic and cook, stirring often, until lightly browned, 1 to 2 minutes. Add zucchini and cook until limp, 2 to 3 minutes.

3. Add half-and-half, salt, and cayenne. Cook until sauce is heated through, about 3 minutes.

4. Drain pasta. Transfer to a serving bowl and toss with pesto. Add walnut pieces and sauce. Serve hot with grated Parmesan on the side.

Chapter 6

Pizzas, Pies, and Vegetable Tarts

There is nothing quite so satisfying, from a cook's standpoint, as bringing to the table a savory pie or flaky turnovers hot from the oven. The best-known pie in America (with the possible exception of apple) is probably pizza, which, like pasta, has undergone a dramatic transformation since avant-garde chefs began to top their designer creations with anything from fruits to nuts. The proliferation of ready-to-bake crusts, whether frozen or fresh, has turned pizza-making practically into child's play, and toppings for these quintessential American creations need only be limited by the cook's imagination.

In this chapter, Charlie's Pizza is smothered with a wonderful combination of fresh spinach leaves and slices of crisp Bosc pears. A trip to Hawaii inspired the more exotic Hawaiian Pizza crowned with fresh slices of mango and fresh pineapple. Pizza Primavera, an Italian classic, simply takes advantage of the fresh vegetables of the season.

Tarts follow the same easy-to-make principle. Here again, frozen pie crusts provide an excellent base for your tart, although if you have time, this chapter offers a recipe for making your own pastry, as for Glazed Vegetable Tart. Store-bought pie crusts can also serve as the base for Onion Tart and Fresh Tomato Tart, two savory French specialties, which I learned to make from my mother.

Turnovers like Quick Spinach Ricotta Calzone or Cornish Pasties are both heartwarming treats. You can make them up ahead of time and freeze them. To do that, freeze the uncooked pasties or turnovers on a baking sheet individually. Then wrap them up tightly in foil and place them in the freezer. Smaller versions can be loosely stacked in an airtight container. No need to thaw them, but do allow 10 to 15 extra minutes of baking time for the dough to cook through.

156   CHARLIE'S PIZZA
Prep: 10 minutes   Cook: 12 to 15 minutes   Serves: 4

My brother-in-law Charles Morse serves this up for a quick family supper. It goes so fast he often has to return to the kitchen to make a second one!

1½ cups prepared pizza sauce
1 (12-inch) thin pizza crust
1 (1-pound) bunch of fresh spinach
2 firm Bosc pears, peeled, cored, and very thinly sliced

2 Bermuda onions, very thinly sliced, separated into rings
1 cup pecan pieces (4 ounces)
2 cups shredded mozzarella cheese

1. Preheat oven to 425°F. Spoon pizza sauce evenly over pizza crust.

2. Rinse and dry spinach leaves. Remove stems. Coarsely tear up leaves and spread over pizza sauce. Arrange pear slices decoratively over spinach. Cover with onion rings. Sprinkle pecan pieces on top and cover with mozzarella.

3. Bake 12 to 15 minutes, until pizza crust is crispy and golden. Serve at once.

157   PIZZA PRIMAVERA
Prep: 15 minutes   Cook: 13 to 18 minutes   Serves: 2

2 tablespoons olive oil
1 large onion, chopped
1 cup cauliflower florets, coarsely chopped
½ cup broccoli florets, coarsely chopped
1 small carrot, shredded
½ teaspoon salt
⅛ teaspoon pepper

1 garlic clove, minced
1 teaspoon dried oregano
2 (6-inch) Boboli Italian bread shells
1 cup prepared pizza sauce
2 medium mushrooms, sliced
¼ cup prepared basil pesto
½ cup grated Asiago cheese

1. Preheat oven to 450°F. In a large frying pan, heat oil over medium-high heat. Add onions and cook, stirring occasionally, until softened, 2 to 3 minutes. Add cauliflower, broccoli, and carrot. Reduce heat to medium. Cook, stirring occasionally, until vegetables are crisp-tender, 3 to 5 minutes. Season with salt, pepper, garlic, and oregano.

2. Meanwhile, set pizza crusts on a baking sheet. Spoon pizza sauce evenly over crusts. Arrange sliced mushrooms over sauce. Spoon cooked vegetables over mushrooms. Drizzle on pesto sauce. Top with Asiago cheese.

3. Bake 8 to 10 minutes, until cheese melts and crust is crisp.

158   HAWAIIAN PIZZA
Prep: 30 minutes   Cook: 24 to 32 minutes   Serves: 4 to 6

Fresh pineapple is preferable for this island-style pizza. Choose a mango that is still a little green so it won't disintegrate while cooking. You can serve this as an entree or cut it into small squares to offer as an hors d'oeuvre.

½ fresh ripe pineapple
1 firm mango
1 cup sliced water chestnuts
¼ cup teriyaki sauce
2 tablespoons butter

3 large sweet onions, very thinly sliced
1 (10-ounce) package ready-to-bake thin pizza crust
½ cup hoisin sauce (see Note)
1 cup macadamia nut pieces

1. Preheat oven to 425°F. Cut skin off pineapple; remove any remaining "eyes." Core pineapple and cut into 1-inch chunks. Peel mango. Slice fruit away from pit and cut into ½-inch dice. In a medium bowl, combine pineapple, mango, water chestnuts, and teriyaki sauce. Marinate at room temperature 20 minutes; drain.

2. Meanwhile, in a large nonstick frying pan, melt butter over medium-high heat. Add onions and cook, stirring often, until golden brown, 12 to 15 minutes. Remove onions to a bowl.

3. In same pan, stir-fry drained pineapple, mango, and water chestnuts 2 minutes. Set aside.

4. On a lightly floured surface, roll out crust to a 10 × 15-inch rectangle. Transfer to a lightly oiled baking sheet. Spread hoisin sauce evenly over crust. Top with a layer of onions. Spoon sautéed fruit over onions. Sprinkle macadamia nuts on top.

5. Bake pizza 10 to 15 minutes, until crust is crisp. Serve hot.

NOTE: *Hoisin sauce is available in the Asian foods section of many supermarkets and in Chinese markets.*

159   ORIENTAL RICE PIZZA

Prep: 35 minutes   Cook: 59 to 1 hour 12 minutes   Serves: 6

Enoki mushrooms are slender white Japanese mushrooms that look a little like a flower bud. You can eat them raw or cooked. Substitute white button mushrooms if enoki are not available. Chinese five-spice powder and hoisin sauce are available in the Asian section of supermarkets.

1 teaspoon salt	12 Chinese pea pods, strings
1 cup long-grain white rice	removed
(not converted)	1 cup fresh bean sprouts
⅛ teaspoon Chinese five-spice	1 tablespoon cornstarch
powder	1 cup vegetable broth or
3 eggs	reduced-sodium chicken
4 garlic cloves, minced	broth
2 teaspoons Asian sesame oil	2 tablespoons soy sauce or
2 tablespoons vegetable oil	tamari
1 bunch of scallions, cut into	¼ cup hoisin sauce
2-inch pieces	1 (6-ounce) can sliced water
2 cups spinach leaves, cleaned	chestnuts, drained
and broken up	1 (3-ounce) package enoki
	mushrooms

1. In a medium saucepan, bring 2 cups water and ½ teaspoon of salt to a boil. Add rice. Reduce heat to medium-low. Cover and cook until rice is tender and water is absorbed, 15 to 20 minutes. Remove from heat and fluff with a fork. Set aside to cool slightly.

2. Preheat oven to 400°F. In a medium bowl, combine cooked rice, five-spice powder, eggs, half of minced garlic, sesame oil, and remaining ½ teaspoon salt. Mix well. With a spatula, spread rice mixture evenly over a generously oiled 10-inch pizza pan.

3. Bake 25 to 30 minutes, until rice is slightly crusty and golden. Set aside. Reduce oven temperature to 350°F.

4. While crust is baking, in a large nonstick frying pan or wok, heat vegetable oil. Add scallions and cook over medium heat, stirring occasionally, until soft, 2 to 3 minutes. With a slotted spoon, transfer to a small bowl. Add remaining garlic and spinach leaves to same pan and cook, stirring, until spinach wilts, about 1 minute. With a slotted spoon, transfer to a separate small bowl.

5. In same pan, stir-fry pea pods over medium-high heat until bright green, about 2 minutes. With a slotted spoon, transfer to a medium bowl. Add bean sprouts and baby corn and toss.

6. In a small bowl, dissolve cornstarch in ½ cup broth. Add to frying pan and bring to a boil, stirring until mixture thickens slightly, about 2 minutes. Add remaining broth, soy sauce, hoisin sauce, and water chestnuts. Cook sauce, stirring, until hot, about 2 minutes longer.

7. When rice crust is baked, sprinkle with scallions. Top with spinach, pea pods, and bean sprouts. Spread raw enoki mushrooms over top. Spoon sauce and water chestnuts over vegetables.

8. Bake 10 to 12 minutes, until heated through. Serve hot.

160 PESTO RICOTTA PIE
Prep: 10 minutes   Cook: 20 to 25 minutes   Serves: 4

You can also serve this pie as an appetizer by cutting into 1-inch squares.

5 eggs
⅓ cup prepared pesto sauce
⅓ cup ricotta cheese
1 tablespoon finely diced
   sun-dried tomatoes

½ cup half-and-half
1 (9-inch) frozen pie shell,
   thawed

1. Preheat oven to 400°F. In a medium bowl, beat eggs until blended. Add pesto, ricotta, sun-dried tomatoes, and half-and-half and blend well. Pour into pie shell.

2. Bake 20 to 25 minutes, until pie is set. Let cool 10 minutes before cutting.

161 CARROT AND WALNUT PIE
Prep: 20 minutes   Cook: 40 to 45 minutes   Serves: 6

1 pound carrots, peeled and
   sliced
1 garlic clove, minced
½ teaspoon pepper
4 eggs
3 tablespoons flour
¼ cup half-and-half

1 tablespoon curry powder
½ teaspoon grated nutmeg
1 cup walnut pieces (4 ounces)
2 tablespoons butter, melted
½ teaspoon garlic salt
1 (9-inch) frozen deep-dish pie
   shell, thawed

1. Preheat oven to 350°F. In a medium saucepan, combine carrots, garlic, pepper, and ¼ cup water. Cover and cook over medium heat until carrots are tender, about 10 minutes. Remove from heat and let cool 5 minutes.

2. In a blender or food processor, puree carrots, adding eggs one at a time, until smooth. Transfer puree to a medium bowl. Whisk in flour, half-and-half, curry powder, and nutmeg.

3. In a small bowl, mix walnuts with melted butter and garlic salt. Line bottom of pie crust with walnuts, pressing them well into dough. Fill crust with carrot puree.

4. Bake 30 to 35 minutes, until toothpick inserted in center comes out clean. Serve hot or at room temperature.

162   CALIFORNIA ARTICHOKE PIE
Prep: 20 minutes   Cook: 42 to 48 minutes   Serves: 6

2 (9-inch) frozen pie crusts, thawed
1 (6-ounce) jar marinated artichoke hearts, coarsely chopped
½ pound mushrooms, coarsely chopped

2 garlic cloves, minced
1 tablespoon finely diced sun-dried tomatoes
4 eggs
2 cups shredded sharp provolone cheese
⅛ teaspoon cayenne

1. Preheat oven to 400°F. Reserve 1 unbaked pie shell. Invert second crust onto a lightly floured surface and roll out to an 11-inch round.

2. In a large frying pan, cook marinated artichoke hearts, mushrooms, and garlic over medium heat, until mushrooms are barely tender, 2 to 3 minutes. Stir in sun-dried tomatoes.

3. In a large bowl, beat eggs lightly. Mix in provolone cheese and cayenne. Stir in artichoke mixture. Pour filling into reserved pie shell. Cover with rolled-out second shell. Crimp edges of pie to seal. With a sharp knife, make 4 slits in center of top shell.

4. Bake 40 to 45 minutes, until crust is golden. Serve hot or at room temperature.

163   ONION TART
Prep: 10 minutes   Cook: 36 to 44 minutes   Serves: 6

This cheesy *tarte à l'oignon* is a French classic. I often make it to take along on a picnic, or serve it with a green salad for a complete meal.

2 tablespoons butter
1½ pounds sweet onions, thinly sliced
2 tablespoons flour
2 eggs, lightly beaten
1 cup sour cream
½ cup milk
1 teaspoon Worcestershire sauce

1 cup shredded Swiss cheese
⅛ teaspoon grated nutmeg
½ teaspoon salt
¼ teaspoon pepper
1 frozen (9-inch) deep-dish pastry shell, thawed

1. Preheat oven to 425°F. In a large frying pan, melt butter over medium heat. Add onions, and cook, stirring occasionally, until golden, 5 to 7 minutes. Sprinkle on flour and cook, stirring, 1 to 2 minutes.

2. Transfer onions to a bowl and add beaten eggs. Mix in sour cream, milk, Worcestershire, cheese, nutmeg, salt, and pepper.

3. Pour onion filling into pastry shell. Bake until tart is puffy and brown, 30 to 35 minutes. Let stand 10 minutes before slicing. Serve hot or at room temperature.

164   VEGETABLE POTPIE

Prep: 20 minutes   Cook: 40 to 47 minutes   Serves: 6

2 tablespoons butter
1 medium onion, finely
  chopped
2 garlic cloves, minced
1 cup broccoli florets
1 cup frozen peas, thawed
1 medium carrot, sliced
½ cup cut-up green beans
½ pound potatoes, peeled and
  cut into ½-inch dice
1 (10½-ounce) can condensed
  cream of mushroom soup
¼ pound mushrooms, coarsely
  chopped

1 tablespoon sweet paprika
½ cup vegetable broth or
  reduced-sodium chicken
  broth
2 tablespoons chopped
  parsley
1 tablespoon fines herbes
1 teaspoon salt
1 cup buttermilk biscuit mix
⅓ cup cornmeal
⅓ cup shredded sharp
  Cheddar cheese
⅓ cup buttermilk

1. Preheat oven to 350°F. In a large saucepan, melt butter over medium heat. Add onion and garlic, and cook, stirring occasionally, until soft, 2 to 3 minutes. Add broccoli florets, peas, carrot, green beans, and potatoes. Cook, stirring occasionally, 5 minutes. Reduce heat to low. Stir in cream of mushroom soup, mushrooms, paprika, broth, parsley, fines herbes, and salt. Cover and cook 10 minutes. Remove from heat.

2. Transfer cooked vegetables to a 2-quart casserole dish. In a bowl, blend biscuit mix with cornmeal, cheese, and buttermilk. On a lightly floured surface, knead dough until it loses its stickiness, 3 to 4 minutes. On a layer of wax paper or plastic wrap, roll out dough to size of baking dish.

3. Carefully lift rolled-out cornmeal dough and invert to cover casserole dish. Remove paper or plastic wrap. Crimp edges to side of casserole to cover tightly.

4. Bake 20 to 25 minutes, until crust is golden brown.

165   MINTY POTATO PIE WITH YOGURT SAUCE
Prep: 15 minutes   Cook: 53 to 64 minutes   Serves: 4

2 tablespoons olive oil	¾ cup milk
3 medium potatoes, peeled and cut into ¼-inch slices	1 cup frozen peas, thawed
1 garlic clove, minced	¼ cup walnut pieces
1 teaspoon salt	1 tablespoon chopped fresh mint or 2 teaspoons dried
½ teaspoon pepper	2 (9-inch) frozen pie crusts, thawed
2 tablespoons butter	
1 tablespoon flour	1 cup plain yogurt

1. Preheat oven to 375°F. In a large frying pan, preferably nonstick, heat olive oil over medium heat. Add potatoes, cover, and cook, turning occasionally, until tender, 15 to 20 minutes. Stir in garlic, salt, and pepper. Remove from heat.

2. In a small saucepan, melt butter over medium heat. Sprinkle in flour and cook, whisking constantly, 1 minute. Add milk all at once and cook, whisking, until sauce boils and thickens, 2 to 3 minutes. Stir in peas and walnut pieces. Season with one-third of mint. Remove from heat and set aside.

3. To assemble pie, sprinkle half of remaining chopped mint on bottom of pie crust. Layer half of potatoes inside crust and top with creamed peas. Top with remaining potatoes. Cover pie with second pie crust. Trim to size and crimp edges tightly, as you would for apple pie. With a sharp knife, cut 4 small slits in center of top crust.

4. Bake until crust is golden, 35 to 40 minutes. Let stand 10 minutes before cutting.

5. Meanwhile, in a small bowl, mix yogurt with remaining mint. Serve potato pie with yogurt sauce on the side.

166   FRESH TOMATO TART
Prep: 10 minutes   Cook: 20 to 25 minutes   Serves: 4

Just accompany this tomato tart with a fresh green salad, and presto! Dinner's ready.

1 (9-inch) frozen pie shell, thawed	½ cup heavy cream
	½ cup shredded Swiss cheese
2 teaspoons Dijon mustard	1 teaspoon dried basil
1 large tomato, seeded and thinly sliced	½ teaspoon salt
	¼ teaspoon pepper
3 eggs	

1. Preheat oven to 400°F. With tines of a fork, prick holes all over pie shell. With a knife, spread mustard over bottom of shell. Line pie shell with tomato slices.

2. In a medium bowl, whisk eggs with cream until frothy. Blend in cheese, basil, salt, and pepper. Pour over tomato slices.

3. Bake tart 20 to 25 minutes, until puffy and lightly browned. Let stand 10 minutes before serving.

167 GLAZED VEGETABLE TART
Prep: 20 minutes   Cook: 31 to 38 minutes   Serves: 4 to 6

This lovely tart is abloom with broccoli and cauliflower florets.

1 carrot, peeled and sliced	**½ teaspoon salt**
1 bunch of broccoli, broken into florets	**2 teaspoons cornstarch**
1 small head of cauliflower, broken into florets	**1 cup cold vegetable broth or reduced-sodium chicken broth**
1 cup flour	**1 cup mayonnaise**
4 tablespoons butter	**⅓ cup prepared basil pesto**

1. Preheat oven to 375°F. In a large saucepan filled with boiling water, cook carrot, broccoli, and cauliflower florets until barely tender, 4 to 5 minutes. Drain and rinse under cold running water. Place in a colander to drain.

2. In a food processor, combine flour, butter, salt, and 3 tablespoons water. Pulse on and off 10 times, or until mixture resembles coarse crumbs. (Or with a pastry blender or 2 knives used scissor fashion, cut pastry until it resembles coarse crumbs.) Add 1 tablespoon more water if mixture is too dry. Transfer dough to a medium bowl and shape into a ball. Refrigerate 10 minutes.

3. In a small bowl, mix cornstarch with 2 tablespoons of cold broth. Set aside. In a small saucepan, heat remaining broth over medium heat. Stir in cold cornstarch mixture and bring to a boil, stirring until mixture thickens, 2 to 3 minutes. Set glaze aside to cool.

4. On a 6 × 10-inch rectangle of plastic wrap, roll out chilled dough to cover. Lift plastic wrap and carefully transfer dough rectangle to an oiled cookie sheet. Invert and discard wrap. With tines of fork, prick crust all over. With fingers, raise up edges of crust and crimp to form ½-inch sides.

5. Bake 25 to 30 minutes, until crust is golden. Let cool 10 minutes. Carefully slide crust onto a serving platter.

6. Meanwhile, in a small bowl mix mayonnaise with pesto. With a spatula, spread herbed mayonnaise over baked crust. Top with an arrangement of broccoli and cauliflower florets. Use carrot slices as dividers. Spoon glaze lightly over vegetables. Serve at room temperature.

168   TORTA MILANESE
Prep: 20 minutes   Cook: 44 to 57 minutes   Serves: 4 to 6

This wonderful torta is good hot or cold. I often make it to take along on a picnic. If time is of the essence, substitute a jar of roasted red pepper strips for the bell pepper and begin with step 2.

1 large red bell pepper	2 tablespoons grated
3 tablespoons butter	Parmesan cheese
1 (10-ounce) package frozen	6 fresh basil leaves, shredded,
chopped spinach, thawed	or 1 teaspoon dried
and squeezed dry	2 (9-inch) frozen pie crusts,
1 tablespoon flour	thawed
¼ cup milk	1½ cups shredded mozzarella
½ teaspoon salt	cheese
¼ teaspoon pepper	2 tablespoons imitation bacon
2 tablespoons olive oil	bits
1 medium onion, chopped	2 hard-boiled eggs, sliced
¼ pound mushrooms, sliced	

1. Preheat broiler. Set pepper on a small baking sheet and broil as close to heat as possible, turning occasionally, until skin blisters all over, 6 to 8 minutes. Seal pepper in a paper bag and let steam 10 minutes. Peel and seed pepper under running water. Cut into 1-inch strips. Place in a colander to drain. Reduce oven temperature to 425°F.

2. In a medium saucepan, melt butter over medium heat. Add spinach and cook until hot, 2 to 3 minutes. Sprinkle on flour and cook, stirring, 1 to 2 minutes longer. Add milk, salt, and pepper. Bring to a boil, stirring occasionally, until mixture thickens slightly, 3 to 4 minutes. Remove from heat.

3. In a large frying pan, heat olive oil. Add onions and cook over medium heat, stirring occasionally, until beginning to color, 3 to 5 minutes. Add mushrooms and cook, stirring occasionally, until most of liquid evaporates, 4 to 5 minutes. Set aside.

4. To assemble torta, sprinkle Parmesan cheese and basil over bottom of 1 pie crust. Spread spinach over cheese-covered crust. Sprinkle with half of mozzarella. Sprinkle bacon bits over cheese. Cover evenly with onions and mushrooms. Sprinkle with remaining mozzarella. Cover with hard-boiled eggs and top with roasted pepper strips. On a lightly floured surface, carefully invert other crust and roll out wide enough to cover bottom pie shell. Carefully cover torta with rolled-out pastry crust. Crimp bottom and top edges of torta to seal. With a sharp knife, cut 4 slits in top crust.

5. Bake 25 to 30 minutes, until torta is nice and brown. Let cool 10 minutes before cutting.

169   QUICK SPINACH RICOTTA CALZONE

Prep: 20 minutes   Cook: 20 to 26 minutes   Makes: 6

These savory turnovers are filling enough to serve as a complete meal. You can usually purchase freshly made bread dough from an Italian baker, or buy the frozen variety in supermarkets. For a thinner crust, use an unbaked pizza crust.

⅓ cup extra-virgin olive oil
¼ pound mushrooms, sliced
1 cup frozen chopped
    spinach, thawed and
    drained
1 cup ricotta cheese
1 tablespoon grated Parmesan
    cheese
2 tablespoons minced onion
2 garlic cloves, minced

¾ cup shredded mozzarella
    cheese
1 teaspoon dried basil
½ teaspoon salt
¼ teaspoon pepper
1 pound frozen bread dough,
    thawed
1 egg, beaten with 1
    tablespoon water

1. Preheat oven to 400°F. In a large frying pan, heat 2 tablespoons olive oil. Add mushrooms and cook over medium heat, stirring occasionally, until mushrooms are limp and liquid evaporates, 4 to 5 minutes. Add drained spinach and cook, stirring, 1 minute. Set mixture in a colander to drain.

2. In a medium bowl, mix ricotta cheese with Parmesan, onion, garlic, mozzarella, basil, salt, and pepper. Mix in spinach and mushrooms.

3. Separate dough into 6 equal parts. On a lightly floured surface, roll out each part to a 6-inch circle. With fingertips or a small brush, paint each circle lightly with some olive oil. Divide spinach-mushroom filling equally among 6 circles. Brush edges with egg wash, fold calzones over, and press to seal. Paint tops of calzones with a little olive oil. Transfer to a lightly oiled baking sheet.

4. Bake 15 to 20 minutes, until calzones are golden brown. Serve at once.

170   PUFFED SPINACH SQUARES

Prep: 15 minutes   Cook: 20 to 22 minutes   Makes: about 20

1 (14-ounce) package frozen
    creamed spinach
½ teaspoon grated nutmeg
⅔ cup ricotta cheese
2 tablespoons dried basil
1 teaspoon lemon pepper
½ teaspoon salt

3 eggs, lightly beaten
1 rectangle frozen puff pastry
    sheet (½ a 17¼-ounce
    package), thawed
2 cups shredded Gruyère
    cheese

1. Preheat oven to 450°F. In a medium saucepan, prepare creamed spinach according to package directions. Remove from heat and stir in nutmeg, ricotta, basil, lemon pepper, and salt. Add eggs, one at a time, stirring to blend well.

2. On a lightly floured surface, roll out puff pastry sheet to form a 14 × 11-inch rectangle. Carefully transfer sheet to a lightly oiled baking sheet. With a sharp knife, cut off a ½-inch strip along each edge. With fingers, lightly wet top edges of puff pastry sheet with water. Carefully set strips around edge to form a shell.

3. With a spatula, spread spinach mixture evenly over puff pastry shell. Sprinkle with Gruyère cheese.

4. Bake 20 to 22 minutes, until puff pastry is golden and spinach mixture sets. Let cool before cutting into squares. This pie is best served warm.

171   RED LENTIL TURNOVERS WITH MUSHROOM WINE SAUCE

Prep: 10 minutes   Cook: 45 to 56 minutes   Makes: 10 to 12

1 tablespoon vegetable oil
1 medium onion, chopped
1 medium carrot, chopped
1 cup red lentils, rinsed and
    picked over
½ teaspoon dried thyme leaves
1 bay leaf
1 (14½-ounce) can vegetable
    broth or reduced-sodium
    chicken broth
½ teaspoon pepper
½ teaspoon salt

1 (17¼-ounce) package frozen
    puff pastry, at room
    temperature
1 egg, lightly beaten
3 tablespoons butter
½ pound mushrooms, sliced
1 tablespoon flour
¼ cup dry red wine
1 tablespoon Worcestershire
    sauce
2 teaspoons ketchup
1 teaspoon dried tarragon

1. In a medium saucepan, heat oil over medium-high heat. Add onions and cook, stirring occasionally, until soft, 2 to 3 minutes. Add carrot, lentils, thyme, bay leaf, broth, and pepper. Reduce heat to medium. Cover and cook until lentils are tender, 25 to 30 minutes. Drain and discard bay leaf. Season with salt. Set aside to cool.

2. Meanwhile, preheat oven to 400°F. On a floured surface, roll out thawed puff pastry sheet to ⅛-inch thickness. Using a 5-inch saucer as a template, cut out 10 or 12 circles. With fingers, dampen edge of each circle with beaten egg. Fill each circle with a scant ¼ cupful of lentils. Fold over to form a turnover. Crimp edges to seal. With a sharp knife, make 2 slits at top of puff to allow steam to escape. Set on oiled baking sheet.

3. Bake 12 to 15 minutes, or until turnovers are puffy and golden.

4. In a medium saucepan, melt butter. Add mushrooms and cook until limp, 3 to 4 minutes. With a slotted spoon, transfer mushrooms to a small bowl.

5. Add flour and ¼ cup wine to same saucepan. Cook, whisking, until mixture boils and thickens, 3 to 4 minutes. Whisk in ¼ cup water, Worcestershire, ketchup, and tarragon. Return mushrooms to sauce and heat through. Top baked lentil turnovers with mushroom sauce and serve hot.

172   PEAR AND BLUE CHEESE PASTRY
Prep: 20 minutes   Cook: 30 to 40 minutes   Serves: 4 to 6

When working with filo dough, be sure to keep sheets covered with a damp towel, or the dough will turn brittle.

1 **stick (4 ounces) butter, melted**	½ **cup crumbled Roquefort cheese (about 2 ounces)**
2 **firm Bosc pears, peeled, cored, and thinly sliced**	1 **teaspoon salt**
1 **cup walnuts, chopped**	¼ **teaspoon dried rosemary**
	8 **filo sheets, thawed**

1. In a large frying pan, melt 2 tablespoons butter over medium-low heat. Add pears and cook until soft and slightly caramelized, 10 to 15 minutes. Set aside to cool.

2. Meanwhile, in a small bowl, mix walnuts with crumbled cheese, salt, and rosemary. Set filo sheets on a dampened towel and cover with another damp towel.

3. Cut filo sheets into 12-inch rounds. (Make a paper template or use a 12-inch pizza pan to help you cut.) Layer 4 filo sheets on a large buttered baking sheet or 12-inch pizza pan, buttering each sheet generously. Cover fourth sheet evenly with walnut mixture. Top with cooked pears, arranging fruit as you would for an apple pie. Fold sides of bottom layers of filo over filling. Cover with remaining 4 buttered filo sheets. Butter top sheet well, and carefully fold sheets under pie, as you would a bedsheet. At this point, filo pie can be refrigerated up to 8 hours or overnight.

4. Preheat oven to 375°F. Bake pie until filo is crisp and golden, 20 to 25 minutes. Cut into wedges and serve immediately or pie will turn soggy.

173   ONION POPOVERS
Prep: 5 minutes   Cook: 45 minutes   Serves: 4 to 6

Serve these for brunch or as an accompaniment to soups or stews. Be sure you use eggs graded large for the correct proportions in this batter.

Vegetable oil or cooking
   spray
2 eggs
1 cup milk
1 cup flour

¼ teaspoon salt
⅛ teaspoon cayenne
1 tablespoon dry onion flakes,
   crushed

1. Preheat oven to 450°F. Generously grease 8 to 10 muffin tins. Heat muffin tins in oven.

2. In a blender or food processor, combine eggs, milk, flour, salt, cayenne, and onion flakes. Blend until smooth.

3. Pour batter into hot tins. Bake 10 minutes. Reduce oven temperature to 350°F. Bake 35 minutes longer, or until tops of popovers are nicely browned. Serve popovers while they are hot.

174   HERBED RICOTTA AND LEEK PASTRY
Prep: 15 minutes   Cook: 18 to 23 minutes   Serves: 6

1 (17¼-ounce) package frozen
   puff pastry dough,
   thawed
1 egg, lightly beaten
2 leeks (white and tender
   green), well rinsed and
   finely chopped

2 tablespoons vegetable oil
1 small onion, chopped
2 garlic cloves, minced
¼ teaspoon dried rosemary
4 ounces feta cheese
½ cup ricotta cheese

1. Preheat oven to 400°F. On a lightly floured surface, carefully unfold each puff pastry rectangle. Lightly roll out to a smooth dough. Transfer rectangles to a large nonstick baking sheet. With a sharp knife, cut a ½-inch strip of dough from all around edges. With fingers, moisten cut edges of rectangles. Stick cut strip of dough around edges to form 2 pastry shells. With a sharp knife, make several slits in bottoms of each dough rectangle.

2. Bake until golden and puffy, 10 to 12 minutes. Remove from oven; leave oven on.

3. Meanwhile, soak chopped leeks in cold water to remove all grit. Drain. In a large frying pan, heat vegetable oil over medium heat. Add leeks, onion, garlic, and rosemary, cover, and cook until onion is soft, 2 to 3 minutes. Remove from heat.

4. In a small bowl, mix feta cheese with ricotta, mashing cheese with a fork. Spread cooked leek mixture over baked pastry shells. Dot with feta mixture. Return to oven and bake 6 to 8 minutes, until heated through. Serve hot.

175   MOROCCAN-STYLE B'STEEYA
Prep: 25 minutes   Cook: 24 to 29 minutes   Serves: 6

This is my meatless adaptation of b'steeya, the traditional flaky filo pie best characterized as the crowning dish in the Moroccan culinary repertoire. Make it for a smashing first course or for a light dinner. Dress it up even further by using exotic mushrooms, such as shiitake or oyster mushrooms, in place of the white button mushrooms called for below.

2 sticks (8 ounces) butter,
    melted
1 bunch of scallions, chopped
1 pound white button
    mushrooms, sliced
2 garlic cloves, minced

½ teaspoon salt
¼ teaspoon pepper
½ cup chopped parsley
2 tablespoons bread crumbs
8 filo sheets, thawed

1. In a medium frying pan, heat 2 tablespoons butter and cook scallions over medium-high heat, stirring occasionally, until soft, about 2 minutes.

2. Add mushrooms and garlic. Cook, stirring occasionally, 2 minutes. (Mushrooms will not be cooked through at this point.) Stir in salt, pepper, parsley, and bread crumbs. Set aside to cool.

3. Set filo sheets on a dampened towel and cover with another damp towel. (Rewrap sheets remaining in package and refreeze for later use.)

4. Set one filo sheet on a well-oiled 10-inch pizza pan. With a brush, paint sheet with melted butter. Proceed in similar manner with next 3 sheets, painting each one generously with melted butter. Spread cooled mushroom mixture evenly on top. Fold outside edges of filo over mushrooms, shaping it into a pie. Cover with remaining 4 filo sheets, buttering each one. Carefully fold top filo sheets under pie, as you would a bedsheet. Generously butter top sheet. Cover with foil. At this point, b'steeya can be refrigerated up to 8 hours or overnight. Do not freeze.

5. To bake, preheat oven to 375°F. Remove foil. Bake b'steeya 20 to 25 minutes, until top crust is flaky and golden brown. Serve immediately, or filo will become soggy.

176   ASPARAGUS TURNOVERS
Prep: 25 minutes   Cook: 27 to 35 minutes   Serves: 6

There is nothing quite like puff pastry to dress up a mundane meal. For this dish, use frozen puff pastry shells, thaw them out, and then roll them to the size you need. These light and airy turnovers can be served as a first course or as a light meal.

1 **pound fresh asparagus, trimmed and cut in 1-inch pieces**	⅛ **teaspoon freshly ground pepper**
2 **teaspoons lemon juice**	1 **cup shredded Emmenthaler cheese**
2 **teaspoons dried tarragon**	1 **(17¼-ounce) package frozen puff pastry sheets, thawed**
2 **tablespoons butter**	
2 **tablespoons flour**	
1 **cup milk**	1 **egg, lightly beaten**
¼ **teaspoon salt**	

1. Preheat oven to 400°F. In a medium saucepan filled with lightly salted boiling water, cook asparagus until just tender, 2 to 3 minutes; drain. Rinse under cold water. Drain again and transfer to a small bowl. Add lemon juice and tarragon, toss, and set aside.

2. In a medium saucepan, melt 2 tablespoons butter over medium heat. Whisk in flour and cook, stirring, 1 to 2 minutes. Add milk all at once and bring to a boil, whisking, until sauce is thick and smooth, 2 to 3 minutes. Add salt, pepper, and cheese and cook, stirring until cheese melts, about 2 minutes. Stir in asparagus. Remove from heat and let cool 5 minutes.

3. Meanwhile, on a floured surface, cut each sheet into 3 equal parts and roll out each piece into a 6-inch square. Place ⅓ cup asparagus mixture in center of each square. Brush edges with beaten egg and fold over diagonally opposite corners to form a turnover. Crimp with a fork to seal. Lightly brush each turnover with additional beaten egg.

4. Set on a baking sheet. Bake 20 to 25 minutes, until turnovers are golden brown. Serve immediately, with remaining asparagus sauce, heated, on the side.

177 CORNISH PASTIES
Prep: 30 minutes   Chill: 1 hour   Cook: 54 to 65 minutes   Serves: 6

The Cornish pasty (pronounced PASS-tee) dates back to eighteenth-century Cornwall, England, where it was a standard workingman's lunch. To make these tasty turnovers in record time, purchase a pie crust mix and begin with step 2.

3 cups flour
1 teaspoon salt
1 cup vegetable shortening, at room temperature
7 to 8 tablespoons ice water
2 tablespoons butter
2 medium onions, chopped
2 small potatoes, peeled and cut into ½-inch dice
2 small turnips, peeled and cut into ½-inch dice

¼ pound mushrooms, coarsely chopped
2 tablespoons Worcestershire sauce
1 tablespoon ketchup
½ teaspoon salt
¼ teaspoon pepper
2 teaspoons dried dill weed
1 egg, lightly beaten

1. In a large bowl, mix flour with salt. In a food processor, with a pastry mixer or with 2 knives used scissor fashion, cut in shortening until mixture resembles coarse crumbs. Add water gradually, mixing well between each addition, until dough holds together. With your hands, shape dough into a ball. Cover with plastic wrap and refrigerate 1 hour.

2. Meanwhile, in a large frying pan, melt butter over medium heat. Cook onions, stirring occasionally, until golden, 4 to 5 minutes. Reduce heat to medium-low. Add potatoes, turnips, and mushrooms. Cover and cook, stirring occasionally, until potatoes are tender, 20 to 25 minutes. Stir in Worcestershire sauce, ketchup, salt, pepper, and dill. Remove from heat. Let cool 10 minutes.

3. Preheat oven to 400°F. To make pasties, cut chilled dough into 6 equal parts. On a floured surface, roll out each piece to 6 inches in diameter. Place ½ to ¾ cup filling in center of each circle. Moisten edges with beaten egg. Fold over and press edges with tines of a fork to seal. With a sharp knife, make 2 slits on top of each pasty. Set on a generously greased baking sheet.

4. Bake 30 to 35 minutes, until pasties are golden brown. Serve hot or at room temperature.

Chapter 7

Say It with Salads

Rare is the menu item that lends itself to as much creative variety as a salad. Whether hot or cold, a salad can assume as many identities as a quick change artist, from appetizers to main dishes and even desserts. Need a quick bean fix for a family get-together? How about a salad with a continental flair, such as Parisian Three-Bean Salad? For a light dessert, spice-tingling Cajun Fruit Cup will tickle adventurous palates.

In summer, when fresh vegetables are abundant, a colorful salad is a welcome sight at lunch or dinner. A summer luncheon with a French accent might include a colorful platter piled high with the makings for a Salade Niçoise, from market-fresh green beans and tender boiled potatoes to juicy, vine-ripened tomatoes. If a Mexican-style salad is in order, I often assemble a hearty Taco Bean Salad with Chili Yogurt Dressing. Crushed peanuts and fresh lime juice add an exciting twist to Crunchy Vietnamese Salad, which along with Cabbage Salad Orientale, an Asian-style slaw, counts among our family favorites. Fattoosh, a salad of Lebanese origins, is an unusual counterpart to the better-known Caesar salad.

In many countries around the world, a traditional meal always begins with an assortment of cooked and raw salads scattered around the table in small saucers, each seasoned with its own special dressing—a sort of vegetarian antipasto or tapas. Peppers are a tasty example. Some salads are best when left to marinate an hour or two, like German Potato Salad or the turmeric-flavored Peruvian Potatoes with Goat Cheese Dressing. Salads blending raw fruits and vegetables also make wonderful combinations, such as Chilied Orange and Fennel Salad or the Exotic Waldorf Salad studded with raisins and grapes.

Whatever you choose to prepare, use the freshest possible ingredients. Nothing is less appetizing than vegetables or fruits past their prime. Leafy greens should be washed carefully under running water, drained, and dried thoroughly before being tossed into the salad bowl.

Equally versatile as the ingredients in a salad is the choice of dressing, which can range from a simple vinaigrette to a creamy, herb-accented blend. Vinegars and oils now come in a variety of herb-infused flavors, with mild and low-acid balsamic and rice vinegars strong competitors to red wine or white vinegars. Specialty oils, such as virgin or extra-virgin olive oil (the difference is in the number of pressings), command almost as much space on the supermarket shelves these days as plain vegetable oil.

Like salads, dressings call for a dash of imagination: You can add your own signature to a lackluster dressing with fresh or dried herbs, such as parsley, tarragon (my favorite), or basil. When a creamy dressing is called for, try mixing mayonnaise and plain yogurt in equal quantities to lower the calorie count. Plain yogurt also makes an excellent low-fat substitute for sour cream in dips and cold sauces.

178 ASPARAGUS WALNUT SALAD

Prep: 15 minutes   Cook: 13 to 15 minutes   Serves: 6 to 8

Corkscrew pasta, or rotelle, is available in supermarkets. If you can find the tricolored variety—white, green, and orange—it will add extra color to this tasty salad.

8 ounces corkscrew pasta, preferably tricolored
½ pound asparagus, trimmed and cut into 2-inch pieces
8 ounces mozzarella cheese, cut into ½-inch cubes
2 medium tomatoes, seeded and diced

½ pound mushrooms, sliced
1 cup walnut pieces (about 4 ounces)
¼ cup olive oil
⅓ cup balsamic vinegar
1 (1-ounce) envelope Italian salad dressing mix

1. In a large saucepan filled with lightly salted boiling water, cook noodles until tender but still firm, 10 to 12 minutes. Drain and rinse under cold running water. Drain again and place in a large serving bowl.

2. In a medium saucepan of boiling water, cook asparagus until just tender, about 3 minutes. Drain, rinse under cold running water, and drain again. Transfer to bowl with pasta. Add mozzarella, tomatoes, mushrooms, and walnut pieces.

3. In a small bowl, whisk together olive oil, vinegar, and dressing mix. Pour dressing over salad and toss to coat evenly. Serve at room temperature or chilled.

179   EAST-WEST AVOCADO HALVES
Prep: 5 minutes   Cook: 2 minutes   Serves: 2

This is my husband Owen's favorite way of eating a ripe avocado. If you like spicy food, add a drop or two of Tabasco to the dressing.

2 tablespoons tomato ketchup
1 tablespoon dry white wine
2 tablespoons rice vinegar

2 tablespoons teriyaki sauce
2 tablespoons honey
2 large ripe avocados

1. In a small nonreactive saucepan, combine ketchup, wine, vinegar, teriyaki sauce, and honey. Cook over medium heat, stirring, until hot and well blended, about 2 minutes.

2. Meanwhile, peel avocados and cut in half. Rotate halves in opposite directions to loosen seed. Discard seed.

3. Set avocado halves on serving plates. Spoon equal amounts of warm sauce in each avocado cavity and serve.

180   TACO BEAN SALAD WITH CHILI YOGURT DRESSING
Prep: 20 minutes   Cook: none   Serves: 8 to 10

1 small head of iceberg lettuce, torn into bite-size pieces
1 (8¾-ounce) can kidney beans, drained
1 (8¾-ounce) can garbanzo beans, drained
1 (15-ounce) can white hominy, drained
1 medium onion, chopped
6 radishes, finely diced
2 celery ribs, finely diced
1 medium carrot, shredded
½ cup chopped cilantro
3 tablespoons balsamic vinegar

1 (4-ounce) can diced green chiles, drained
½ cup mayonnaise
1 (8-ounce) container plain yogurt
1 tablespoon chili powder
2 garlic cloves, crushed through a press
½ teaspoon salt
¼ teaspoon pepper
Grated zest and juice of ½ lime
1 (9-ounce) package seasoned tortilla chips, broken up

1. In a large salad bowl, combine lettuce, kidney beans, garbanzo beans, hominy, onion, radishes, celery, carrot, cilantro, and balsamic vinegar. Toss to mix, cover, and refrigerate until ready to serve.

2. In a medium bowl, mix chiles with mayonnaise, yogurt, chili powder, garlic, salt, pepper, lime zest, and lime juice.

3. Toss vegetables with tortilla chips just before serving. Pass chili yogurt dressing on the side.

181   CABBAGE SALAD ORIENTALE
Prep: 20 minutes   Cook: 1 to 2 minutes   Serves: 4 to 6

Let the Japanese enoki mushrooms marinate in the sauce for a few minutes to absorb the flavors of the dressing.

¼ cup slivered almonds	2 garlic cloves, minced
1 (3-ounce) packet ramen dry noodle soup with seasoning packet	1 teaspoon sugar
	⅓ cup sliced water chestnuts
2 tablespoons vegetable oil	1 (3-ounce) package enoki mushrooms, trimmed and separated
2 tablespoons Asian sesame oil	
2 tablespoons rice vinegar	1 small head of cabbage, shredded
1 tablespoon soy sauce or tamari	3 scallions, chopped
½ teaspoon minced fresh ginger	1 medium carrot, shredded

1. In a dry medium frying pan, toast almonds over medium heat, tossing, until they turn golden, 1 to 2 minutes. Set aside. In a small bowl, break up ramen noodles, reserving seasoning packet.

2. In a medium bowl, whisk together vegetable oil, sesame oil, vinegar, soy sauce, ginger, garlic, and sugar. Add contents of seasoning packet. Stir in water chestnuts and enoki mushrooms. Set aside to marinate 10 minutes.

3. In a large bowl, combine cabbage, scallions, and shredded carrot. Add mushroom mixture and marinade and toss to mix well. Just before serving, toss with broken-up ramen noodles and toasted almonds.

182   BELGIAN ENDIVE WITH ROQUEFORT DRESSING
Prep: 10 minutes   Cook: none   Serves: 4

French tradition warrants that this salad be served on Christmas or New Year's Eve in French homes, a tradition which my French-born grandmother used to follow. The slightly bitter taste of the tear-shaped Belgian endive marries itself well with Roquefort cheese and a strong-flavored vinaigrette. To clean endives, wipe them with a damp cloth. Don't soak them, since they tend to absorb water in the process.

2 teaspoons Dijon mustard	¼ teaspoon pepper
2 tablespoons raspberry vinegar	3 Belgian endives, sliced ½ inch thick
3 tablespoons walnut oil	¼ cup walnut pieces
1 garlic clove, minced	¼ cup crumbled Roquefort cheese
½ teaspoon salt	

1. In a small bowl, whisk mustard with vinegar. Add oil, garlic, salt, and pepper, and whisk until vinaigrette thickens.

2. In a large bowl, toss endives, walnuts, and Roquefort cheese with dressing. Serve chilled.

---

183   MEXICAN SLAW
Prep: 20 minutes   Cook: 1 to 2 minutes   Serves: 8 to 10

¾ cup cider vinegar	1 medium green bell pepper, thinly sliced
½ cup sugar	
2 teaspoons dry mustard	1 medium red bell pepper, thinly sliced
1 teaspoon celery seed	
1 teaspoon salt	1 (8-ounce) can whole-kernel corn, drained
⅛ teaspoon cayenne	
½ cup vegetable oil	½ cup sliced black olives
1 medium head of green cabbage, shredded	½ cup pimiento-stuffed green olives, sliced
1 large Bermuda onion, thinly sliced	1 (7-ounce) can diced green chiles, drained

1. In a medium nonreactive saucepan, combine vinegar, sugar, dry mustard, celery seed, salt, and cayenne. Bring to a boil over medium heat. Cook, stirring, until sugar dissolves, 1 to 2 minutes. Remove from heat and let cool. Whisk in oil.

2. Meanwhile, in a large serving bowl, combine cabbage, onion, green and red peppers, corn, black and green olives, and diced green chiles. Pour on dressing and toss. Cover and refrigerate until serving time.

---

184   CELERY ROOT RÉMOULADE
Prep: 20 minutes   Cook: none   Chill: 1 hour   Serves: 4

This classic French salad is one of my favorites. Celery root is a large, daunting root, which requires some patience to peel. The resulting salad is worth every effort, however. The vinaigrette should be quite highly spiced.

1 (2-pound) celery root	1 tablespoon chopped parsley
2 tablespoons lemon juice	1 garlic clove, minced
1 tablespoon Dijon mustard	1 hard-boiled egg, finely diced
1 tablespoon red wine vinegar	
¾ cup vegetable oil	½ teaspoon salt

1. With a brush, scrub celery root under running water. Peel root with a sharp stainless steel paring knife. With large holes of a hand-held grater, shred root and place in a medium serving bowl. Toss with lemon juice so root doesn't darken.

2. In a small bowl, whisk together mustard and vinegar until thickened. Add 1 tablespoon water and blend well. Gradually whisk in oil in a stream until dressing is consistency of mayonnaise. Stir in parsley, garlic, egg, and salt. Mix with celery root. Cover and refrigerate until chilled, at least 1 hour.

185 FATTOOSH

Prep: 20 minutes   Cook: 4 to 6 minutes   Serves: 4 to 6

This is an unusual salad of Lebanese origins—a sort of Middle Eastern Caesar salad. You can use either French bread or sourdough to make the bread cubes. The parsley, cilantro, and mint leaves are left whole to create a more interesting texture.

1 small eggplant	1 head of romaine lettuce, torn
½ cup extra-virgin olive oil	into bite-size pieces
½ small cucumber, peeled and	4 cups fresh bread cubes,
sliced	toasted
4 cups loosely packed Italian	2 garlic cloves, minced
flat-leaf parsley, rinsed	¼ cup raspberry or red wine
and patted dry	vinegar
12 whole mint leaves, rinsed	2 teaspoons lemon juice
and patted dry	½ teaspoon salt
¼ cup loosely packed cilantro	¼ teaspoon pepper
leaves, rinsed and patted	
dry	

1. Preheat broiler. Cut eggplant lengthwise in slices ¼ inch thick. Paint slices lightly with olive oil. Set in a single layer on a foil-lined baking sheet. Broil until light brown, turning carefully with tongs, 2 to 3 minutes on each side. Transfer slices to platter or cutting board and allow to cool. Cut each slice into ½-inch strips.

2. In a salad bowl, mix cucumber, parsley, mint leaves, cilantro, and lettuce. In a medium bowl, toss bread cubes with garlic.

3. In a small bowl, whisk vinegar, remaining olive oil, lemon juice, salt, and pepper until blended.

4. Just before serving, add eggplant strips and garlic croutons to salad. Pour on dressing and toss.

186 INDONESIAN GADO GADO WITH PEANUT SAUCE

Prep: 25 minutes   Cook: 26 to 36 minutes   Serves: 6 to 8

Any seasonal vegetables can star in this colorful Indonesian main-course salad.

12 small new potatoes, cut in half
1 medium head of cauliflower, broken into florets
1 pound fresh green beans
3 large zucchini, cut into ½-inch-thick slices
1 head of romaine lettuce, separated into leaves
1 large cucumber, peeled, seeded, and sliced
4 hard-boiled eggs, cut into quarters

4 ounces fresh bean sprouts
¼ cup creamy peanut butter
2 garlic cloves, minced
¼ to ½ teaspoon red chili flakes
¾ cup vegetable or reduced-sodium chicken broth
1 tablespoon soy sauce or tamari
2 teaspoons brown sugar
1 tablespoon lemon juice
1 cup crushed peanuts
1 (2.8-ounce) can French-fried onion rings, crushed

1. In a large saucepan filled with boiling water, cook potatoes, covered, until tender, 15 to 20 minutes; drain. Let cool, then peel. Set aside.

2. Meanwhile, in another large saucepan filled with lightly salted boiling water, cook cauliflower until tender, 3 to 5 minutes. With a slotted spoon, transfer to a medium bowl.

3. In same pan, return water to a boil. Add green beans and cook 2 minutes. Add zucchini and cook until both vegetables are barely tender, 3 to 4 minutes. Drain in colander, then let cool.

4. Arrange lettuce leaves to cover bottom of a large serving platter. Set cooked vegetables on top of leaves. Intersperse with cucumber slices and hard-boiled eggs. Top with sprouts.

5. In a medium saucepan, heat peanut butter over medium-low heat. Add garlic, chili flakes, and broth and cook, stirring, until sauce thickens, 3 to 5 minutes. Add soy sauce, brown sugar, and lemon juice. Stir to dissolve sugar and remove from heat.

6. To serve, sprinkle crushed peanuts and onion rings over top of salad. Serve at room temperature, with warm peanut sauce on the side.

NOTE: *If peanut sauce thickens upon standing, reheat with a little water to thin.*

187   PARISIAN THREE-BEAN SALAD

Prep: 15 minutes   Cook: 2 to 3 minutes   Serves: 4

For this salad, use the smallest, tenderest green beans you can find, preferably the slender French variety known as *haricots verts*.

¼ pound thin green beans
1 (10-ounce) package frozen baby lima beans, thawed
½ cup olive oil
2 tablespoons tarragon-flavored vinegar
1 teaspoon Dijon mustard
1 garlic clove, minced
½ teaspoon sugar

¼ teaspoon salt
¼ teaspoon pepper
1 (15-ounce) can cannellini beans, drained
1 large sweet onior , very thinly sliced
1 tablespoon chopped chives

1. In a medium saucepan filled with boiling water, cook green beans and lima beans until green beans are crisp-tender, 2 to 3 minutes. Drain and rinse under running water. Set aside to cool.

2. In a small bowl, make dressing by whisking together olive oil, vinegar, 1 tablespoon water, mustard, garlic, sugar, salt, and pepper until well blended.

3. In a serving bowl, mix green beans and lima beans with cannellini beans and sliced onion. Toss with dressing. Sprinkle with chives. Serve at room temperature.

188   GAZPACHO ASPIC WITH WATERCRESS MAYONNAISE

Prep: 20 minutes   Cook: 5 to 7 minutes   Chill: 12 hours
Serves: 6 to 12

3 envelopes unflavored gelatin
½ cup dry vermouth
3½ cups canned tomato or V8 juice
2 tablespoons Worcestershire sauce
1 tablespoon balsamic vinegar
2 garlic cloves, minced
½ cup finely diced cucumber
½ medium carrot, shredded
3 scallions, finely chopped

1 celery rib, finely diced
2 radishes, sliced
2 tablespoons chopped parsley
½ teaspoon pepper
1 bunch of watercress, stems removed
½ cup mayonnaise
½ cup plain yogurt
2 teaspoons lemon juice
Lettuce leaves
Pitted olives, for decoration

1. In a small bowl, sprinkle gelatin over vermouth. Stir well. Place bowl inside a pan filled with 2 inches of water over medium heat. Heat, stirring, until gelatin dissolves, 5 to 7 minutes.

2. In a large bowl, combine gelatin with tomato juice, Worcestershire sauce, balsamic vinegar, and garlic. Stir well. Add cucumber, carrot, scallions, celery, radishes, parsley, and pepper. Pour gazpacho into a generously oiled 6-cup ring mold. Cover and refrigerate 12 to 24 hours.

3. In a blender or food processor, puree watercress with mayonnaise, yogurt, and lemon juice. Transfer watercress mayonnaise to a small bowl. Cover and refrigerate until serving time.

4. To serve, unmold aspic by running a knife around inside of pan and dipping mold in warm water 10 to 20 seconds. Invert onto a platter lined with lettuce leaves. Decorate with pitted olives. Serve with watercress mayonnaise on the side.

---

189 FRESH BEAN MEDLEY WITH MARINATED BABY CORN

Prep: 20 minutes   Stand: 30 minutes   Cook: 4 to 6 minutes
Serves: 4 to 6

This salad is one of the inspirations of Andrea Peterson, a farmer in San Diego County who specializes in gourmet produce. Purple beans are sometimes available in farmers' markets or specialty food stores. If not, just double the amount of fresh green beans.

¼ cup olive oil	½ pound yellow wax beans
3 tablespoons balsamic vinegar	½ pound green beans
1 teaspoon sugar	½ pound purple beans (or use more green beans)
1 tablespoon soy sauce or tamari	¼ cup pine nuts
½ teaspoon pepper	4 ounces crumbled feta cheese (about 1 cup)
6 ears of canned baby corn	

1. In a small bowl, mix olive oil, vinegar, sugar, soy sauce, and pepper. Add drained baby corn to marinade and set aside 30 minutes.

2. Meanwhile, in a large pot filled with lightly salted boiling water, blanch yellow, green, and purple beans until crisp-tender, 2 to 3 minutes; drain.

3. In a dry nonstick medium frying pan, toast pine nuts over medium heat, shaking pan several times, until lightly browned, 2 to 3 minutes. Transfer to a small bowl.

4. Just before serving, in a large salad bowl, toss beans with marinated corn, crumbled feta cheese, and pine nuts. Serve at room temperature or slightly chilled.

190   GRUYÈRE SALAD
Prep: 15 minutes   Cook: none   Chill: 1 hour   Serves: 4

This is often part of the assortment of salads that opens a traditional French meal.

½ pound Gruyère cheese, cut into ½-inch cubes
2 celery ribs, finely diced
½ large sweet onion, finely diced
2 garlic cloves, minced
2 tablespoons chopped chives
¾ cup finely chopped parsley
4 radishes, thinly sliced

1 tablespoon balsamic vinegar
2 tablespoons olive oil
1 teaspoon Dijon mustard
⅓ cup bottled horseradish sauce
8 lettuce leaves
⅓ cup broken-up walnut pieces

1. In a medium bowl, combine cheese, celery, onion, garlic, chives, parsley, and radishes. Toss to mix.

2. In a small bowl, whisk together vinegar, olive oil, mustard, and horseradish sauce. Pour dressing over cheese mixture and toss to coat. Cover and refrigerate at least 1 hour, until chilled.

3. To serve, spoon salad onto lettuce leaves and garnish with walnut pieces.

191   FANCY MACARONI SALAD
*Prep: 10 minutes   Cook: 8 to 10 minutes   Chill: 1 hour
Serves: 8 to 10*

Add the avocado at the last minute to prevent it from turning brown.

1 (16-ounce) package elbow macaroni
1 (16-ounce) container fresh Mexican salsa or homemade (page 260)
1 (7-ounce) jar marinated artichoke hearts, coarsely chopped

3 scallions, finely chopped
1 ripe avocado, peeled and diced
¼ cup chopped Italian parsley

1. In a medium saucepan filled with lightly salted boiling water, cook macaroni until tender but still firm, 8 to 10 minutes. Drain and rinse under cold running water. Drain well. Transfer to a serving bowl.

2. Add salsa, artichoke hearts, and scallions. Toss to mix. Cover and refrigerate until chilled, 1 to 2 hours. Just before serving, toss with avocado and sprinkle with chopped parsley.

192 MEDITERRANEAN SALAD WITH ARTICHOKE HEARTS AND FETA CHEESE

Prep: 15 minutes   Cook: none   Serves: 2

For a more pungent vinaigrette, make your own garlic oil by steeping 4 cloves of crushed garlic overnight in 2 cups of extra-virgin olive oil. This is a main-course salad. As a first course, it would serve four.

½ small head of romaine lettuce, torn into bite-size pieces
1 Belgian endive, sliced
½ cup diced (½-inch) artichoke hearts
1 tablespoon capers, drained
1 (4-ounce) package crumbled feta cheese, preferably herb-flavored

1 teaspoon Dijon mustard
2 tablespoons rice wine vinegar
¼ cup olive oil
2 garlic cloves, minced
⅛ teaspoon pepper
⅛ teaspoon salt
¼ cup chopped parsley
1 tablespoon walnut pieces

1. On a serving platter or 2 large plates, arrange lettuce and Belgian endive. Top with artichoke hearts, capers, and feta cheese.

2. In a small bowl, whisk together mustard and vinegar until smooth. Whisk in olive oil, garlic, pepper, and salt until well blended. Stir in chopped parsley.

3. Spoon dressing over salads and sprinkle walnut pieces on top.

193 CAJUN FRUIT CUP

Prep: 15 minutes   Cook: none   Chill: 1 hour   Serves: 6

1 medium honeydew melon
1 small cantaloupe
1 large slice of watermelon
1 medium cucumber
1 tablespoon lime juice

1½ tablespoons finely chopped fresh mint
2 teaspoons Cajun seasoning
2 teaspoons candied ginger, finely diced

1. Cut honeydew and cantaloupe melons in half and scoop out seeds. With a melon baller, scoop out melon balls and place them in a large serving bowl. Proceed in same manner with watermelon.

2. Peel and finely dice cucumber. Add to melon balls.

3. Add the lime juice, mint, and Cajun seasoning. Cover and refrigerate at least 1 hour, until well chilled. Sprinkle candied ginger on top.

194   CONFETTI PEPPERS
Prep: 20 minutes   Cook: 6 to 8 minutes   Serves: 6 to 8

This cumin-accented pepper salad is a Moroccan classic. For a more festive appearance, use a combination of red, yellow, and green bell peppers.

8 large green, yellow, and/or red bell peppers	2 teaspoons ground cumin
2 tablespoons olive oil	½ teaspoon salt
2 garlic cloves, minced	¼ teaspoon pepper
	2 tablespoons lemon juice

1. Preheat broiler. Set peppers on a baking sheet. Broil as close to heat as possible, turning, until skins blister evenly, 6 to 8 minutes. Transfer peppers to a bag and seal. Let steam 10 minutes. When cool enough to handle, peel and seed peppers under running water. Set in a colander to drain.

2. Finely dice peppers and place in a serving bowl. Mix with olive oil, garlic, cumin, salt, pepper, and lemon juice. Serve chilled.

195   PERUVIAN POTATOES WITH GOAT CHEESE DRESSING
Prep: 20 minutes   Cook: 20 to 25 minutes   Serves: 4 to 6

Turmeric adds a bright yellow tint to the goat cheese dressing, which dresses up this unusual Peruvian specialty. Select the creamiest potatoes you can find, such as small red potatoes or, better yet, buttery Yukon Golds. The length of cooking time will depend on the quality and size of the potatoes.

1½ pounds small red or white potatoes	½ teaspoon ground cumin
1 (5⅓-ounce) package soft goat cheese	6 ears of canned baby corn
⅛ teaspoon turmeric	½ cup diced red bell pepper
2 garlic cloves, minced	2 hard-boiled eggs, sliced
2 tablespoons lemon juice	12 kalamata olives
2 tablespoons plain yogurt	2 tablespoons chopped parsley
1 jalapeño pepper, seeded and minced	

1. In a large saucepan of boiling salted water, cook potatoes until tender, 20 to 25 minutes. Drain and let cool. Quarter potatoes.

2. Meanwhile, in a blender or food processor, combine goat cheese, turmeric, garlic, lemon juice, yogurt, jalapeño pepper, and cumin. Puree goat cheese dressing until smooth.

3. To assemble, in a medium bowl, combine potatoes, baby corn, and red pepper. Add dressing and toss to coat. Arrange salad on a large serving platter. Top with sliced egg and olives. Garnish with chopped parsley. Serve chilled or at room temperature.

196   GERMAN POTATO SALAD
Prep: 15 minutes   Cook: 31 to 38 minutes   Serves: 6

My mother-in-law, Letty Morse, is a Wisconsin native whose German-style potato salad is a must at every family picnic. In this adapted version of Letty's specialty, toss the warm potatoes with the dressing for best results.

2 pounds red potatoes, scrubbed	½ cup sugar
1 large sweet onion, chopped	¼ teaspoon liquid smoke (optional)
1 teaspoon salt	¼ cup chopped parsley
2 tablespoons cornstarch	½ cup imitation bacon bits
½ cup cider vinegar	2 hard-boiled eggs, quartered

1. In a large saucepan filled with boiling water, cook potatoes until tender but not mushy, 25 to 30 minutes; drain. When potatoes are cool enough to handle, peel and cut into 1-inch cubes. Transfer to a serving bowl and toss with onion and salt. Cover and set aside.

2. Meanwhile, in a medium saucepan, bring 1½ cups water to a boil. In a small bowl, dissolve cornstarch in ½ cup cold water. Add to boiling water, stirring constantly until mixture thickens somewhat, 1 to 2 minutes. Reduce heat to medium-low. Add vinegar and sugar and stir until mixture thickens, 5 to 6 minutes. Stir in liquid smoke.

3. Pour hot dressing over potatoes, add chopped parsley, and toss to coat evenly. Sprinkle bacon bits on top and decorate with egg quarters. Serve at room temperature.

197   NICOLE'S MARINATED MUSHROOMS
Prep: 10 minutes   Cook: none   Chill: 1 hour   Serves: 4

These marinated mushrooms are one of my mother's specialties. Pick out the freshest, firmest button mushrooms available for this tasty salad.

1 pound small fresh button mushrooms	½ teaspoon salt
2 tablespoons lemon juice	¼ teaspoon pepper
¼ cup chopped parsley	¼ cup olive oil
½ teaspoon dried tarragon	Lettuce leaves

1. Wipe whole button mushrooms clean with a damp cloth. Place in a medium bowl. Add lemon juice and toss to coat. Add parsley, tarragon, salt, pepper, and olive oil. Stir well. Cover and refrigerate for at least 1 hour until ready to serve, stirring occasionally.

2. To serve, spoon equal amounts of mushrooms onto individual plates lined with lettuce leaves.

198 SPINACH SALAD WITH PARSLEY MAYONNAISE

Prep: 20 minutes   Cook: none   Serves: 4

1 pound fresh spinach leaves
1 large sweet onion, sliced
   into paper-thin rings
1 red bell pepper, sliced into
   ¼-inch rings
2 hard-boiled eggs, quartered
1 cup mayonnaise
½ cup plain yogurt
3 scallions, chopped

2 garlic cloves, minced
1 tablespoon capers, drained
1 teaspoon Dijon mustard
2 tablespoons balsamic
   vinegar
¾ cup chopped parsley
2 medium tomatoes, halved
   and sliced

1. Rinse spinach well under cold running water, taking care to remove all grit. Spin or pat dry. Tear leaves into bite-size pieces. Arrange spinach leaves on 4 individual salad plates. Top with onion rings, pepper rings, and hard-boiled eggs.

2. In a blender or food processor, combine mayonnaise, yogurt, scallions, garlic, capers, mustard, vinegar, and parsley. Puree until smooth.

3. To serve, arrange tomato slices in a scallop fashion around each plate. Spoon dressing over salad. Serve chilled.

199 CHILLED ORANGE AND FENNEL SALAD

Prep: 20 minutes   Cook: none   Serve: 8

This salad calls for sweet onions, such as Maui or Vidalia, and the sweetest oranges possible.

8 small sweet seedless
   oranges
½ cup vegetable oil
2 tablespoons balsamic
   vinegar
1 teaspoon ground cumin
1 teaspoon chili powder

1 head of romaine lettuce,
   shredded
2 medium sweet onions, very
   thinly sliced
1 fennel bulb, cut into ¼-inch
   rings

1. Peel oranges, removing all bitter white pith. Cut oranges into ¼-inch slices.

2. In a small bowl, whisk together oil, vinegar, cumin, and chili powder. Set dressing aside.

3. Spread a layer of shredded romaine on a large serving platter. Cover with a layer of orange slices. Cover liberally with onion slices. Top with fennel rings. Spoon dressing over salad. Serve chilled.

200 ROASTED POTATO SALAD WITH CAPERS AND BALSAMIC VINEGAR

Prep: 10 minutes   Cook: 20 to 25 minutes   Serves: 4 to 6

2 pounds russet potatoes, peeled and cut into 1-inch cubes
¼ cup olive oil
3 garlic cloves, minced
3 tablespoons balsamic vinegar

¼ medium sweet onion, chopped
1 tablespoon capers, drained
¼ teaspoon salt
½ teaspoon freshly ground pepper

1. Preheat oven to 400° F. In a medium bowl, toss diced potatoes with olive oil and garlic. Place potatoes in a single layer on a large baking sheet. Roast 20 to 25 minutes, tossing occasionally, until potatoes are tender. Set aside to cool.

2. Transfer potatoes to a serving bowl. Toss with balsamic vinegar, onion, capers, salt, and pepper. Serve at room temperature or chilled.

201 SPINACH GRAPEFRUIT PLATE

Prep: 10 minutes   Cook: none   Serves: 4

2 pink grapefruit
2 teaspoons ground cumin
1 teaspoon salt
1 pound fresh spinach
½ cup olive oil

2 tablespoons balsamic vinegar
1 cup oil-cured black olives, pitted

1. Peel and seed grapefruit. Separate into sections, removing skin and white membrane. Cut into chunks. Transfer to a small bowl and toss with cumin and salt.

2. Rinse spinach well under cold running water, taking care to remove all grit. Tear off tough stems. Pat or spin dry. Arrange spinach leaves on 4 individual serving plates. In a small bowl, whisk together olive oil and balsamic vinegar.

3. To serve, spoon equal amounts of grapefruit over spinach. Sprinkle with dressing. Top with black olives. Serve chilled.

202   SALADE NIÇOISE

Prep: 10 minutes   Cook: 25 to 33 minutes   Serves: 4 to 6

This classic composed French salad hails from Nice, a town in the south of France. Canned or frozen vegetables are not recommended, since the flavors depend on using the freshest seasonal produce available. Tiny French marinated olives are available in specialty food stores, although Greek kalamata olives are fine substitutes.

6 red or white potatoes, 1 to 1½ inches in diameter	½ teaspoon salt
1 red bell pepper	¼ teaspoon pepper
1 pound fresh green beans	2 large ripe tomatoes, sliced
2 teaspoons Dijon mustard	1 cucumber, peeled and sliced
2 tablespoons rice wine vinegar	1 sweet Bermuda onion, thinly sliced
1 teaspoon lemon juice	1 fennel bulb, cut into ½-inch rings (optional)
2 garlic cloves, minced	2 hard-boiled eggs, quartered
1 teaspoon dried tarragon	½ cup French or Greek olives
¾ cup extra-virgin olive oil	2 tablespoons capers, drained
1 teaspoon sugar	

1. In a large saucepan filled with boiling salted water, cook potatoes until tender, 15 to 20 minutes. Drain and set aside.

2. Preheat broiler. Place pepper on a baking sheet and broil as close to heat as possible, turning occasionally, until skin blisters evenly, 6 to 8 minutes. Or roast directly over a gas flame for about 5 minutes. Transfer to a bag and seal. Let steam 10 minutes. Peel and seed pepper under running water. Cut into strips and set aside.

3. Meanwhile, in another large saucepan of boiling water, cook beans until crisp-tender, 4 to 5 minutes. Drain and rinse under cold running water. Drain well.

4. To make dressing, place mustard, vinegar, lemon juice, garlic, tarragon, olive oil, sugar, salt, and pepper in a blender or food processor. Blend until smooth and thickened.

5. To serve, arrange all salad ingredients attractively on a large serving platter. Top with pepper strips. Sprinkle with capers. Serve with dressing on the side.

203   VEGETABLE AIOLI

Prep: 15 minutes   Cook: 51 to 63 minutes   Serves: 4 to 6

Aioli is a pungent garlic-flavored mayonnaise traditionally served in the south of France as a condiment for a composed salad of cooked and raw vegetables. It is also the name of the assembled dish. Serve as a first course or side dish.

2 pounds small red or white potatoes	4 medium carrots, sliced
½ pound small beets	4 ripe tomatoes, sliced
1 large head of cauliflower, broken into florets	⅔ cup mayonnaise
1 pound zucchini or yellow crookneck squash, sliced crosswise on a diagonal	½ cup extra-virgin olive oil
	5 garlic cloves, crushed through a press
	1½ tablespoons lemon juice
½ pound green beans	2 teaspoons capers, drained
	⅛ teaspoon pepper

1. In a large saucepan of boiling water, cook potatoes until tender, 20 to 25 minutes. Drain and set aside.

2. Meanwhile, in a medium saucepan of boiling water, cook beets until tender, 20 to 25 minutes. Drain and let cool. Peel and cut into ¼-inch-thick slices.

3. In another large saucepan of boiling salted water, cook cauliflower until barely tender, about 5 minutes. Scoop out with a skimmer or slotted spoon, place in a colander, and rinse under cold running water; drain well. Add zucchini to same pan and cook until barely tender, 2 to 3 minutes. Scoop out, transfer to colander, rinse briefly, and drain well. Add green beans and carrots to pan and cook until crisp-tender, 4 to 5 minutes. Drain and set aside.

4. Arrange all vegetables decoratively on a large serving platter. Garnish with tomato slices.

5. In a blender or food processor, combine mayonnaise, olive oil, garlic, lemon juice, capers, and pepper. Transfer to a serving bowl. Serve vegetables at room temperature, with aioli sauce on the side.

204 CRUNCHY VIETNAMESE SALAD
Prep: 20 minutes   Stand: 30 minutes   Cook: 2 to 3 minutes
Serves: 4 to 6

My husband and I are particularly fond of Vietnamese food, and this is one of our favorite salads. It looks smashing on a buffet table!

4 ounces bean threads or cellophane noodles
2 eggs
4 teaspoons soy sauce or tamari
5 garlic cloves, minced
1 tablespoon butter
4 scallions, coarsely chopped
1 cup bean sprouts
1 (3-ounce) package enoki mushrooms, cleaned, separated, and trimmed

2 tablespoons finely chopped fresh mint
½ small cabbage, finely shredded
½ medium sweet onion, sliced paper thin
6 tablespoons fresh lime juice
3 tablespoons Asian sesame oil
1 teaspoon Chinese chili paste
2 tablespoons sugar
½ cup dry-roasted peanuts, crushed

1. In a medium bowl, soak cellophane noodles in warm water 30 minutes. Drain well. With scissors, cut noodles into 2-inch pieces. Set aside.

2. Meanwhile, in a small bowl, beat eggs with 1 teaspoon soy sauce and 1 minced garlic clove. In a medium frying pan, melt butter over medium heat. Add eggs and swirl mixture around pan to cover bottom. Cook until set, 2 to 3 minutes. Slide onto a plate and let cool. Carefully roll up omelet jelly-roll fashion and slice into ¼-inch-wide strips.

3. Arrange a bed of cellophane noodles on bottom of a large serving platter. Sprinkle with chopped scallions. Spread bean sprouts over scallions. Arrange enoki mushrooms over bean sprouts. Top with half of chopped mint leaves. Cover with half of omelet strips. Top with all of cabbage, onion rings, and remaining omelet strips. Garnish with remaining mint.

4. In a small bowl, combine remaining 3 teaspoons of soy sauce, lime juice, sesame oil, Chinese chili paste, sugar, remaining garlic, and 3 tablespoons water. Mix until well blended. Spoon dressing over salad. Top with crushed peanuts. Serve chilled.

205 EXOTIC WALDORF SALAD
Prep: 20 minutes   Cook: none   Chill: 1 hour   Serves: 8

1 tablespoon bottled creamy
   horseradish sauce
¾ cup mayonnaise
¼ cup plain yogurt
1 tablespoon honey
   Grated zest of ½ orange
3 tart apples, peeled, cored,
   and diced
2 bananas, sliced
¼ cup orange juice

1 fresh pineapple, peeled,
   cored, and cut into 1-inch
   cubes
1 cup seedless grapes
1 cup golden seedless raisins
1 tablespoon candied ginger,
   finely diced
4 kiwifruit, peeled and sliced
½ cup crushed macadamia
   nuts

1. In a small bowl, mix horseradish, mayonnaise, yogurt, honey, and orange zest. Set aside.

2. In a medium bowl, toss diced apples and sliced bananas with orange juice. Set aside.

3. In a serving bowl, mix pineapple, grapes, raisins, and candied ginger. Toss with dressing. Stir in apples and bananas. Decorate with kiwi slices. Cover and refrigerate at least 1 hour. Sprinkle with macadamia nuts before serving.

Chapter 8

Creative Ways with Rice and Other Grains

The choice of grains now available in supermarkets and in health food stores can be overwhelming. The myriad varieties of white and brown rice, newly rediscovered and commercialized "heirloom" grains such as quinoa (pronounced KEEN-wah), or foreign imports like couscous, a cracked durum wheat semolina, make it easier to meet the guidelines of the USDA's Food Guide Pyramid, which recommends a daily intake of 6 to 11 servings of pasta, bread, cereal, or rice. This gives you a lot of leeway when planning a nutritionally well-balanced meal.

The most popular grain to grace the American table is still white rice. Yet Americans consume a mere twenty pounds per person per year compared to the Chinese, who eat many times that amount. Long-grain rice, as its name implies, is a longer and more slender grain. It is the most commonly available and is used in most of the rice recipes included in this book. Brown rice, the most wholesome rice product because it is the least refined, is often labeled as a health food because of its higher fiber and oil content. When the kernels are milled until their protective layers of bran disintegrate, the end product is white or polished rice. Be sure to store brown rice in the refrigerator or freezer, since it can turn rancid.

Wild rice, the only grain native to North America, is not a rice at all, but rather the seed of an aquatic grass (*Zizania aquatica*), grown mainly in California and Minnesota. One thing to remember when cooking wild rice is that it will plump up to four times its original size, and needs to cook until the kernels literally burst open. Other grains, such as wheat berries and millet, add a hearty consistency to soups and stews, while the aptly named pearl barley cooks up to the appearance of small pearls. Thanks to its high fiber content, it is reputed to help reduce levels of fat and cholesterol in the bloodstream. A quick rinse under cold running water before cooking rice or other grains is recommended to get rid of any impurities.

The dishes built around grains in this chapter will take you on a whirlwind tour around the world from West African Jolof Rice to Italy's Risotto with Peas.

For this Casablanca-born cook, there is no comfort food more appealing than a platter piled high with Seven-Vegetable Couscous, while the light Herb and Garlic Cheese Grits Soufflé hails from my midwestern husband's side of the family. Why not try a tasty, nutritious grain dish on your own family?

206   JAMBALAYA PIQUANT

Prep: 10 minutes   Cook: 26 to 33 minutes   Serves: 4

3 cups vegetable broth or
   reduced-sodium chicken
   broth
1½ cups long-grain white rice
2 tablespoons olive oil
2 medium onions, chopped
½ medium red bell pepper,
   finely diced
2 fresh green chiles, minced
3 garlic cloves, minced
1 (16-ounce) can Cajun-style
   stewed tomatoes

2 celery ribs, finely diced
1 (11-ounce) can whole-kernel
   corn, liquid reserved
2 tablespoons capers, drained
2 tablespoons Worcestershire
   sauce
⅛ teaspoon cayenne
1 medium avocado, cubed
1 tablespoon lemon juice

1. In a medium saucepan, bring broth to a boil. Stir in rice, cover, and cook over medium-low heat until tender, 15 to 20 minutes. Remove from heat and fluff with a fork.

2. Meanwhile, in a large frying pan, heat olive oil over medium heat. Add onions and cook, stirring occasionally, until softened, 3 minutes. Add bell pepper, green chiles, and garlic. Cook, stirring occasionally, for 3 minutes.

3. Add tomatoes and celery. Reduce heat to low, cover, and cook, until celery softens, 3 to 4 minutes. Add corn with its liquid, capers, Worcestershire sauce, and cayenne. Stir and remove from heat until rice is ready.

4. In a small bowl, toss avocado cubes with lemon juice. Add fluffed rice to tomato mixture in pan. Stir to blend all ingredients. Heat through for 2 to 3 minutes. Top with avocado cubes and serve immediately.

207   MOST EXCELLENT FRIED RICE

Prep: 10 minutes   Cook: 7 to 11 minutes   Serves: 2

This is a terrific recipe to make when you have leftover cooked rice. If you're doing it from scratch, begin with ⅔ cup raw rice and 1⅓ cups water and cook, covered, 15 to 20 minutes. Cool slightly before proceeding.

2 dried Chinese mushrooms
2 tablespoons Asian sesame
   oil
2 eggs, lightly beaten
1 small onion, chopped
2 cups cooked rice
2 tablespoons soy sauce or
   tamari

⅛ teaspoon Chinese five-spice
   powder (optional)
⅛ teaspoon sugar
½ cup frozen green peas,
   thawed
½ cup roasted peanuts

1. In a small bowl, soak mushrooms in warm water until softened, about 10 minutes. Drain, reserving mushroom water. Discard woody stems. Cut cap into thin strips.

2. In a wok or large frying pan, heat 1 tablespoon sesame oil over medium heat. Pour in beaten eggs, tipping pan to form a thin omelet. Cook until omelet is set, 2 to 3 minutes. Slide omelet onto a plate. Roll up jelly-roll style and cut into ¼-inch-thick strips.

3. In same pan, heat remaining 1 tablespoon oil over medium heat. Add onion and cook until golden, 2 to 3 minutes. Stir in cooked rice, mushroom strips, soy sauce, five-spice powder, sugar, and peas. Cover and cook until heated through, 3 to 5 minutes. If rice is too dry, add 1 tablespoon reserved mushroom soaking water.

4. To serve, mound fried rice on a platter. Top with egg strips and roasted peanuts.

NOTE: *Chinese five-spice powder is available in the Asian foods section of supermarkets or ethnic markets.*

---

208 BENGALI RICE WITH SWEET TOMATO SAUCE

Prep: 15 minutes   Cook: 1 hour 13 minutes to 1½ hours   Serves: 4

½ cup slivered almonds
1 (8-ounce) can crushed unsweetened pineapple
2 tablespoons vegetable oil
1 medium onion, chopped
½ green bell pepper, diced
1 cup brown rice, rinsed and drained
2½ cups vegetable broth or reduced-sodium chicken broth

¼ teaspoon turmeric
½ teaspoon grated nutmeg
1 cinnamon stick
½ teaspoon ground cardamom
½ cup raisins
1 (28-ounce) can peeled plum tomatoes, drained and coarsely chopped
1 teaspoon cinnamon
2 garlic cloves, minced
¼ cup honey

1. In a small nonstick frying pan over medium-high heat, toast almonds, tossing often, until they turn light brown, 1 to 1½ minutes. Set aside.

2. Drain pineapple, reserving juice. In a heavy medium saucepan, heat vegetable oil over medium heat, add onion, and cook, stirring occasionally, until softened, 2 to 3 minutes. Add green pepper and crushed pineapple and cook 5 minutes. Add brown rice, broth, reserved pineapple juice, turmeric, nutmeg, cinnamon stick, cardamom, and raisins. Cover, reduce heat to medium-low, and cook until rice is tender and liquid is absorbed, 40 to 45 minutes.

3. Meanwhile, place tomatoes, cinnamon, and garlic in a medium frying pan. Cover and cook over low heat, stirring occasionally, 15 to 20 minutes. Stir in honey and continue to cook, uncovered, until tomatoes lose most of their liquid and attain a jamlike consistency, 10 to 15 minutes. Set aside.

4. When rice is cooked, discard cinnamon stick. Fluff with a fork and blend in toasted almonds. Spoon tomato sauce over rice and serve hot.

209   RICE CRUST WITH SPINACH AND HERB CHEESE

Prep: 10 minutes   Cook: 45 to 57 minutes   Serves: 4 to 6

⅔ cup long-grain white rice
1 cup shredded Emmenthaler
   or Gruyère cheese
2 eggs, lightly beaten
1 (10-ounce) package chopped
   frozen spinach, thawed

2 (4-ounce) packages herbed
   cream cheese
1 teaspoon pepper

1. In a medium saucepan, bring 1⅓ cups of lightly salted water to a boil. Stir in rice. Reduce heat to medium-low. Cover and cook until rice is tender, 15 to 20 minutes. Remove from heat and fluff with a fork. Set aside to cool slightly.

2. Preheat oven to 400°F. Add cheese and eggs to rice and mix well. Spread rice mixture over a lightly greased 9-inch pie pan, flattening with a spatula to cover bottom and sides of dish. Bake 25 to 30 minutes, until rice crust turns golden brown. Reduce oven temperature to 375°F.

3. With your hands, squeeze spinach to remove as much liquid as possible. Mix spinach with half of herbed cheese and spread over cooked rice shell. Season with pepper. Dot with remaining cheese. Bake 5 to 7 minutes, until cheese melts slightly and pie is hot. Serve hot or at room temperature.

210   WEST AFRICAN JOLOF RICE

Prep: 20 minutes   Cook: 23 to 27 minutes   Serves: 6

This rice dish was inspired by Peri Klemm, a young friend of mine who spent a year studying in Ghana. This is my version of the traditional specialty from West Africa. Because this is served right out of the pan it is cooked in, choose an attractive flameproof casserole or deep skillet.

2 tablespoons olive oil
1 bunch of scallions, finely
   chopped
2 garlic cloves, minced
1¾ cups vegetable broth or
   reduced-sodium chicken
   broth
3 teaspoons curry powder
2 teaspoons turmeric
¼ teaspoon cayenne

1 (16-ounce) can stewed diced
   tomatoes
1¾ cups instant brown rice
1 (16-ounce) package frozen
   mixed vegetables, thawed
8 ounces firm tofu, drained
1 medium plantain
¼ cup flour
½ cup vegetable oil
1 cup banana chips

1. In a large flameproof casserole, heat olive oil over medium-high heat. Cook scallions, stirring occasionally, until soft, about 2 minutes. Add garlic and cook, stirring, 1 minute.

2. Add broth, 2 teaspoons curry powder, turmeric, cayenne, tomatoes, and brown rice. Stir well. Add mixed vegetables. Cover and reduce heat to medium. Cook until rice is tender, according to package directions, 10 to 12 minutes.

3. Meanwhile, pat tofu dry. Dice tofu and plantain to size of a peanut. In a large bowl, toss tofu and plantain with flour until coated.

4. In a large frying pan, heat vegetable oil over medium-high heat. Add tofu and plantain and fry, stirring occasionally, until golden, 10 to 12 minutes. With a slotted spoon, remove tofu and plantain and drain on paper towels. Transfer to a bowl and toss with remaining 1 teaspoon curry powder.

5. When rice is cooked, fluff with a fork. Mix in fried tofu and plantain. Garnish with banana chips and serve while hot.

---

211   RISOTTO WITH ROASTED PEPPERS
Prep: 15 minutes   Cook: 43 to 54 minutes   Serves: 4

Loretta Scott, an accomplished cook and fellow food writer, often serves this risotto for a light supper.

1 **red bell pepper**	2½ **cups vegetable broth or**
1 **green bell pepper**	**reduced-sodium chicken**
1 **stick (4 ounces) butter**	**broth**
½ **medium onion, chopped**	½ **teaspoon freshly ground**
2 **garlic cloves, minced**	**pepper**
1 **cup medium-grain or**	2 **tablespoons capers, drained**
Arborio rice	½ **cup grated Parmesan cheese**
½ **cup Marsala wine**	

1. Preheat broiler. Place peppers on a small baking sheet. Broil as close to heat as possible, turning, until skins blister evenly, 6 to 8 minutes. Seal in a paper bag and let steam 10 minutes. Peel and seed peppers under running water. Cut into ½-inch strips.

2. In a heavy medium saucepan, melt 4 tablespoons butter over medium heat. Add onion and garlic and cook, stirring occasionally, until softened, about 3 minutes. Add rice and cook, stirring, 1 to 2 minutes. Add Marsala and cook, stirring, until it is absorbed, 3 to 4 minutes. Stir in 1 cup broth and pepper. Reduce heat to medium-low. Cook, stirring gently, until broth is almost completely absorbed, 5 to 7 minutes. Slowly stir in remaining broth. Cover and cook without disturbing rice until grain is tender but not mushy, 25 to 30 minutes.

3. Stir in capers, cheese, remaining butter, and half of pepper strips. Decorate rice with remaining roasted pepper strips and serve immediately.

212   RISOTTO WITH PEAS

Prep: 10 minutes   Cook: 35 to 44 minutes   Serves: 4

A good risotto makes for a most satisfying first course or side dish. Left-over risotto can be used for stuffing vegetables or to make a crust for a rice pizza (page 124).

1 **stick (4 ounces) butter**	6 **saffron threads, crushed**
½ **medium onion, chopped**	½ **teaspoon dried thyme leaves**
2 **garlic cloves, minced**	½ **teaspoon white pepper**
1 **cup Arborio rice**	½ **cup frozen petite peas,**
½ **cup dry white wine**	**thawed**
2½ **cups vegetable broth or**	½ **cup grated Romano cheese**
reduced sodium chicken	
broth	

1. In a medium saucepan, melt 4 tablespoons butter over medium heat. Add onion and garlic and cook, stirring occasionally, until softened, 2 to 3 minutes. Add rice and cook, stirring, until grains are coated with butter, about 1 minute. Add wine and cook, stirring, until absorbed, 2 to 3 minutes.

2. Add 1 cup broth, saffron, thyme, and pepper. Reduce heat to medium-low. Cook, stirring gently, until broth is almost completely absorbed, 5 to 7 minutes. Slowly add remaining broth and stir to blend. Cover and cook without stirring until rice is tender but not mushy, 25 to 30 minutes.

3. Stir in peas, cheese, and remaining butter. Add more butter if a creamier consistency is desired. Serve immediately.

213   RISOTTO WITH EXOTIC MUSHROOMS

Prep: 10 minutes   Cook: 32 to 40 minutes   Serves: 4

1 **stick (4 ounces) butter**	6 **saffron threads, crushed**
2 **shallots, minced**	½ **teaspoon salt**
3 **shiitake mushrooms, sliced**	½ **teaspoon pepper**
3 **oyster mushrooms, sliced**	1 **cup shredded fontina cheese**
1 **cup medium-grain rice,**	1 **tablespoon chopped parsley**
rinsed and drained	
½ **cup dry vermouth**	
2½ **cups vegetable broth or**	
reduced-sodium chicken	
broth	

1. In a heavy medium saucepan, melt 4 tablespoons butter over medium heat. Add shallots and cook, stirring occasionally, until softened, 2 minutes. Add mushrooms and cook, stirring occasionally, 3 minutes, until they begin to give up their juices. Add rice and cook, stirring, until rice is pale golden and liquid is absorbed, 1 to 2 minutes. Add vermouth and stir until it is absorbed, about 1 minute.

2. Add 1 cup broth, saffron, salt, and pepper. Reduce heat to medium-low. Cook, stirring, until broth is absorbed, 5 to 7 minutes. Slowly add remaining broth, stirring continuously. Cover and cook without disturbing rice until grain is tender but not mushy, 20 to 25 minutes.

3. Stir in cheese and remaining butter. Sprinkle with parsley and serve immediately.

---

214   PERSIAN RICE PILAF WITH DILLED SOUR CREAM

Prep: 10 minutes   Cook: 36 to 45 minutes   Serves: 4 to 6

My friend Iran Jewett hails from Iran, formerly known as Persia. During one of our food talks, she waxed nostalgic about a rice dish she used to eat as a child. This is my interpretation. I use frozen baby lima beans instead of the traditional fresh baby fava beans.

1 cup sour cream	2 tablespoons olive oil
2 tablespoons chopped fresh dill or 1½ teaspoons dried	1 cup long-grain white rice, rinsed and drained
2 teaspoons lemon juice	4 tablespoons butter
1 teaspoon turmeric	1 large onion, chopped
⅛ teaspoon Chinese five-spice powder	1 (10-ounce) package frozen baby lima beans, thawed
8 saffron threads, crushed	2 garlic cloves, minced
1 (14½-ounce) can vegetable broth or reduced-sodium chicken broth	½ teaspoon salt
	½ cup slivered almonds

1. Preheat oven to 325° F. In a serving bowl, mix sour cream with 1 tablespoon chopped dill and lemon juice. Cover and refrigerate until ready to use. In a medium bowl, stir turmeric, five-spice powder, and saffron into broth.

2. In a medium saucepan, heat olive oil. Add rice and cook over medium-high heat, stirring to prevent scorching, until rice turns golden brown, 8 to 10 minutes.

3. Slowly stir spiced broth into browned rice and cook, uncovered, stirring constantly, until half of liquid is absorbed, 3 to 4 minutes. Reduce heat to low. Cover and cook until rice is tender, 12 to 15 minutes.

4. Meanwhile, in a medium frying pan, melt butter. Add onion and cook over medium heat, stirring occasionally, until soft, 2 to 3 minutes. Add lima beans, remaining dill, garlic, and salt. Cook, stirring, until heated through, about 3 minutes.

5. Spoon half of cooked rice over bottom of a generously oiled 8-inch square baking dish. Cover evenly with lima bean mixture. Top with remaining rice. Dot with butter and sprinkle with almonds.

6. Bake 8 to 10 minutes, until heated through. Serve with dilled sour cream on the side.

215   WILD RICE WITH BUTTERNUT SQUASH AND BLACKENED PECANS

Prep: 10 minutes   Cook: 1 hour 4 minutes to 1 hour 11 minutes
Serves: 2 to 4

1 cup wild rice	⅛ teaspoon salt
1½ pounds butternut squash	1 stick (4 ounces) butter
½ cup port wine	1 cup pecan pieces (about
⅛ teaspoon grated nutmeg	4 ounces)

1. In a medium saucepan filled with lightly salted boiling water, cook wild rice, covered, until kernels burst open but rice is still firm, 40 to 45 minutes.

2. Meanwhile, peel butternut squash and cut into 1-inch cubes. (This is more easily accomplished if squash is microwaved on High for 6 minutes. Let cool before peeling and proceed with recipe.)

3. In a large saucepan, simmer squash in port wine, covered, until tender, 9 to 10 minutes. (If squash has not been microwaved, this will take about 10 to 15 minutes longer.) Add nutmeg and salt. Cook 5 minutes.

4. In a small frying pan, melt butter over medium-high heat. Add pecan pieces and cook, stirring, until butter turns golden brown, 4 to 5 minutes. Immediately remove from heat.

5. To serve, spoon hot butternut squash over cooked wild rice. Top with blackened pecan sauce.

216   HUNGARIAN SAUERKRAUT STEW WITH MUSHROOMS AND BARLEY

Prep: 10 minutes   Cook: 1 hour 18 minutes to 1 hour 23 minutes
Serves: 6

6 small red potatoes, scrubbed	1 (14½-ounce) can vegetable
4 tablespoons butter	broth or reduced-sodium
1 large sweet onion, finely	chicken broth
diced	1 cup dry white wine
1 pound mushrooms, sliced	1 teaspoon poppy seeds
8 ounces fresh sauerkraut,	½ cup pearl barley
rinsed and drained	1 cup sour cream
1 large tart apple, peeled,	2 tablespoons chopped
seeded, cored, and cut	parsley
into 1-inch chunks	

1. Preheat oven to 375°F. In a large saucepan filled with boiling water, cook potatoes until barely tender, 10 to 15 minutes. Drain and let cool, then peel and cut in half.

2. Meanwhile, in a large frying pan, melt butter over medium-high heat. Add onions and cook, stirring occasionally, until softened, about 3 minutes. Add mushrooms and cook until lightly browned, about 5 minutes.

3. Add sauerkraut, cooked potatoes, apple, broth, wine, poppy seeds, and barley. Cover tightly and bake 1 hour.

4. To serve, stir in sour cream and garnish with parsley.

---

217 ZUCCHINI-OATMEAL FRITTERS WITH KASSERI CHEESE AND MINTY TOMATO SAUCE

Prep: 15 minutes   Cook: 21 to 27 minutes   Serves: 3 to 4

Kasseri cheese is similar to feta, but with a sharper flavor.

2 medium zucchini, shredded	½ teaspoon dried mint
1 teaspoon salt	3 eggs
2 tablespoons olive oil	4 scallions, chopped
½ medium onion, chopped	2 tablespoons crumbled
1 (14-ounce) can Italian peeled tomatoes, drained and chopped	kasseri or feta cheese
	½ cup rolled oats
1 teaspoon sugar	⅛ teaspoon cayenne
	Vegetable oil, for frying

1. Place grated zucchini in a colander, sprinkle with ½ teaspoon salt, and toss lightly. Let drain 10 to 15 minutes.

2. Meanwhile, in a large nonreactive frying pan, heat olive oil over medium-high heat. Add onion and cook, stirring occasionally, until golden, about 2 to 3 minutes. Add tomatoes, sugar, remaining ½ teaspoon salt, and mint. Reduce heat to medium-low. Cook partially, until tomato sauce is slightly thickened, 15 to 20 minutes.

3. With your hands, squeeze out all liquid from grated zucchini. In a medium bowl, beat eggs. Add zucchini, scallions, onion, kasseri cheese, oats, and cayenne.

4. Preheat oven to 200°F. Line a baking sheet with a double layer of paper towels. In a large frying pan, heat 1 inch of oil to 375°F. Drop batter by heaping tablespoons into hot oil. Fry fritters in batches until golden brown, turning carefully with a spatula, about 2 minutes on each side. Transfer to baking sheet to drain. Keep warm in oven while cooking remaining fritters.

218   BULGUR AND WALNUT SALAD

Prep: 10 minutes   Cook: 15 to 18 minutes   Serves: 4

2 teaspoons soy sauce
½ cup bulgur wheat
1¼ cups frozen baby peas,
   thawed
½ cup plain yogurt
¼ cup mayonnaise
1 teaspoon balsamic vinegar
⅛ teaspoon pepper

½ cup walnut pieces
¼ cup chopped parsley
1 tablespoon grated Parmesan
   cheese
4 scallions, chopped
1 (2-ounce) can diced
   pimientos, drained

1. In a medium saucepan, bring 1½ cups water and soy sauce to a boil over medium heat. Add bulgur wheat and cover. Reduce heat to medium-low and cook until bulgur is tender, 15 to 18 minutes. Remove from heat and fluff with a fork. Transfer to a bowl and let bulgur stand for 10 minutes to cool.

2. Add peas, yogurt, mayonnaise, vinegar, pepper, walnuts, parsley, Parmesan cheese, scallions, and pimientos. Mix well. Serve chilled.

219   ARTICHOKES AND WILD RICE AU GRATIN

*Prep: 5 minutes   Cook: 1 hour 18 minutes to 1 hour 23 minutes
Serves: 4 to 6*

Wild rice adds an elegant touch to this delicious casserole. The nutty-flavored wild rice must cook undisturbed until the grain breaks open.

⅔ cup wild rice
2 tablespoons butter
1 medium onion, chopped
1 cup sliced mushrooms
1 (15-ounce) can quartered
   artichoke hearts, drained

½ cup chopped parsley
1 cup milk
2 eggs, lightly beaten
2 cups shredded sharp
   Cheddar cheese

1. Rinse wild rice under running water. Place in a medium saucepan filled with 4 cups boiling water. Reduce heat to medium. Cover and cook undisturbed until rice is tender and grains break open, 40 to 45 minutes.

2. Meanwhile, in a medium frying pan, melt butter. Add onion and cook over medium heat, stirring often, until softened, about 3 minutes. Add mushrooms and artichoke hearts. Cook, stirring occasionally, until mushrooms are limp, about 5 minutes. Remove from heat and stir in parsley.

3. When rice is cooked, drain to remove any liquid, if necessary. Preheat oven to 350°F. In a medium bowl, mix cooked rice with milk, beaten eggs, and cheese. Stir in artichoke mixture.

4. Pour rice into a lightly oiled 2-quart baking dish or casserole. Cover and bake 30 minutes.

220 TABBOULEH TOMATOES
Prep: 10 minutes   Cook: 3 minutes   Chill: 1 hour   Serves: 6

Tabbouleh is a Middle Eastern specialty that usually calls for bulgur wheat. I like to use couscous, which is sometimes referred to in this country as Moroccan pasta. Couscous is available in instant form in supermarkets or in bulk in health food stores. The flavors of mint and lemon juice should be quite pronounced.

1 cup instant couscous	½ teaspoon salt
1½ cups vegetable broth or reduced-sodium chicken broth	⅛ teaspoon pepper
	1 teaspoon minced fresh ginger
1 tablespoon butter	⅓ cup cooked fresh or thawed frozen petite peas
1 cup chopped Italian flat-leaf parsley	
	1 tablespoon pine nuts
½ cup chopped mint leaves plus 6 whole mint leaves	Grated zest of ½ lemon
	1 tablespoon extra-virgin olive oil
4 scallions, chopped	
1 garlic clove, minced	6 large tomatoes
½ cup lemon juice	

1. In a medium saucepan, cook couscous according to package directions, using broth instead of water. Stir in butter. Let stand 5 minutes. Fluff couscous with a fork.

2. In a medium bowl, mix cooked couscous with parsley, mint leaves, scallions, garlic, lemon juice, salt, pepper, ginger, peas, pine nuts, lemon zest, and olive oil. Cover and refrigerate 1 hour.

3. Meanwhile, cut off tops of tomatoes. With a spoon, scoop out pulp, leaving ½-inch shell intact. Dice tomato pulp and add to couscous mixture,

4. Fill each tomato with tabbouleh. Decorate with a mint leaf. Serve chilled.

221   CRUNCHY BARLEY MOLD

Prep: 20 minutes   Cook: 40 to 45 minutes   Chill: 8 hours
Serves: 4 to 6

Pearl barley swells up to four times its size when cooked and still retains a flavorful crunch. This pretty ring is ideal for picnics.

1 cup raw pearl barley
2 celery ribs, finely diced
2 scallions, chopped
1 medium carrot, shredded
½ cup bread and butter
   pickles, finely diced
½ medium bell pepper, finely
   diced

2 (1.6-ounce) envelopes
   buttermilk-style salad
   dressing
1 cup plain yogurt
½ cup sour cream

1. In a medium saucepan, bring 4 cups of water to a boil. Add barley and reduce heat to medium. Cover and cook until barley is tender, 40 to 45 minutes. Remove from heat and fluff with a fork. Transfer to a large bowl.

2. Add celery, scallions, carrot, pickles, and red bell pepper to barley. Toss to mix. In a medium bowl, blend dressing mix with yogurt and sour cream. Pour over barley mixture and stir to blend.

3. Press barley mixture firmly into a lightly oiled 4-cup ring mold. Refrigerate 8 hours or overnight. Before serving, unmold onto a platter and garnish as desired.

222   WILD RICE PANCAKES

Prep: 10 minutes   Cook: 11 to 15 minutes   Serves: 4 to 6

1½ cups cooked wild rice
1 cup cooked white rice
3 scallions, sliced
½ cup sour cream
½ teaspoon salt
1 teaspoon dried rosemary
   leaves, crushed

½ cup shredded Cheddar
   cheese
2 eggs
6 tablespoons butter
1 pound button mushrooms,
   sliced

1. Preheat oven to 200°F. In a medium bowl, combine wild rice, white rice, scallions, sour cream, salt, rosemary, cheese, and eggs. Stir batter until well mixed.

2. In a large nonstick frying pan, melt 2 tablespoons butter over medium-high heat. Using about 3 tablespoons batter for each pancake, fry pancakes in batches. Ladle batter into pan and pat down with spatula to make pancakes 3 to 4 inches in diameter. Cook, turning once, until pancakes are crisp, 4 to 5 minutes on each side. With a spatula, transfer cooked pancakes to an ovenproof platter and keep warm in the oven. Repeat until all batter is used, adding up to 2 tablespoons more butter when pan becomes dry.

3. In same frying pan, melt 2 tablespoons butter over medium heat. Add mushrooms and cook, stirring frequently, until tender and lightly browned, 3 to 5 minutes. Spoon mushrooms over pancakes and serve.

223   SEVEN-VEGETABLE COUSCOUS
Prep: 30 minutes   Cook: 35 to 42 minutes   Serves: 6 to 8

In Morocco, where couscous is a staple, this particular couscous is a specialty of Casablanca—my hometown.

2 (14½-ounce) cans vegetable broth or reduced-sodium chicken broth
8 saffron threads, crushed
1 teaspoon turmeric
½ bunch cilantro, rinsed and tied with string
1 bunch of parsley, rinsed and tied with string
3 medium carrots, peeled, quartered lengthwise, and cut into 3-inch sticks
3 turnips, peeled and quartered

6 scallions, cut into 3-inch pieces
3 medium zucchini
4 celery ribs, cut into 3-inch pieces
1 cup frozen baby lima beans
1 cup canned garbanzo beans, drained
½ teaspoon salt
½ teaspoon pepper
1 (12-ounce) package instant couscous
2 tablespoons butter
Hot pepper sauce

1. In a 5- to 6-quart soup pot or a Dutch oven, bring broth to a simmer. Add saffron, turmeric, cilantro, and parsley. Cover and simmer 10 to 12 minutes.

2. Add carrots, turnips, and scallions. Cook over medium heat, covered, 15 to 20 minutes, or until just tender.

3. Meanwhile, trim zucchini and halve crosswise. Then cut lengthwise into slices ¼ inch thick. When carrots and turnips are tender, add zucchini, celery, lima beans, and garbanzo beans to pot. Season with salt and pepper. Cover and simmer until zucchini is soft, about 10 minutes. Remove and discard bunches of cilantro and parsley.

4. Meanwhile, prepare couscous according to package directions. Add butter and fluff with a fork.

5. To serve, mound couscous on a serving platter. With a slotted spoon, remove vegetables from broth and arrange over the grains. Serve with broth and hot sauce on the side, so couscous can be moistened and seasoned according to individual preference.

224 CITRUSY COUSCOUS TIMBALES WITH PISTACHIOS AND GOLDEN RAISINS

Prep: 20 minutes   Cook: 3 minutes   Chill: 1 hour   Serves: 5

Whole wheat couscous, a variation on the regular white or cracked wheat semolina, is available in packaged form in large supermarkets or in bulk in health food stores.

1 cup whole wheat couscous	2 tablespoons pistachio nuts
1 cup vegetable or chicken broth	¼ cup chopped parsley
½ cup orange juice	½ medium cucumber, finely diced
2 tablespoons butter	1 celery rib, very finely diced
2 teaspoons lemon juice	1 tablespoon vegetable oil
½ teaspoon minced fresh ginger	1 medium tomato, finely diced
2 tablespoons golden raisins, plumped in warm water and drained	1 large avocado, finely diced
	5 fresh mint leaves

1. Cook couscous according to package directions, using broth and orange juice instead of water. Stir in butter. Transfer couscous to a large bowl and fluff with a fork. Add lemon juice, ginger, raisins, pistachios, parsley, cucumber, and celery.

2. Lightly oil five ½-cup custard molds or ramekins. Spoon couscous mixture inside molds, patting down tightly. Cover and refrigerate at least 1 hour, or until ready to serve.

3. To serve, carefully unmold each timbale onto a plate. Top each timbale with some diced tomato, some diced avocado, and a mint leaf. Serve cold.

225 COUSCOUS CHINOISE

Prep: 15 minutes   Cook: 10 to 15 minutes   Serves: 4

To add extra texture to the tofu, I sometimes fry the tofu cubes in ½ cup vegetable oil until they turn golden. I then drain them well before adding them to the sauce.

1 large eggplant	1 (16-ounce) package firm tofu, drained and cut into ½-inch cubes
2 tablespoons olive oil	
3 tablespoons butter	
½ pound mushrooms, sliced	1 (12-ounce) package whole wheat couscous
2 tablespoons oyster sauce	Parsley sprigs
1 tablespoon soy sauce	
1 (14½-ounce) can vegetable broth or reduced-sodium chicken broth	

1. Preheat broiler. Slice unpeeled eggplant lengthwise in ¼-inch slices. Pat dry and set in a single layer on ungreased baking sheet.

2. With a brush, paint slices with olive oil. Broil as close to heat as possible until lightly browned, 1 to 2 minutes on each side, turning with tongs. Cool, then cut into ½-inch strips. Set aside.

3. In a medium saucepan, melt butter over medium heat. Cook mushrooms, stirring occasionally, until mushrooms turn limp, 2 to 3 minutes. Add oyster sauce, soy sauce, and broth. Cook, stirring to blend, 1 to 2 minutes. Add eggplant strips and tofu cubes. Cook, covered, 5 to 6 minutes.

4. Meanwhile, in a medium saucepan, prepare couscous according to package directions. Mix in remaining butter and fluff couscous with a fork.

5. To serve, mound couscous on a serving platter. Top with tofu and eggplant mixture. Decorate with parsley sprigs. Serve hot.

---

226 SWEET COUSCOUS STUFFING
Prep: 10 minutes   Cook: 4 to 5 minutes   Serves: 4

This sweet couscous hails from Morocco, where it is used as a stuffing for chicken or squab. I like to use it to stuff a Thanksgiving turkey. You can also use it as a side dish, however. Orange blossom water is available in Middle Eastern markets and in the gourmet foods section of some supermarkets.

¼ cup raisins	¼ cup brown sugar
4 tablespoons butter	2 tablespoons orange blossom
1 medium onion, chopped	water
2 tablespoons slivered	1 teaspoon cinnamon
almonds	¼ teaspoon grated nutmeg
1 cup instant couscous	2 tablespoons chopped dates
1¼ cups vegetable or reduced-	½ teaspoon salt
sodium chicken broth	¼ teaspoon pepper
6 saffron threads	

1. Place raisins in a small bowl filled with warm water and let stand until ready to use. Drain.

2. In a medium frying pan, melt 2 tablespoons butter over medium heat. Add onions and almonds and cook, stirring occasionally, until onions are golden and almonds are lightly toasted, 4 to 5 minutes. Set aside.

3. In a large saucepan over medium-high heat, bring broth, remaining 2 tablespoons butter, and saffron to a boil. Add couscous all at once, stirring to blend. Remove pan from heat. Cover and let stand 5 minutes.

4. Fluff couscous with a fork and transfer to a serving bowl. Stir in onion mixture, brown sugar, orange blossom water, cinnamon, nutmeg, chopped dates, salt, and pepper. Sprinkle raisins on top for decoration. Serve hot.

227 HERB AND GARLIC CHEESE GRITS SOUFFLÉ

Prep: 5 minutes   Cook: 45 to 50 minutes   Serves: 4 to 6

This light and airy soufflé remains quite firm when taken out of the oven. The next day, cut any leftovers into squares and sauté them in butter for a tasty breakfast treat.

1 teaspoon salt	1 (8-ounce) package cream
1 cup quick grits	cheese with garlic
2 tablespoons chopped sun-	and herbs
dried tomatoes	2 eggs
	½ cup milk

1. Preheat oven to 375°F. In a large saucepan, bring 4 cups water and salt to a boil. Gradually add grits in a stream, stirring constantly to dissolve any lumps. Add sun-dried tomatoes. Cook over medium heat, stirring occasionally, until thickened, about 5 minutes. Remove from heat and stir in cream cheese until melted.

2. In a small bowl, beat eggs. Beat in milk until well mixed. Add to grits and stir vigorously to blend well.

3. Transfer grits to a generously oiled 2-quart baking dish. Bake 40 to 45 minutes, until soufflé is puffy and golden. Serve immediately.

228 POLENTA PIE WITH MUSHROOM-WINE SAUCE

Prep: 15 minutes   Cook: 35 to 44 minutes   Serves: 6

2¼ cups vegetable broth or	Salt and freshly ground
reduced-sodium chicken	pepper
broth	1 tablespoon flour
¾ cup yellow cornmeal or	¼ cup dry red wine
polenta	1 tablespoon Worcestershire
2 tablespoons grated	sauce
Parmesan cheese	1 tablespoon soy sauce or
1 stick (4 ounces) butter	tamari
1 medium onion, sliced	1 teaspoon ketchup
1 pound mushrooms, sliced	1 garlic clove, cut in half

1. Preheat oven to 350°F. In a medium saucepan, bring broth to a boil over medium heat. Add polenta in a slow stream, stirring constantly. Add Parmesan cheese. Reduce heat to low and cook, stirring frequently, until mixture thickens, 10 to 15 minutes. Stir in 2 tablespoons butter.

2. Meanwhile, in a large skillet, melt 2 tablespoons butter. Add onion and cook over medium heat, stirring occasionally, until soft, 3 to 5 minutes. Add mushrooms and cook until limp, 4 to 5 minutes. Remove from heat. Season with salt and pepper to taste.

3. In a medium saucepan, melt remaining butter. Whisk in flour and cook, stirring, 1 minute. Add wine and cook, stirring, until mixture boils and thickens, 2 to 3 minutes. Stir in Worcestershire, soy sauce, and ketchup. Add mushrooms and onion. Remove from heat.

4. Rub bottom and sides of 2-quart baking dish with cut garlic. Lightly butter dish. Spoon half of polenta mixture on bottom. Top with half of mushroom sauce. Cover with remaining polenta and finish with a layer of mushroom sauce. Cover and bake 15 minutes.

---

229   POLENTA GNOCCHI AL FORNO

Prep: 30 minutes   Cook: 27 to 33 minutes   Chill: 4 hours
Serves: 4 to 6

4 cups milk	1 cup cornmeal
½ teaspoon salt	2 tablespoons grated
¼ teaspoon grated nutmeg	Parmesan cheese
¼ teaspoon pepper	2 eggs, lightly beaten
2 tablespoons dry onion flakes	1 (30-ounce) jar prepared spaghetti sauce
1 tablespoon diced sun-dried tomatoes	3 ounces Asiago or fontina cheese, thinly sliced

1. In a large saucepan, combine milk, salt, nutmeg, pepper, onion flakes, and sun-dried tomatoes. Bring to a low boil over medium heat. Add cornmeal in a stream, stirring continuously with a wooden spoon until mixture becomes cohesive. Be careful, for polenta will spatter. Reduce heat to low and continue to cook, stirring, until all liquid is absorbed, 4 to 5 minutes. Remove from heat.

2. Let cool 3 minutes. Stir in Parmesan and eggs until well blended.

3. With a spatula, spread warm polenta mixture evenly over a baking sheet lined with oiled aluminum foil. Cover and refrigerate until completely chilled, at least 4 and up to 24 hours.

4. Preheat oven to 350°F. To prepare gnocchi, with a sharp knife, cut polenta into 2 × 2-inch squares. With a spatula, transfer squares to an oiled 9 × 13-inch baking dish. Spoon spaghetti sauce over gnocchi. Layer sliced cheese over top.

5. Bake gnocchi 20 to 25 minutes, until cheese is bubbly and browned.

230   BASIL-MINT MILLET SALAD

Prep: 10 minutes   Cook: 56 to 67 minutes   Serves: 3 to 4

This herb-scented salad acquires additional taste from the nutty flavor of toasted millet grains.

1 cup millet
2½ cups vegetable broth or reduced-sodium chicken broth
¼ cup golden raisins
1 tablespoon finely chopped fresh basil

2 teaspoons chopped fresh mint
2 tablespoons lemon juice
1 small onion, finely chopped
2 celery ribs, finely chopped

1. In a large nonstick skillet, toast millet over high heat, shaking pan often to prevent scorching, until grains begin to pop, 1 to 2 minutes. Transfer grains to a medium saucepan.

2. Add broth to toasted millet. Cover and bring to a boil; reduce heat to low. Cook 35 minutes. Uncover and cook 5 minutes longer. Remove millet from heat. Fluff with a fork and let cool 10 to 15 minutes.

3. Meanwhile, in a small bowl, soak golden raisins in hot water to cover until soft and plumped, about 15 minutes; drain.

4. In a serving bowl, gently blend millet with basil, mint, lemon juice, onion, golden raisins, and celery. Stir to blend. Cover and refrigerate until ready to serve.

231   WHEAT BERRY MEDLEY

Prep: 15 minutes   Cook: 50 minutes to 1 hour   Serves: 6 to 8

1 cup wheat berries
2 ounces crumbled feta cheese
1 large shallot, minced
4 scallions, chopped
1 small cucumber, peeled, seeded, and finely diced
1 large carrot, shredded
2 celery ribs, finely diced
4 radishes, finely diced

½ fennel bulb, finely diced (optional)
½ cup chopped parsley
½ cup orange juice
½ cup extra-virgin olive oil
3 tablespoons lemon juice
2 teaspoons salt
1 teaspoon pepper
10 pitted black olives

1. In a large saucepan filled with lightly salted boiling water, cook wheat berries, covered, over medium heat until tender, 50 minutes to 1 hour. Drain well. Allow to cool.

2. In a large serving bowl, mix wheat berries with feta cheese, shallot, scallions, cucumber, carrot, celery, radishes, fennel, parsley, orange juice, olive oil, lemon juice, salt, and pepper.

3. Decorate with black olives. Cover and refrigerate until ready to serve.

232   QUINOA EGG ROLLS

Prep: 20 minutes   Cook: 22 to 27 minutes   Makes: 14 to 16

The tiny, slightly crunchy grains of quinoa give these egg rolls an unexpected crunch. Quinoa is available in bulk in health food stores and specialty markets and in packages in some supermarkets. Chinese five-spice powder, black bean sauce, and oyster sauce are available in Asian markets and in the Asian foods section of large supermarkets.

1   (14½-ounce) can vegetable broth or reduced-sodium chicken broth
¾   cup quinoa, rinsed and drained
3   dried Chinese mushrooms
4   scallions, coarsely chopped
1   teaspoon minced fresh ginger
¼   cup thinly slivered water chestnuts
¼   cup thinly slivered bamboo shoots

½   teaspoon Chinese five-spice powder
2   garlic cloves, minced
2   tablespoons soy sauce
1   (16-ounce) package egg roll wrappers
    Vegetable oil, for frying
2   tablespoons Chinese black bean sauce
1   teaspoon dry mustard
1   tablespoon oyster sauce

1. In a medium saucepan, bring 1½ cups broth to a boil. Add quinoa, cover, reduce heat to medium-low, and cook until tender, 15 to 20 minutes. Remove from heat and let stand, covered, 5 minutes. Fluff quinoa with a fork and set aside to cool slightly.

2. In a medium bowl, soak dried mushrooms in warm water for 10 minutes, or until soft; drain. Discard woody stems and cut caps into thin slivers. Return mushrooms to bowl and add scallions, ginger, water chestnuts, bamboo shoots, five-spice powder, garlic, and soy sauce. Mix in quinoa.

3. Set egg roll wrappers on a flat surface. Place 1 heaping tablespoon cooled filling along bottom quarter of wrapper. Fold wrapper over filling, fold in sides, and roll up to form a "cigar" about 5 inches long and ½ inch in diameter. Repeat with remaining wrappers and filling.

4. In a wok or deep skillet, heat 1 inch vegetable oil over medium-high heat until oil is hot but not smoking (350°F). With tongs, carefully set egg rolls in hot oil. Deep-fry in batches without crowding, turning once, until golden brown, about 2 minutes on each side. With a slotted spoon, transfer egg rolls to paper towels to drain. (If not serving immediately, keep warm in a 200°F oven.)

5. In a small saucepan, mix black bean sauce, ½ cup broth, dry mustard, and oyster sauce. Cook over medium heat until heated through, about 3 minutes. Serve as a dip for egg rolls.

233 KASHA CALIFORNIA

Prep: 10 minutes   Cook: 36 to 45 minutes   Serves: 4 to 6

Arthur and Anna Devine, Southern California fruit growers, regularly enjoy this casserole. "It's one of my husband's favorites," says Anna. Roasted buckwheat groats are available in health food stores.

2½ cups vegetable broth or reduced-sodium chicken broth	2 tablespoons olive oil
1 cup roasted whole buckwheat groats	1 large onion, chopped
2 tablespoons soy sauce or tamari	1 red bell pepper, finely diced
2 teaspoons dried basil	2 small zucchini, sliced
1 teaspoon paprika	½ pound mushrooms, sliced
1 teaspoon curry powder	2 garlic cloves, minced
	2 cups shredded sharp Cheddar cheese (8 ounces)

1. Preheat oven to 350°F. In a medium saucepan, bring 2¼ cups broth to a boil over medium-high heat. Add groats, soy sauce, basil, paprika, and curry powder. Reduce heat to medium, cover, and cook until groats are tender, about 10 minutes. Remove from heat and fluff with a fork.

2. Meanwhile, in a large frying pan, heat olive oil over medium-high heat. Add onion and bell pepper and cook, stirring occasionally, until softened, 3 to 5 minutes. Add zucchini slices, mushrooms, garlic, and remaining ¼ cup broth. Cover and cook until zucchini turns soft, 3 to 5 minutes.

3. Spread half of groat mixture on bottom of a well-oiled 9-inch square baking dish. Cover with vegetables and mushrooms. Top with half of cheese. Cover with remaining groats. Sprinkle remaining cheese over top.

4. Bake 20 to 25 minutes, until cheese is bubbly. Let stand 10 minutes before serving.

Chapter 9

Stuffed, Wrapped, and Rolled

Stuffed vegetables or jumbo pasta shells, savory fillings wrapped in cabbage leaves or rolled up in thin tortillas or crepes are great ways to enjoy meatless dining. Many are a complete meal in themselves. In this chapter I have adapted a host of international recipes, including Stuffed Chard Leaves in a lemon-accented sauce, which I serve hot but also enjoy cold the next day. Soul-satisfying Barley Cabbage Rolls are an adaptation of the meat-filled classic. For Stuffed Zucchini Mexicana I use refried beans as a stuffing—a tasty alternative to rice. Acorn Squash Stuffed with Ricotta is ideally suited to a light dinner. So is Stuffed Eggplant Española.

Soft flour tortillas serve as edible envelopes for the flavor-packed Asparagus Fajitas and for my adaptation of the Chinese-influenced Moo Shu Vegetables, usually served in rice flour pancakes. Tofu Lettuce Rolls are a fresh and light unusual Chinese specialty wrapped in lettuce leaves. For a festive brunch, I would serve Ratatouille-Filled Parmesan Crepes, Pretty Pepper Rings, or Stuffed Pasta Shells à la Russe—for the latter, don't forget the vodka!

In some parts of the world, such as the Middle East, stuffed vegetables often serve as openers to a multicourse meal. Eggplant, seasonal squash, tomatoes, or bell peppers are often filled with a savory rice or couscous mixture. Sometimes the stuffing is made from leftovers, chopped very finely and accented with fresh herbs. Many of these specialties are simmered in fragrant sauces. Others are simply baked and placed under the broiler to brown at the last minute. Whenever possible, I include the diced part of my edible container in the stuffing, so nothing goes to waste.

234   ASPARAGUS FAJITAS

Prep: 20 minutes   Stand: 30 minutes
Cook: 13 to 17 minutes   Serves: 4

Fajitas have taken the country by storm. This meatless version is bursting with a rainbow of quick-cooked vegetables, among them tender asparagus spears. Serve with salsa and rice.

1 **pound small asparagus spears, cut into 2-inch pieces**
1 **large red bell pepper, cut into ¼-inch strips**
1 **large green bell pepper, cut into ¼-inch strips**
4 **scallions, cut into 2-inch pieces**
1 **medium zucchini, cut into matchsticks**
2 **garlic cloves, minced**
1 **tablespoon lime juice**
1 **(1¼-ounce) envelope dry fajita spice mix (3 tablespoons)**
8 **(10-inch) flour tortillas**
⅓ **cup vegetable oil**

1. In a medium bowl, combine asparagus, red and green pepper strips, scallions, zucchini, garlic, lime juice, and fajita spice mix. Toss well. Set aside to marinate for 30 to 60 minutes.

2. Preheat oven to 275°F. Wrap tortillas in aluminum foil and heat in oven until warm, 7 to 10 minutes.

3. Meanwhile, in a large frying pan or a wok, heat oil over medium heat. With a slotted spoon, drain marinated vegetables. Place in pan and cook, stirring often, 6 to 7 minutes. Add some of the marinade if mixture seems too dry.

4. Wrap equal amounts of hot vegetables in warm tortillas. Serve immediately.

235   ASPARAGUS ENCHILADAS

Prep: 15 minutes   Cook: 27 to 34 minutes   Serves: 6

12 **(10-inch) flour tortillas**
2 **pounds fresh asparagus**
4 **tablespoons butter**
¼ **cup flour**
3 **cups vegetable broth or reduced-sodium chicken broth**
1 **cup sour cream**
1 **(8-ounce) jar mild green jalapeño salsa**
2 **cups shredded Swiss cheese**
1 **large white onion, finely chopped**
1 **cup chopped parsley**

1. Preheat oven to 350°F. Wrap tortillas in aluminum foil and keep warm in oven until ready to fill.

2. Cut asparagus spears into 2-inch pieces. In a large pot filled with lightly salted boiling water, cook asparagus until barely tender, 3 minutes. Drain, rinse under cold running water, and drain again.

3. In a large saucepan, melt butter over medium heat. Add flour and cook, stirring, 1 to 2 minutes. Add broth all at once and bring to a boil, whisking, until sauce is thick and smooth, 3 to 4 minutes. Remove from heat. Stir in sour cream, salsa, and cheese.

4. Remove warm tortillas from oven. Increase heat to 400°F. Cover bottom of a 9 x 13-inch baking dish with a thin layer of sauce.

5. Fill each tortilla with 2 tablespoons asparagus pieces, 1 teaspoon chopped onion, a little parsley, and 1 tablespoon cheese sauce. Roll up carefully and set snugly in baking pan. Proceed in similar fashion until all tortillas are used. Cover enchiladas with remaining sauce.

6. Cover with aluminum foil and bake 20 to 25 minutes, until bubbly. Serve hot.

236 BARLEY CABBAGE ROLLS

Prep: 45 minutes   Cook: 1 hour 22 minutes to 1 hour 33 minutes
Serves: 6

1 (14½-ounce) can vegetable broth or reduced-sodium chicken broth	2 teaspoons dried thyme leaves
1 cup pearl barley	2 teaspoons dried basil
1 large cabbage, cored	1 (14½-ounce) can Italian-style stewed tomatoes
1 envelope dry onion soup mix	2 cups spaghetti sauce
½ cup toasted walnuts	½ cup dry red wine
1 large carrot, shredded	2 cups half-and-half
1 cup chopped parsley	1 cup sour cream

1. In a medium saucepan, bring broth to a boil. Add barley, cover, and cook over medium heat until barley is tender, 30 to 35 minutes. Set aside to cool.

2. Meanwhile, in a large pot of boiling water, cook cabbage until leaves are tender, 10 to 15 minutes; drain. Plunge cooked cabbage into large bowl filled with cold water. Drain again. Carefully separate each cabbage leaf. With a paring knife, cut out a V shape from core at base of each leaf to ease rolling.

3. In a large bowl, mix cooked barley, onion soup mix, toasted walnuts, carrot, parsley, thyme, and basil. Fill each cabbage leaf with 2 tablespoons filling, fold sides over, and roll up.

4. In a large nonreactive saucepan or Dutch oven, combine stewed tomatoes, spaghetti sauce, and red wine. Bring to a simmer. Gently add cabbage rolls to sauce. Cover and cook 40 minutes.

5. About 5 minutes before serving, add half-and-half. Stir gently until heated through, 2 to 3 minutes. Serve cabbage rolls garnished with parsley. Pass sour cream on the side.

237   ACORN SQUASH STUFFED WITH RICOTTA
Prep: 10 minutes   Cook: 1 hour to 1 hour 10 minutes   Serves: 4

2 small acorn squash
1 tablespoon soy sauce or
   tamari
1 (16-ounce) container ricotta
   cheese
1 egg

2 tablespoons dry onion
   flakes
2 tablespoons chopped chives
1 (1-ounce) envelope ranch
   salad dressing mix

1. Preheat oven to 375°F. Bake acorn squash 35 to 40 minutes, until barely tender. Remove from oven and cut in half. Let cool 10 minutes. With a large spoon, scoop out seeds. Sprinkle squash cavities with soy sauce. Set, cut-side up, in a 9 x 13-inch baking dish.

2. Meanwhile, in a medium bowl, mix ricotta with egg, onion flakes, chives, and ranch dressing. Mound mixture equally inside acorn squash halves.

3. Bake 15 to 20 minutes, until filling is hot and puffy.

238   SAVORY STUFFED APPLES
Prep: 10 minutes   Cook: 30 to 35 minutes   Serves: 6 to 8

This pretty dish will dress up any holiday table. For best results, use a tart apple, such as a Granny Smith.

6 to 8 large apples
1 teaspoon salt
½ teaspoon pepper
3 to 4 tablespoons butter
1 (6-ounce) package seasoned
   stuffing mix
1 celery rib, finely diced

2 scallions, chopped
¼ teaspoon liquid smoke
   (optional)
1 (14½-ounce) can vegetable
   broth or reduced-sodium
   chicken broth

1. Preheat oven to 350°F. With an apple corer, core apples, taking care to leave a plug at base. With a spoon or small end of a melon baller, remove apple from center, leaving a ¾-inch shell. Dice removed apple very fine and set aside.

2. Sprinkle each apple cavity with salt and pepper. Place 1 teaspoon butter in each. Set apples in a 9 x 13-inch baking dish. Bake 15 minutes. Remove from oven.

3. Meanwhile, prepare stuffing according to package directions. Add diced apple, celery, scallions, and liquid smoke. Mix well.

4. Fill each apple cavity with equal amounts of stuffing. Return apples to baking dish. Pour broth around apples. Bake 15 to 20 minutes, until apples are nice and soft and stuffing is heated through.

239   JIFFY CHILES RELLENOS

Prep: 20 minutes   Cook: 40 to 45 minutes   Serves: 4

These simple chiles rellenos are easily assembled from prepared ingredients. If the prepackaged rice and beans are not available, substitute 2 cups cooked rice mixed with 1 cup canned red kidney beans.

1 (8-ounce) package red bean and rice mix	2½ cups shredded Monterey Jack cheese
2 (7-ounce) cans whole green chiles	1 teaspoon chili powder
1 (14½-ounce) can Mexican-style stewed tomatoes	8 scallions, finely chopped
	2 cups crushed salsa-flavored tortilla chips

1. Preheat oven to 375°F. In a medium saucepan, prepare bean and rice mix according to package directions. Cook, covered, 20 minutes.

2. Meanwhile, drain green chiles and rinse under running water. Carefully slit one side of green chiles open.

3. Layer stewed tomatoes on bottom of a shallow 2½-quart baking dish. With a soup spoon, stuff each chile with 2 tablespoons bean and rice mixture. Set chiles atop stewed tomatoes. Cover with half of cheese. Sprinkle with chili powder and top with scallions. Cover with remaining cheese and crushed tortilla chips.

4. Bake 20 to 25 minutes, until cheese is melted and casserole is bubbly.

240   STUFFED EGGPLANT ESPAÑOLA

Prep: 10 minutes   Cook: 40 to 53 minutes   Serves: 2

1 (6-ounce) package Spanish-style rice mix	2 garlic cloves, minced
1 large eggplant	5 plum tomatoes, chopped
3 tablespoons olive oil	¼ cup shredded Jarlsberg cheese

1. In a medium saucepan, cook rice according to package directions, 15 to 20 minutes.

2. Meanwhile, preheat broiler. Cut eggplant lengthwise in half. With a spoon or grapefruit knife, scoop out eggplant, leaving ½-inch shell intact. Cut eggplant into ½-inch dice.

3. Broil eggplant shells until lightly browned, 5 to 6 minutes. Transfer to a small baking dish. Reduce oven temperature to 375°F.

4. In a large frying pan, heat olive oil over medium-high heat. Add diced eggplant, garlic, and tomatoes. Cook, stirring occasionally, until eggplant is tender, 5 to 7 minutes.

5. Mix cooked eggplant with cooked rice. Stuff reserved shells with equal amounts of rice mixture. Sprinkle cheese on top.

6. Bake until golden brown, 15 to 20 minutes.

241   CASHEW APPLE EGGPLANT
Prep: 10 minutes   Cook: 1 hour to 1 hour 10 minutes   Serves: 2

1 medium eggplant
2 tablespoons olive oil
1 small onion, chopped
1 medium tomato, seeded
  and diced
1 tart apple, peeled, cored,
  and diced

¼ cup chopped parsley
2 garlic cloves, minced
1 teaspoon paprika
¼ teaspoon pepper
⅓ cup cashew pieces

1. Preheat oven to 350°F. With tines of a fork, prick eggplant skin in several places. Place eggplant in a small baking pan and bake until tender, 25 to 30 minutes. Cut in half lengthwise and let cool 10 minutes. With a spoon, scoop out flesh, leaving ½-inch shells intact. Place shells in a small baking dish. Coarsely dice flesh.

2. Meanwhile, in a large frying pan, heat oil over medium-high heat. Add onion and cook, stirring occasionally, until golden, 4 to 5 minutes. Add tomato and apple and cook, stirring, until apple softens, 3 to 5 minutes. Add diced eggplant, parsley, garlic, paprika, and pepper. Cook, stirring occasionally, until most of liquid evaporates, 8 to 10 minutes.

3. Add cashews to cooked eggplant. Stuff eggplant shells equally with mixture. Cover with aluminum foil. Bake 20 minutes. Serve immediately.

242   TOFU LETTUCE ROLLS
Prep: 20 minutes   Cook: 3 minutes   Serves: 4

The secret to these crunchy rolls is to dice the soybean cake and the mushrooms to the size of half a peanut. The ingredients are usually available in the Asian foods section of large supermarkets as well as in Chinese markets.

4 dried Chinese mushrooms
½ cup dry-roasted peanuts
1 tablespoon Asian sesame oil
1 (4-ounce) package baked
  soybean cake, finely
  diced
2 tablespoons soy sauce or
  tamari
1 tablespoon oyster sauce

3 garlic cloves, minced
1 teaspoon Chinese black
  bean paste
2 tablespoons rice wine or dry
  sherry
½ cup hoisin sauce
1 head of green leafy lettuce,
  separated into leaves

1. In a small bowl, soak mushrooms in warm water for 10 minutes. Drain. Cut off woody stems and discard. Finely dice mushroom caps. Set aside.

2. Place peanuts in blender or food processor and chop coarsely. Transfer to a small bowl and set aside.

3. In a medium frying pan, heat sesame oil over medium heat. Add diced bean cake and mushrooms and cook, stirring occasionally, until hot, about 2 minutes. Add soy sauce, oyster sauce, garlic, bean paste, and rice wine. Cook, stirring constantly, 1 minute. Stir in ground peanuts. Remove from heat.

4. To serve, spread a dab of hoisin sauce on each lettuce leaf. Top with 1 tablespoon filling. Roll up each leaf as you would a burrito. Serve with additional hoisin sauce on the side.

---

243 STUFFED CHARD LEAVES

Prep: 35 minutes   Cook: 1 hour 5 minutes to 1 hour 10 minutes
Serves: 3 to 4

2½ cups vegetable broth or reduced-sodium chicken broth
1 tablespoon soy sauce or tamari
1 cup brown rice
2 scallions, chopped
½ cup walnuts, coarsely chopped
¼ cup raisins
2 tablespoons chopped parsley

Grated zest of 1 lemon
6 large chard leaves
2 tablespoons olive oil
1 teaspoon minced garlic
1 teaspoon ground ginger
1 teaspoon ground cardamom
½ teaspoon pepper
2 tablespoons lemon juice
Lemon wedges, for garnish

1. In a medium saucepan, bring broth and soy sauce to a boil over medium heat. Add brown rice. Reduce heat to low, cover, and simmer until rice is tender, 40 to 45 minutes. Transfer to a medium bowl and let cool 5 minutes. Add scallions, walnuts, raisins, parsley, and lemon zest. Mix well.

2. Meanwhile, in a large saucepan filled with boiling water, cook chard leaves until they are tender, 4 to 5 minutes. Drain leaves, reserving cooking liquid. Carefully cut off thick chard stems and place them at bottom of a large skillet. Cut each leaf into 3-inch pieces. Stuff each piece of chard leaf with 2 tablespoons brown rice mixture. Roll up into a small bundle. Set bundles in skillet on top of chard stems. Drizzle olive oil over stuffed leaves.

3. In a small bowl, mix 1 cup reserved chard cooking liquid with garlic, ginger, cardamom, pepper, and lemon juice. Pour over stuffed leaves. Cover and cook over medium-low heat 20 minutes. Serve hot, with lemon wedges on the side.

244   TWICE-BAKED STUFFED PEPPERS
Prep: 15 minutes   Cook: 46 to 50 minutes   Serves: 6

3 large green bell peppers, cut
in half lengthwise and
seeded
6 cups prepared instant
mashed potatoes
⅓ cup plain yogurt

1 envelope dry vegetable soup
mix
2 egg whites, stiffly beaten
1 (10¾-ounce) can cream of
mushroom soup
¾ cup bread crumbs

1. Preheat oven to 450°F. Set halved green peppers on a baking sheet and bake until soft, 8 to 10 minutes. Remove from oven. Set peppers snugly in a 9 x 13-inch baking dish. Reduce oven temperature to 350°F.

2. Meanwhile, in a large bowl, mix prepared mashed potatoes with yogurt and soup mix. With a spatula, gently fold in egg whites.

3. In a medium saucepan, prepare mushroom soup according to directions.

4. Fill pepper halves equally with potato mixture. Pour mushroom soup around peppers. Bake 30 minutes. Remove from oven and sprinkle bread crumbs on top. Bake until bread crumbs turn brown, 8 to 10 minutes. Serve hot.

245   STUFFED PASTA SHELLS À LA RUSSE
Prep: 20 minutes   Cook: 12 to 15 minutes   Serves: 3 to 4

Jumbo pasta shells are sometimes hard to find in mainstream supermarkets but Italian delis usually have them in stock. Serve these shells for a light luncheon, or take them to a picnic (provided they are kept chilled). Substitute black olives for the capers, if you prefer.

10 jumbo pasta shells
1 (10-ounce) package frozen
peas and carrots, cooked
according to directions
and drained
1 tablespoon capers, drained
2 tablespoon pecan pieces,
coarsely chopped
2 shallots, minced

1 tablespoon dried dill weed
1 celery rib, finely diced
1 tablespoon finely diced sun-
dried tomatoes
½ cup mayonnaise
¼ cup plain yogurt
1 tablespoon Dijon mustard
¼ cup chopped parsley

1. In a large pot filled with lightly salted boiling water, cook shells until tender but still firm, 12 to 15 minutes. Drain. Rinse under cold running water. Transfer to a serving platter.

2. Meanwhile, in a large bowl, mix cooked vegetables, capers, pecans, shallots, dill, celery, and sun-dried tomatoes.

3. In a medium bowl, combine mayonnaise, yogurt, Dijon mustard, and chopped parsley. Stir into vegetables.

4. Fill shells generously with mixture. Decorate with parsley sprigs. Set on individual plates or on serving platter lined with lettuce leaves. Chill until ready to serve.

246 RATATOUILLE-FILLED PARMESAN CREPES
Prep: 30 minutes   Cook: 53 to 68 minutes   Serves: 4 to 5

This dish serves equally well for a dinner or brunch.

⅓ cup olive oil	1 tablespoon dried rosemary
2 small onions, diced	1 teaspoon dried thyme leaves
2 small eggplants, peeled and cut into ½-inch cubes	1 bay leaf
1 red bell pepper, seeded and diced	4 garlic cloves, minced
	1 teaspoon salt
1 green bell pepper, seeded and diced	⅛ teaspoon cayenne
	1 cup flour
1 (15-ounce) can diced stewed tomatoes	1½ cups milk
	2 eggs, lightly beaten
2 yellow crookneck squash, cut into ½-inch slices	¼ cup grated Parmesan cheese
	2 tablespoons melted butter

1. Preheat oven to 375°F. In a large skillet, heat olive oil over medium heat. Add onion and cook, stirring occasionally, until golden, 2 to 3 minutes. Add eggplant and cook, stirring, until lightly browned, 4 to 5 minutes. Add red and green pepper and cook, stirring, until soft, 4 to 5 minutes.

2. Add tomatoes, squash, rosemary, thyme, bay leaf, and garlic. Partially cover and cook until vegetable mixture thickens somewhat, 20 to 25 minutes. Discard bay leaf. Stir in salt and cayenne. Set ratatouille aside to cool.

3. Meanwhile, prepare crepes. In a medium bowl, whisk together flour, milk, eggs, Parmesan cheese, and melted butter.

4. Lightly grease a medium skillet to prevent crepes from sticking to pan. Heat skillet over medium heat. Pour ⅓ cup batter into skillet and swirl around to cover bottom. Cook until underside is golden, 2 to 3 minutes. Flip crepe over and cook until spotted brown on other side, 1 to 2 minutes. Do not let edges turn crisp. Repeat with remaining batter. As crepes are made, transfer to a dinner plate and stack.

5. To assemble, spoon a thin layer of ratatouille to cover bottom of a 9 x 13-inch baking dish. Place ⅓ to ½ cup ratatouille filling at bottom edge of each crepe. Roll up, jelly-roll style. Set snugly inside baking dish.

6. Bake 20 to 25 minutes, until bubbly.

247 BAKED STUFFED POTATOES

Prep: 12 minutes   Cook: 1 hour 4 minutes to 1 hour 13 minutes
Serves: 4

4 large baking potatoes,
  scrubbed
1 tablespoon olive oil
1 medium onion, chopped
2 garlic cloves, minced
2 tablespoons minced sun-
  dried tomatoes
½ finely diced green bell
  pepper

½ cup diced black olives
1 teaspoon salt
½ teaspoon pepper
1 cup shredded mozzarella
  cheese
Paprika

1. Preheat oven to 375°F. Wrap potatoes in foil. With tines of fork, prick potatoes in several places. Bake 55 minutes to 1 hour, until tender.

2. Meanwhile, in a medium frying pan, heat oil over medium heat. Add onion, garlic, sun-dried tomatoes, green pepper, and olives. Cook, stirring occasionally, until vegetables soften, 3 to 5 minutes. Remove from heat.

3. When potatoes are cooked, slice one-quarter off top lengthwise. Let cool 5 minutes. Carefully scoop out potatoes, leaving 1-inch-thick shells. Sprinkle shells with salt and pepper.

4. Divide vegetable filling equally among potatoes. Top with cheese and a dusting of paprika. Bake until cheese melts, 6 to 8 minutes.

248 PRETTY PEPPER RINGS

Prep: 15 minutes   Chill: 2 hours   Cook: 30 to 35 minutes   Serves: 4

These pepper rings make a lovely garnish around a platter of bulgur or rice. Use a mixture of yellow, red, and green peppers, for more color. The savory filling is delicious hot or at room temperature, and to my mind, tastes even better the next day.

2 medium red bell peppers
2 medium green bell peppers
1½ cups ricotta
⅓ cup grated Parmesan cheese
3 tablespoons imitation bacon
  bits

½ medium onion, chopped
½ teaspoon dried basil
¼ teaspoon pepper
1 egg
1 (14½-ounce) can Italian-style
  stewed tomatoes

1. Cut off tops of peppers. With a spoon, scoop out seeds and rinse peppers under running water. Invert in a colander to drain.

2. In a medium bowl, mix together ricotta, Parmesan cheese, bacon bits, onion, basil, pepper, and egg. Beat until fairly smooth.

3. Stuff each pepper tightly with equal amounts of ricotta mixture. Set stuffed peppers upright in a dish, cover with plastic wrap, and refrigerate at least 2 hours or overnight.

4. Preheat oven to 350°F. Carefully cut each pepper crosswise into ½-inch-thick rings. Set rings in a lightly oiled 9 x 13-inch baking dish. Top each ring with a dollop of stewed tomatoes.

5. Bake 30 to 35 minutes, until filling is set. Arrange slices in alternating colors on a serving dish. Serve hot or at room temperature with warm stewed tomatoes on the side.

---

249   STUFFED POTATO BALLS
Prep: 20 minutes   Cook: 17 to 20 minutes   Serves: 4 to 5

These crunchy potato balls can be served either as a quick snack or for a light meal.

1 **cup frozen green peas**	1 **cup shredded Cheddar**
2 **tablespoons mayonnaise**	**cheese**
⅔ **cup walnut pieces**	2 **eggs**
5 **cups prepared instant**	3 **cups crushed barbecue-**
mashed potatoes	**flavored potato chips**

1. Preheat oven to 400°F. In a small saucepan, cook green peas in 1 cup boiling water for 5 minutes. Drain. Transfer to a small bowl and mash with a fork. Add mayonnaise and walnut pieces. Set aside.

2. In a medium bowl, mixed prepared mashed potatoes with cheese. Set aside.

3. To form potato balls, place potato mixture the size of a large egg in the palm of your hand. Press down to form a 4-inch patty. Place about 1½ teaspoons green pea filling in center. Enclose filling with mashed potatoes, forming a potato ball the size of a tennis ball. Seal tightly. Repeat procedure until all the mashed potatoes are used. Set aside.

4. In a medium bowl, beat eggs with 1 tablespoon water. Place crushed potato chips in another medium bowl.

5. Carefully roll each potato ball in egg, then in crushed chips. Set on a lightly greased baking sheet. Bake until potato balls are heated through, 12 to 15 minutes.

250   ROASTED GARLIC POTATO BOATS

Prep: 15 minutes   Cook: 1 hour 5 minutes to 1 hour 15 minutes
Serves: 2

2 large baking potatoes, scrubbed	5 tablespoons butter
2 heads of garlic, papery husks removed	½ cup plain yogurt
2 tablespoons grated Parmesan cheese	½ teaspoon salt
	¼ teaspoon pepper
	1 teaspoon fines herbes

1. Preheat oven to 375°F. Wrap each potato in aluminum foil. With tines of fork, poke a few holes in potatoes. Wrap heads of garlic in aluminum foil. Bake until potatoes and garlic bulbs are soft, 55 minutes to 1 hour.

2. When potatoes are cooked, slice off top fourth lengthwise. Let cool 5 minutes. With a spoon, scoop out potatoes into a small bowl, leaving ½-inch shell intact. Sprinkle each shell with Parmesan cheese.

3. With a fork, mash potatoes. Add 3 tablespoons butter, yogurt, salt, pepper, and herbs. Unwrap garlic, and gently squeeze out each clove into mashed potato mixture. Mix well.

4. Fill each shell with potato mixture. Dot with remaining 2 tablespoons butter. Return stuffed potatoes to oven and bake until heated through, 10 to 15 minutes.

251   STUFFED PATTYPAN SQUASH WITH ASPARAGUS CREAM SAUCE

Prep: 20 minutes   Cook: 24 to 32 minutes   Serves: 6

6 large pattypan squash (about 4 inches in diameter)	1 tablespoon soy sauce or tamari
2 tablespoons vegetable oil	2 garlic cloves, minced
1 pound mushrooms, chopped	2 tablespoons bread crumbs
1 teaspoon minced fresh ginger	½ teaspoon pepper
	1 (10¾-ounce) can cream of asparagus soup

1. Preheat broiler. Slice off a dime-sized piece from base of each squash to help them sit flat. Cut off lids and reserve. With a small spoon or a melon baller, scoop out and reserve insides, leaving ½-inch shell intact. Set squash shells on a small baking sheet. Broil until lightly browned, 6 to 8 minutes. Remove from oven. Reduce heat to 350°F.

2. Chop scooped-out squash. In a large frying pan, heat oil over medium heat. Add chopped squash and mushrooms and cook, stirring occasionally, until mushrooms give up their liquid, 3 to 4 minutes. With a slotted spoon, transfer to a small bowl. Add ginger, soy sauce, garlic, bread crumbs, and pepper. Mix well.

3. Fill squash shells with equal amounts of stuffing. Transfer stuffed squash to a 7 x 11-inch baking dish. Top each squash with lid. Spoon asparagus soup around squash. Cover tightly with foil.

4. Bake 15 to 20 minutes, until squash is tender.

---

252 MACADAMIA-STUFFED PATTYPAN SQUASH

Prep: 25 minutes   Cook: 20 to 28 minutes   Serves: 4 to 6

Scalloped squash makes a perfect receptacle for this elegant stuffing.

6 **medium pattypan squash**	½ **cup seasoned bread crumbs**
1 **teaspoon salt**	½ **cup crushed macadamia**
1 **cup tomato sauce**	**nuts**
2 **tablespoons olive oil**	⅓ **cup shredded Swiss cheese**
2 **celery ribs, diced**	1 **egg**
3 **scallions, chopped**	⅛ **teaspoon cayenne**

1. Preheat broiler. Cut off a dime-sized piece from base of each squash. Cut off lids and reserve. With a large spoon or a melon baller, scoop out and reserve insides, leaving ½-inch shell intact. Sprinkle cavities with a little salt. Set squash shells on baking sheet. Broil until lightly browned, 6 to 8 minutes. Remove from oven. Reduce heat to 375°F.

2. Cover bottom of a 7 x 11-inch baking dish with tomato sauce. Set squash shells snugly in sauce. Set aside.

3. On a cutting board, finely dice scooped-out squash.

4. In a large frying pan, heat olive oil over medium heat. Cook diced squash, celery, and scallions, stirring occasionally, until vegetables soften, 4 to 5 minutes.

5. In a medium bowl, mix cooked vegetables with bread crumbs, crushed nuts, cheese, egg, and cayenne.

6. Divide stuffing evenly among squash shells. Replace lids on top of each squash.

7. Bake until heated through, 10 to 15 minutes. Serve hot.

253   BULGUR BAKED TOMATOES

Prep: 20 minutes   Cook: 45 to 53 minutes   Serves: 4

½ cup bulgur
4 large tomatoes
2 tablespoons olive oil
½ red bell pepper, finely diced
1 small onion, chopped
2 garlic cloves, minced
½ cup chopped black olives

½ cup crushed walnuts
¾ teaspoon allspice
1 teaspoon salt
½ teaspoon pepper
¼ cup chopped parsley
1 tablespoon finely chopped
   fresh mint

1. Preheat oven to 375°F. In a medium saucepan, bring 1½ cups water to a boil. Add bulgur and reduce heat to medium-low. Cover and cook until bulgur is tender, 15 to 18 minutes. Remove from heat and fluff with a fork. Transfer to a medium bowl.

2. Meanwhile, cut a lid off top of each tomato. With a pointed spoon or a small knife, remove insides, leaving a ½-inch shell. Invert tomatoes in colander to drain. Dice insides of tomatoes and set aside.

3. In a medium frying pan, heat olive oil over medium heat. Add diced tomatoes, bell pepper, and onion and cook, stirring occasionally, until most of liquid evaporates, 4 to 5 minutes. Stir in garlic, olives, walnuts, allspice, salt, pepper, parsley, and mint. Add to cooked bulgur and mix well.

4. Lightly salt and pepper each hollowed-out tomato. Stuff each cavity with equal amounts of bulgur salad. Replace lid atop each tomato.

5. Set tomatoes snugly inside an 8-inch square baking dish. Bake until tomatoes are tender, 30 to 35 minutes.

254   COLD TOMATOES VALENCIANA

Prep: 15 minutes   Cook: 15 to 20 minutes   Serves: 4

1 (6-ounce) package Mexican-
   style rice mix
4 large tomatoes
3 scallions, chopped
1 (2-ounce) jar diced
   pimientos, drained
½ cup frozen peas, thawed
1 (6-ounce) jar marinated
   artichoke hearts, chopped

2 tablespoons lemon juice
½ cup extra-virgin olive oil
2 teaspoons Dijon mustard
½ teaspoon salt
¼ teaspoon pepper
½ cup chopped parsley

1. In a medium saucepan, cook rice according to package directions, 15 to 20 minutes. Set aside to cool.

2. Meanwhile, cut a lid off top of each tomato. With a pointed spoon or a small knife, hollow out tomato, leaving a ½-inch shell intact. Invert tomatoes in a colander to drain. Dice removed tomato.

3. In a large bowl, mix cooled rice with scallions, pimientos, peas, artichoke hearts and their marinade, and diced tomato.

4. In a small bowl, whisk lemon juice, olive oil, mustard, salt, and pepper. Add dressing to rice and mix well.

5. Fill each tomato with equal amounts of rice mixture. Sprinkle with parsley. Replace lids. Serve chilled.

---

255 ZUCCHINI ENCHILADAS ROJAS
Prep: 30 minutes   Cook: 48 to 56 minutes   Serves: 8

Make this dish for a crowd ahead of time and freeze it. To reheat, there is no need to thaw the casserole. Just add a little liquid to the dish before popping it in the oven.

¼ **cup plus 2 tablespoons vegetable oil**
16 **(7-inch) corn tortillas**
1 **large onion, diced**
2 **medium zucchini, cut into ½-inch cubes**
8 **ounces mushrooms, chopped**
1 **(7-ounce) can diced green chiles**
⅓ **cup wheat germ**
1 **(10-ounce) can mild Mexican red chili sauce**
2 **(10¾-ounce) cans cream of mushroom soup**
⅔ **cup milk**
½ **teaspoon dried oregano**
1 **cup plain yogurt**
3 **cups shredded Cheddar cheese**

1. Preheat oven to 375°F. In a large frying pan, heat ¼ cup vegetable oil over medium-high heat until a small piece of tortilla when dropped in turns to an instant crisp. Holding tortillas with tongs, fry each one 8 to 10 seconds. Do not let tortillas get crisp. Transfer to paper towels to drain.

2. Pour off oil and wipe pan clean with paper towels. In same pan, put remaining 2 tablespoons vegetable oil. Add onion and cook over medium heat, stirring occasionally, until softened, 2 to 3 minutes. Add zucchini and cook, stirring, until soft, 2 to 3 minutes. Add mushrooms and diced green chiles and cook, stirring, until they turn limp, 2 to 3 minutes. Transfer vegetables to a large bowl. Mix in wheat germ and ½ cup red chili sauce.

3. In a medium saucepan, prepare 2 cans mushroom soup according to directions on can. Remove from heat and stir in milk, oregano, yogurt, and remaining red chili sauce.

4. Spoon some sauce on bottom of two 9 x 13-inch baking dishes. Fill each tortilla with equal amounts of vegetable mixture. Roll tortillas jelly-roll style. Set, seam-side down, in baking dishes. Cover with mushroom/chili sauce. Sprinkle 1½ cups shredded cheese over each dish. Cover tightly with aluminum foil.

5. Bake 40 to 45 minutes, until bubbly.

256 STUFFED ZUCCHINI MEXICANA
Prep: 20 minutes   Cook: 29 to 38 minutes   Serves: 4

If Mexican flavors excite your palate, try using seasoned refried beans as a stuffing for vegetables.

8 medium zucchini	½ cup dry white wine
1 teaspoon salt	1 cup vegetable broth or
2 tablespoons olive oil	reduced-sodium chicken
½ medium onion, chopped	broth
1 (16-ounce) can refried beans	2 cups shredded pepper Jack
2 teaspoons ground cumin	cheese
1 teaspoon dried thyme leaves	

1. Preheat broiler. Cut zucchini in half lengthwise. Scoop out insides, leaving a ½-inch shell intact. Reserve scooped-out zucchini for another use or discard.

2. Set shells on a small baking sheet. Broil until shells are lightly browned, 4 to 5 minutes. Reduce heat to 350°F. Transfer shells to a 9 x 13-inch baking dish. Sprinkle lightly with salt.

3. In a medium frying pan, heat olive oil over medium-high heat. Add onion and cook, stirring occasionally, until golden, 2 to 3 minutes. Remove from heat and transfer to a medium bowl. Add refried beans, cumin, and thyme. Mash lightly with a fork.

4. Fill each zucchini shell with equal amounts of bean mixture. Pour wine and broth around shells.

5. Cover tightly with aluminum foil. Bake 15 to 20 minutes, until shells are tender. Remove foil, sprinkle shells with cheese, and bake until lightly browned, 8 to 10 minutes.

257 MOO SHU VEGETABLES

Prep: 30 minutes   Stand: 30 minutes   Cook: 6 to 9 minutes
Serves: 4 to 6

This classic Chinese pancake is filled with savory stir-fried vegetables. For convenience's sake, I've substituted flour tortillas for the traditional thin pancakes. Dried Chinese mushrooms and packages of shredded black tree fungus are available in the Asian section of supermarkets, as are tiger lily buds. If no tiger lily buds are available, simply double the amount of mushrooms.

12 (7-inch) flour tortillas
6 dried Chinese mushrooms
¼ cup shredded Chinese black
    tree fungus
1 ounce tiger lily buds
2 tablespoons dry sherry
2 tablespoons soy sauce or
    tamari
1 teaspoon Asian sesame oil
2 tablespoons oyster sauce
1 teaspoon minced fresh
    ginger

1 garlic clove, minced
3 tablespoons vegetable oil
1 large carrot, shredded
2 medium zucchini, cut into
    matchstick pieces
3 scallions, cut into 2-inch
    pieces
4 cups shredded cabbage
½ cup hoisin sauce

1. Preheat oven to 200°F. Wrap tortillas in aluminum foil and keep warm in oven until ready to fill.

2. Soak dried mushrooms, tree fungus, and tiger lily buds in 3 separate bowls each filled with ½ cup warm water for 30 minutes. Drain well, reserving liquid from mushrooms. Cut off woody stems from mushrooms and discard. Cut mushroom caps in slivers.

3. In a small bowl, mix sherry, soy sauce, sesame oil, oyster sauce, ginger, and garlic.

4. In a wok or large frying pan, heat vegetable oil over medium-high heat. Add carrot and cook, stirring occasionally, until barely tender, 2 to 3 minutes. Add zucchini, scallions, cabbage, and prepared sherry/ginger sauce. Cook, stirring, until cabbage wilts, 3 to 4 minutes. Add slivered mushrooms, tree fungus, and tiger lily buds. Cook, stirring, until heated through, 1 to 2 minutes.

5. To serve, spread some hoisin sauce on each warm tortilla. Fill with ½ cup vegetables and roll up, jelly-roll style. Serve immediately with additional hoisin sauce on the side.

258   TWO-SQUASH STUFFED ZUCCHINI

Prep: 25 minutes   Cook: 44 to 58 minutes   Serves: 4

4 medium zucchini, scrubbed and cut in half lengthwise
2 tablespoons olive oil
2 pounds butternut squash, peeled and cut into 2-inch chunks
1½ cups vegetable broth or reduced-sodium chicken broth
½ teaspoon salt
⅓ cup wheat germ
1 egg
1 teaspoon paprika
½ cup walnut pieces
1 envelope dry onion soup mix
¼ cup bread crumbs

1. Preheat broiler. With a spoon or a melon baller, scoop out insides of zucchini, leaving a ½-inch shell intact. Coarsely chop insides. Set shells on a small baking sheet. Broil until shells are lightly browned, 4 to 5 minutes. Reduce oven temperature to 350°F. Transfer shells to a 9 x 13-inch baking dish.

2. In a medium saucepan, heat olive oil over medium heat. Add butternut squash, chopped zucchini, broth, and salt. Cover and cook until butternut squash is tender, 20 to 25 minutes. With a slotted spoon, transfer vegetables to a medium bowl. Mash lightly with a fork. Reserve cooking juices.

3. Add wheat germ, egg, paprika, walnut pieces, and soup mix to mashed squash. Mix well. Fill zucchini halves equally with squash mixture. Pour reserved juices in between shells. Cover tightly with foil.

4. Bake 15 to 20 minutes, until zucchini is tender. Remove foil. Top with bread crumbs and bake until they turn golden brown, 5 to 8 minutes.

Chapter 10

Eggs-cellent Dishes

Eggs are part of a number of dishes in a person's daily diet and, as such, are one of nature's most precious gifts to cooks. Whether beaten to a frothy peak, poached, fried, scrambled, hard-boiled, or baked, eggs add flavor and texture to many a dish, from feathery light soufflés to velvety custards.

A few elementary precautions are prudent to follow when purchasing and cooking eggs. Whenever possible, buy your eggs right at the source at a farmers' market or directly from an egg farmer. Otherwise, purchase eggs from the refrigerated section of supermarkets. Refrigerate the eggs in their original container as soon as you get them home. Discard any egg that is cracked. The freshest eggs are the ones to poach or fry, or to use for soufflés. Eggs over three days old are good for hard-boiled eggs, since the air cell inside the egg expands, thus making it easier to peel. Most recipes call for eggs right out of the refrigerator. If you intend to beat the whites to a stiff peak, let the eggs stand a maximum of 30 minutes at room temperature; this will help them attain a fuller volume.

In this chapter I have assembled a collection of favorites, such as a Spanish Potato Tortilla, which can be cut in wedges or cubes, and Owen's Eggs Sardou, which my husband often prepares for guests. On other occasions, I pop the no-fuss Eight-Hour Mushroom-Spinach Bake in the oven, when guests arrive. To dress up a meal, Asparagus Flans with Blue Cheese Vinaigrette make an elegant substitute for a salad. Picnics take on an international flair with vegetable-stuffed Eggs à la Russe, parsley-flecked Persian Frittata with Greens and Goat Cheese, or the rich Artichoke Frittata.

For a quick breakfast, Watercress Machaca, an unusual Mexican version of scrambled eggs, is guaranteed to wake up your tastebuds, especially when wrapped in a warm burrito. If you feel a little more ambitious, Cheddar Cheese Soufflé with Sun-Dried Tomatoes is a light and flavorful first course.

Those who have opted to cut out eggs from their diet because of health concerns will find a number of egg substitutes on the market. Yet fresh eggs are still one of nature's most perfect foods. Like all things, they are best enjoyed in moderation.

259 ARTICHOKE FRITTATA
Prep: 20 minutes   Cook: 26 to 28 minutes   Serves: 4 to 6

1 (6-ounce) jar marinated
  artichokes
1 small onion, chopped
2 garlic cloves, minced
6 eggs, lightly beaten
¼ cup milk

1 teaspoon dried basil
1 cup grated Asiago cheese
¼ cup plus 1 tablespoon Italian
  bread crumbs
1 teaspoon seasoned salt
½ teaspoon pepper

1. Preheat oven to 350°F. Drain artichoke hearts, reserving marinade. Cut artichokes into ½-inch dice.

2. In a medium frying pan, heat reserved marinade over medium-high heat. Add onion and garlic and cook, stirring occasionally, until soft, about 3 minutes. Add diced artichoke hearts and cook until very lightly browned, 3 to 5 minutes. With a slotted spoon, transfer vegetables to a plate and let cool slightly.

3. In a medium bowl, beat eggs with milk and basil. Stir in grated cheese, ¼ cup bread crumbs, salt, and pepper. Add cooled artichokes.

4. Generously grease a 10-inch pie plate. Dust bottom with 1 tablespoon bread crumbs. Pour egg mixture into pan. Bake 20 minutes, or until puffy and brown. Remove from oven and let stand 10 minutes. Carefully slide frittata onto serving plate. Serve warm, at room temperature, or cold.

260 BASQUE PIPÉRADE
Prep: 10 minutes   Cook: 18 to 25 minutes   Serves: 4 to 6

This Basque variation of a frittata is usually served in the same dish it is cooked in. You can also make individual omelets using the same topping.

3 tablespoons olive oil
1 large onion, thinly sliced
1 green bell pepper, cut into
  ½-inch strips
2 red bell peppers, cut into
  ½-inch strips
2 large tomatoes, seeded and
  coarsely chopped

2 garlic cloves, minced
1 teaspoon salt
⅛ teaspoon cayenne
6 eggs, lightly beaten
1 teaspoon fines herbes
¼ teaspoon pepper

1. In a large nonstick frying pan, heat 2 tablespoons olive oil over medium-high heat. Add onion and cook, stirring occasionally, until golden, 2 to 3 minutes. Add green and red bell peppers. Cook, stirring, until soft, 3 to 5 minutes. Add tomatoes and garlic. Reduce heat to low. Partially cover and simmer until most of liquid evaporates, 8 to 10 minutes. Season with ½ teaspoon of salt and cayenne. With a slotted spoon, transfer peppers to a bowl. Do not rinse pan.

2. In a medium bowl, beat eggs with herbs, pepper, and remaining ½ teaspoon salt. Heat remaining 1 tablespoon oil in frying pan. Pour eggs into frying pan and cook over medium-low heat, stirring gently, until barely set, 5 to 7 minutes. Spoon vegetables over eggs. Heat through but do not mix. Serve hot.

261   ASPARAGUS FLANS WITH BLUE CHEESE VINAIGRETTE

Prep: 20 minutes   Cook: 38 to 40 minutes   Serves: 6

You can unmold these delicate little flans on a bed of lettuce leaves or serve them in their ramekins. This is a good dish for entertaining because it can be served chilled or at room temperature.

½ pound asparagus tips, cut into ½-inch pieces
3 eggs
4 ounces herb-flavored cream cheese
½ cup small-curd cottage cheese
½ teaspoon dried tarragon
½ teaspoon prepared white horseradish
1 tablespoon melted butter

2 teaspoons Dijon mustard
2 tablespoons tarragon vinegar
3 tablespoons vegetable oil
1 tablespoon crumbled blue cheese
1 garlic clove, crushed through a press
½ teaspoon salt
¼ teaspoon pepper
3 cups mixed lettuce leaves

1. Preheat oven to 325°F. In a medium saucepan filled with lightly salted boiling water, cook asparagus tips until tender, 3 to 5 minutes. Drain, rinse briefly under running water, and drain well.

2. In a blender, combine half of cooked asparagus with eggs, cream cheese, cottage cheese, tarragon, and horseradish. Puree until smooth. Transfer to a bowl and stir in remaining asparagus tips.

3. Grease six ⅔-cup ramekins or custard cups with melted butter. Divide mixture equally among ramekins. Set ramekins in a larger baking pan and pour hot water halfway up sides of ramekins.

4. Bake 35 minutes, or until flans are set and knife inserted in center comes out clean. Let cool in mold 10 minutes.

5. Meanwhile, in a small bowl, whisk together mustard, vinegar, oil, crumbled blue cheese, garlic, salt, and pepper.

6. To serve, divide lettuce equally among 6 plates. Unmold a flan on top of each plate. Spoon vinaigrette over all. Serve at room temperature or chilled.

262   SPANISH POTATO TORTILLA
Prep: 10 minutes   Cook: 30 to 38 minutes   Serves: 4 to 8

I often make this to take along on a picnic. In Spain, this tortilla is a thick omelet (not to be confused with the flour or corn tortillas from Mexico). It is usually part of an assortment of *tapas,* or appetizers served with drinks. The number of servings will depend on whether you serve this as an appetizer or as a main course. A nonstick or well-seasoned cast-iron skillet works best when making this omelet. It will keep up to 3 days, wrapped in foil in the refrigerator.

3 tablespoons olive oil	2 garlic cloves, minced
2 medium potatoes, peeled and cut into ¼-inch-thick slices	8 eggs, lightly beaten
	1 tablespoon chopped chives
	1 teaspoon salt
1 small onion, finely diced	½ teaspoon pepper

1. In a medium skillet, heat oil over medium heat. Add potatoes, onion, and garlic. Cover and cook, stirring occasionally, until potatoes are tender, 20 to 25 minutes.

2. In a medium bowl, beat eggs with chives, salt, and pepper. When potatoes are tender, pour egg mixture into pan. Cover and cook over medium heat until eggs are set, 8 to 10 minutes.

3. To cook other side, carefully invert omelet onto a large dinner plate. Gently slide tortilla, uncooked-side down, back into skillet. Cook 2 to 3 minutes. Remove from heat and let cool. Cut in wedges and serve warm or at room temperature.

263   PERSIAN FRITTATA WITH GREENS AND GOAT CHEESE
Prep: 10 minutes   Cook: 23 to 26 minutes   Serves: 4 to 6

You can make this with all sorts of mixed greens, including lettuce leaves, chard, or spinach. If cut into 2-inch squares, this frittata can be served as an hors d'oeuvre.

1 cup arugula leaves	6 scallions, chopped
4 leaves of iceberg lettuce	4 garlic cloves, minced
4 leaves of romaine lettuce	6 eggs
1 cup coarsely chopped parsley	½ cup crumbled goat cheese
	½ teaspoon ground cardamom
1 tablespoon chopped fresh dill or 1½ teaspoons dried	½ teaspoon pepper
	½ teaspoon salt
¼ cup olive oil	½ cup crushed pistachio nuts
	Wedges of lemon

1. Preheat oven to 350°F. Rinse, dry, and coarsely chop arugula, iceberg, and romaine lettuce leaves. Add parsley and dill to greens. Set aside.

2. In a large frying pan, heat 2 tablespoons oil. Add scallions and cook over medium-high heat, stirring occasionally, until softened, 2 to 3 minutes. Add garlic and chopped greens and cook, stirring occasionally, until vegetables turn limp, about 3 minutes. Transfer to a bowl and let cool slightly.

3. In a medium bowl, beat eggs lightly. Mix in goat cheese, cardamom, pepper, and salt. Add cooked greens to egg mixture.

4. Wipe frying pan clean and return to stove. Heat remaining 2 tablespoons olive oil over medium heat. Pour in egg mixture and cook until edges are set, about 2 minutes. Reduce heat to medium-low, cover, and cook without disturbing until frittata is barely set, 6 to 8 minutes.

5. Carefully slide frittata onto a 12-inch pizza pan. Sprinkle crushed pistachios on top. Place in oven and bake 10 minutes, or until top is firm. Let cool. Cut in wedges and serve at room temperature with wedges of lemon.

---

264   BROCCOLI RABE FRITTATA
Prep: 10 minutes   Cook: 13 to 16 minutes   Serves: 4

Broccoli rabe, also called rapini, is a close cousin of everyday broccoli, with a stronger, more mustardy flavor. In season, you will find it in Italian and specialty markets. If broccoli rabe isn't available, substitute broccoli florets broken up into very small pieces. Leftover frittata makes a great filling for sandwiches.

¼ cup olive oil
1 medium onion, chopped
2 garlic cloves, minced
3 cups coarsely chopped
    broccoli rabe
6 eggs
1 tablespoon chopped fresh
    basil or 1½ teaspoons
    dried

½ cup shredded provolone
    cheese
1 tablespoon bread crumbs
½ teaspoon salt
¼ teaspoon pepper

1. In a large frying pan, heat 2 tablespoons olive oil and cook onion, garlic, and broccoli rabe over medium heat, stirring occasionally, until broccoli rabe is barely tender, 5 to 6 minutes. Remove from heat.

2. In a large bowl, beat eggs lightly. Mix in broccoli rabe, basil, provolone, bread crumbs, salt, and pepper.

3. In same large frying pan, heat remaining 2 tablespoons olive oil. Pour in egg mixture. Cover and cook without stirring over medium-low heat until center is almost set, 4 to 5 minutes.

4. Remove pan from heat and carefully invert frittata onto a large plate. Cover with inverted frying pan and carefully flip frittata back into pan. Cook until bottom turns brown, 4 to 5 minutes. Slide onto serving platter and serve hot, warm, or at room temperature.

265 TUNISIAN EGG TURNOVERS
Prep: 15 minutes   Cook: 4 to 5 minutes   Serves: 2

These triangular-shaped turnovers are an adaptation of a specialty called *briks* in Tunisia. They are commonly served at the beginning of a meal or for a light supper. The fillings vary according to the cook's inspiration. Instead of the traditional filolike dough used for brik, I have substituted Chinese egg roll wrappers. Briks must be served hot. They taste best when served with a sprinkle of lemon juice.

3 hard-boiled eggs, coarsely mashed	½ teaspoon salt
½ cup chopped parsley	¼ teaspoon black pepper
8 garlic cloves, minced	½ teaspoon crushed hot red pepper
1 cup shredded imported Swiss or Jarlsberg cheese (4 ounces)	4 (5-inch) egg roll wrappers
	Vegetable oil, for frying
	4 wedges of lemon

1. In a medium bowl, mix eggs, parsley, garlic, cheese, salt, black pepper, and hot pepper with a fork until well blended.

2. Set the egg roll wrappers out on a flat surface. Place ¼ cup egg mixture in center of each wrapper. Fold over to make a triangular turnover, or brik. Rub inside edges with a little water and press to seal well.

3. In a large frying pan, heat 1 inch of vegetable oil over medium heat to 375°F. (Do not overheat oil or wrapper will cook to a crisp and filling will remain cold.) Cook until golden brown on one side, 2 to 3 minutes. With tongs, carefully turn brik over and cook until brown on other side, about 2 minutes. Drain briefly on paper towels. Serve hot, with lemon wedges to squeeze over brik.

266 ZUCCHINI AND BROCCOLI BAKE WITH SMOKED GOUDA CHEESE
Prep: 15 minutes   Cook: 42 to 48 minutes   Serves: 4

4 tablespoons butter	2 tablespoons flour
1 large onion, diced	5 eggs
2 medium zucchini, shredded (about 4 cups)	⅛ teaspoon cayenne
1 cup small broccoli florets	2 cups grated smoked Gouda cheese (8 ounces)
1 envelope dry ranch-style dressing mix	¼ cup bread crumbs

1. Preheat oven to 325°F. In a large frying pan, melt butter over medium heat. Add onion and cook, stirring occasionally, until softened, 2 to 3 minutes.

2. Meanwhile, in a large bowl, toss zucchini and broccoli florets with dressing mix and flour. Add vegetables to onions in pan and stir until moistened. Remove from heat.

3. In a medium bowl, beat eggs lightly. Mix in cayenne and 1 cup grated cheese.

4. Generously grease a 7 x 11-inch baking dish. Sprinkle bottom with bread crumbs. Pour in egg mixture and sprinkle remaining grated cheese on top. Bake until firm, 40 to 45 minutes. Let cool 10 minutes before cutting into squares.

---

267 EIGHT-HOUR MUSHROOM-SPINACH BAKE

Prep: 10 minutes   Stand: 8 hours   Cook: 48 to 55 minutes
Serves: 6 to 8

This great entertaining dish doesn't take eight hours to make. To the contrary, it is quickly prepared at least eight hours or up to a day before serving. Less than an hour before you're ready to serve, the only work you'll do will be to pop it in the oven.

2 tablespoons butter	3 eggs
1 pound mushrooms, sliced	1 teaspoon salt
1 small onion, chopped	¼ teaspoon pepper
1 (10-ounce) package frozen	2 cups milk
chopped spinach, thawed	½ teaspoon grated nutmeg
10 slices of firm-textured white	1 cup shredded Jarlsberg
bread, crusts removed	cheese (4 ounces)

1. In a large frying pan, melt butter. Add mushrooms and onion and cook over medium-high heat until tender, 5 to 7 minutes.

2. With your hands, squeeze out all liquid from spinach. Add to mushrooms. Cook, stirring, 3 minutes. Remove from heat and set aside.

3. Cut bread slices into 1-inch squares. In a medium bowl, beat eggs lightly. Mix in salt, pepper, milk, and nutmeg.

4. Place half of bread squares on bottom of a lightly greased 2-quart glass baking dish. Cover with half of mushroom-spinach mixture. Add half of egg mixture. Continue layering bread, mushrooms, and final layer of egg and cheese. Cover with plastic wrap and refrigerate 8 hours or overnight.

5. Preheat oven to 350°F. Bake until lightly browned on top, 40 to 45 minutes. Serve immediately.

268 EGGS FLORENTINE CASSEROLE
Prep: 15 minutes   Cook: 32 to 39 minutes   Serves: 8

2 tablespoons butter
4 scallions, chopped
1 pound mushrooms, sliced
2 (10-ounce) packages frozen
    chopped spinach, thawed
1 cup shredded sharp
    Cheddar cheese

12 eggs
2 cups half-and-half
½ teaspoon salt
¼ teaspoon pepper
1 cup shredded Swiss cheese
2 teaspoons paprika

1. Preheat oven to 350°F. In a large frying pan, melt butter over medium heat. Add scallions and cook, stirring occasionally, until softened, 2 to 3 minutes. Add mushrooms and cook, stirring occasionally, until mushrooms turn limp, 3 to 4 minutes. Remove from heat.

2. In a large saucepan filled with 2 cups lightly salted boiling water, cook spinach 2 minutes. Transfer to a colander. Rinse under cold running water to cool. With your hands, squeeze out as much liquid as possible.

3. Spread grated Cheddar on bottom of a generously greased 7 x 11-inch baking dish. Top with spinach. Cover with mushroom mixture. In a large bowl, beat eggs with half-and-half, salt, and pepper. Pour over spinach. Sprinkle Swiss cheese and paprika on top.

4. Bake 25 to 30 minutes, until casserole is set. Serve immediately.

269 BOLIVIAN CORN PUDDING
Prep: 10 minutes   Cook: 55 minutes to 1 hour   Serves: 4 to 6

Rita Minguillon was born in Bolivia, where *huminta*, this traditional corn pudding, accompanies Christmas dinner. She still makes it at holiday time every year in her California home.

1 (17-ounce) can cream-style
    corn
3 eggs, lightly beaten
½ teaspoon salt
¼ teaspoon pepper

2 drops of Tabasco
1 tablespoon sugar
½ cup raisins
½ cup diced Monterey Jack
    cheese

1. Preheat oven to 350°F. In a medium bowl, combine cream-style corn, eggs, salt, pepper, Tabasco, and sugar. Beat until well blended. Stir in raisins and cheese. Pour into a lightly oiled 1½-quart baking dish.

2. Bake 55 minutes to 1 hour, until corn pudding feels firm to the touch. Serve hot.

270 EGGS EN COCOTTE

Prep: 30 minutes   Stand: 30 minutes   Cook: 15 to 20 minutes
Serves: 4

4 **large tomatoes**	1 **teaspoon fines herbes**
1 **teaspoon salt**	4 **teaspoons butter**
4 **eggs**	½ **cup grated Gruyère cheese**

1. With a sharp knife, cut a lid off top of each tomato. With a small knife or a pointed spoon, cut out inside of tomatoes, leaving ¾-inch shell intact. Sprinkle each shell with salt. Invert in a colander to drain for 30 minutes.

2. Preheat oven to 375°F. Set tomatoes in individual ovenproof ramekins or small bowls. Break 1 egg inside each tomato. Sprinkle with fines herbes. Top with butter and grated cheese.

3. Bake cocottes 15 to 20 minutes, until eggs are set. Serve in ramekins.

271 BREAKFAST BURRITOS

Prep: 10 minutes   Cook: 6 to 9 minutes   Serves: 3

If you prepare the avocado more than 10 minutes ahead of time, sprinkle it with a little lemon juice to prevent it from turning brown.

6 **(8-inch) flour tortillas**	¼ **cup grated Romano cheese**
2 **tablespoons butter**	1 **teaspoon chili powder**
1 **small onion, chopped**	¼ **teaspoon salt**
1 **cup chopped mushrooms**	1 **avocado, peeled and diced**
(4 ounces)	1 **cup Mexican salsa**
6 **eggs**	

1. Preheat oven to 200°F. Wrap up tortillas in foil and keep warm until serving time.

2. In a large frying pan, melt butter over medium heat. Add onion and cook, stirring occasionally, until soft, 2 to 3 minutes. Add mushrooms and cook, stirring, until mushrooms begin to release their liquid, 2 to 3 minutes.

3. In a medium bowl, beat eggs with cheese, chili powder, and salt. Pour into frying pan over mushrooms. Cook over medium heat, stirring constantly to break up large lumps, until eggs are set, 2 to 3 minutes. Mix in diced avocado and remove from heat.

4. To assemble burritos, wrap up a spoonful of scrambled eggs in a warm tortilla. Serve with salsa on the side.

272 EGGS À LA RUSSE

Prep: 30 minutes   Cook: 20 minutes   Makes: 12

In Russia, tradition calls for downing a shot glass filled with vodka while eating stuffed hard-boiled eggs to help the process along. This recipe was inspired by a memorable dinner "à la Russe" where several stuffed eggs preceded a four-course dinner!

6 **eggs**	½ **cup mayonnaise**
1 **tablespoon capers, drained**	½ **cup plain yogurt**
½ **small onion, very finely diced**	1 **tablespoon white horseradish**
2 **teaspoons dried tarragon**	2 **teaspoons chopped fresh dill or 1 teaspoon dried**
1 **celery rib, finely diced**	**Dill or parsley sprigs, for garnish**
½ **cup frozen petite peas, thawed**	
1 **medium carrot, grated**	

1. In a large saucepan, place eggs in a generous amount of water. Bring to a boil and cook eggs for 5 minutes. Reduce heat to medium-low and continue cooking for 15 minutes. Remove from heat and drain. Let eggs stand in a medium bowl of cold water for 10 minutes. Remove shells.

2. With a very sharp knife, cut eggs in half lengthwise. With a small spoon, carefully remove yolks and transfer to a medium bowl. Set hollowed egg whites on a serving platter.

3. With a fork, mash yolks until fairly smooth. Add capers, onion, tarragon, celery, peas, carrot, mayonnaise, yogurt, horseradish, and dill. Mix until well blended.

4. With a spoon, mound equal amounts of egg mixture into hollowed-out eggs. Decorate each with a sprig of dill. Refrigerate until ready to serve.

273 EGGS AND SPINACH AU GRATIN

Prep: 25 minutes   Cook: 34 to 44 minutes   Serves: 6 to 8

2 **(16-ounce) bags frozen chopped spinach**	½ **teaspoon pepper**
4 **tablespoons butter**	2 **tablespoons white wine Worcestershire sauce**
¼ **cup flour**	1 **cup grated Asiago cheese**
1½ **cups milk**	6 **hard-boiled eggs, cut in half lengthwise**
1 **cup half-and-half**	
¼ **teaspoon grated nutmeg**	½ **cup bread crumbs**

1. Preheat oven to 350°F. Cook spinach according to package directions, 8 to 10 minutes. Drain well, squeezing out as much liquid as possible. Set aside.

2. In a medium saucepan, melt butter over medium-high heat. Whisk in flour and cook until flour turns pale golden, 3 to 4 minutes. Add milk and bring to a boil, whisking, until smooth and thickened, 4 to 5 minutes. Whisk in half-and-half and reduce heat to low. Add nutmeg, pepper, Worcestershire, and cheese. Cook, stirring, until cheese melts, 4 to 5 minutes. Remove cheese sauce from heat.

3. In a medium bowl, blend drained spinach with half of cheese sauce. Spread mixture in bottom of a 7 x 11-inch baking dish.

4. Place egg halves, yolk-side down, over spinach. Cover with remaining cheese sauce. Sprinkle with bread crumbs. Bake until bubbly and brown, 15 to 20 minutes. Serve hot.

---

274   BRIOCHES WITH TEX-MEX SCRAMBLED EGGS

Prep: 20 minutes   Cook: 10 to 14 minutes   Serves: 4

Serve these scrambled eggs in individual French egg brioches, if they are available at your bakery, or substitute French-style rolls.

4 small brioches or crusty rolls	8 eggs, lightly beaten
6 tablespoons butter, softened	1 cup shredded sharp
½ red bell pepper, cut into	Cheddar cheese
¼-inch dice	1 teaspoon salt
1 small onion, chopped	½ teaspoon chili powder
2 tomatoes, seeded and	
coarsely chopped	

1. Preheat oven to 200°F. Prepare brioches by carefully cutting off a small lid from the top. Remove most of the tender dough inside, leaving a ½-inch shell. Use 2 tablespoons butter to lightly butter inside brioches. Reserve lids and set brioches on baking sheet in oven to warm.

2. In a large frying pan, preferably nonstick, melt 2 tablespoons butter over medium heat. Add pepper and onion and cook, stirring occasionally, until soft, 3 to 5 minutes. Add tomatoes and cook 2 minutes. With a slotted spoon, transfer vegetables to a bowl.

3. In a large bowl, beat eggs with cheese, salt, and chili powder. Stir in cooked vegetables.

4. In the same frying pan, melt remaining 2 tablespoons butter. Add egg mixture and cook, stirring, to scramble until eggs are lightly set, 5 to 7 minutes. Fill rolls with scrambled egg mixture. Top with lids and serve immediately.

275   ROQUEFORT QUICHE
Prep: 15 minutes   Cook: 25 to 35 minutes   Serves: 4 to 6

6 ounces Roquefort cheese
3 ounces cream cheese with
   chives, at room
   temperature
3 tablespoons butter, at room
   temperature

3 eggs, lightly beaten
⅓ cup heavy cream
½ teaspoon salt
¼ teaspoon pepper
1 (9-inch) frozen deep-dish pie
   crust, thawed

1. Preheat oven to 375°F. In a medium bowl, combine Roquefort, cream cheese, and butter. Mash with a fork until well blended. With a hand-held electric mixer, beat in eggs, cream, salt, and pepper until fairly smooth. Pour filling into crust.

2. Bake 25 to 35 minutes, until quiche is puffy and brown. Serve immediately; the filling will fall like a soufflé as it cools.

276   BRUNCH SOUFFLÉ WITH APRICOT SAUCE
Prep: 15 minutes   Cook: 58 to 63 minutes   Serves: 6

This soufflé acquires a blintzlike consistency when it is baked. Serve it as soon as it comes out of the oven for best results.

¼ cup plus 1 tablespoon
   brown sugar
6 eggs
1 cup sour cream
   Grated zest of 1 lemon
¾ cup flour
2 teaspoons baking powder
1 (8-ounce) package cream
   cheese, at room
   temperature

1 pint small-curd cottage
   cheese
1 teaspoon vanilla extract
1 tablespoon diced candied
   ginger (optional)
1 cup apricot preserves

1. Preheat oven to 350°F. In a blender or food processor, combine ¼ cup brown sugar, 4 eggs, sour cream, lemon zest, flour, and baking powder. Puree until smooth and well blended. Set batter aside.

2. In a large bowl, combine cream cheese, cottage cheese, vanilla, candied ginger, and remaining 2 eggs. Beat until well blended.

3. Pour half of batter onto bottom of a generously buttered 2-quart baking dish. Cover with cream cheese filling. Top with remaining batter. Sprinkle remaining 1 tablespoon brown sugar on top.

4. Bake 55 to 60 minutes, until puffy and golden. Meanwhile, in a small saucepan, simmer apricot preserves with 2 tablespoons water, stirring, until preserves are hot and melted, about 3 minutes. Serve soufflé hot and spoon apricot sauce over top.

277 MY FAVORITE SPINACH QUICHE

Prep: 15 minutes   Cook: 34 to 46 minutes   Serves: 4 to 6

3 tablespoons butter	1 teaspoon dried thyme leaves
1 large onion, diced	½ teaspoon dried tarragon
1 cup sliced mushrooms	1 teaspoon salt
1 (10-ounce) package frozen chopped spinach, thawed and drained	½ teaspoon pepper
	1½ cups shredded Gruyère cheese
3 eggs	1 (9-inch) frozen pie crust, thawed
½ cup milk	

1. Preheat oven to 375°F. In a large frying pan, melt butter over medium-high heat. Cook onion, stirring occasionally, until soft, about 3 minutes. Add mushrooms and cook, stirring, until barely tender, 3 to 4 minutes. Add drained spinach and cook until moisture evaporates, 3 to 4 minutes. Set aside.

2. In a medium bowl, beat eggs lightly. Mix in milk, thyme, tarragon, salt, pepper, and Gruyère cheese. Add cooked spinach to egg mixture and stir to blend. Pour filling into pie crust.

3. Bake 25 to 35 minutes, until quiche is puffy and golden. Serve warm.

278 CHEDDAR CHEESE SOUFFLÉ WITH SUN-DRIED TOMATOES

Prep: 15 minutes   Cook: 47 to 55 minutes   Serves: 4

2 tablespoons butter	½ teaspoon grated nutmeg
⅓ cup flour	¼ teaspoon pepper
1 cup milk	2 tablespoons finely diced sun-dried tomatoes
1½ cups shredded Cheddar cheese	5 eggs, separated

1. Preheat oven to 350°F. Generously grease a 2-quart soufflé dish and set aside.

2. In a large saucepan, melt butter over medium heat. Add flour and cook, stirring, until it turns a pale golden color, 3 to 4 minutes. Whisk in milk all at once and bring to a boil, stirring, until mixture thickens, 2 to 3 minutes. Stir in shredded cheese, nutmeg, pepper, and sun-dried tomatoes. Continue to cook, stirring, until cheese melts, 2 to 3 minutes. Remove from heat to a bowl and let cool. Stir egg yolks one at a time into cheese mixture until well blended. Set aside.

3. In a large bowl, beat egg whites until stiff but not dry. With a spatula, gently fold beaten egg whites into cheese mixture.

4. Pour into prepared soufflé dish. Bake 40 to 45 minutes, until soufflé is puffed and golden brown. Serve immediately.

279　SPECKLED EGGS BENEDICT

Prep: 20 minutes　Cook: 6 to 8 minutes　Serves: 4

4 eggs
2 English muffins
3 tablespoons butter, softened
8 ounces mushrooms, sliced
½ teaspoon salt

¼ teaspoon pepper
1 (0.9-ounce) envelope
   Hollandaise mix
1 tablespoon imitation bacon
   bits

1. In an egg poacher, poach eggs until whites are set, 3 to 4 minutes.

2. Meanwhile, toast muffins. Spread with 1 tablespoon butter. Keep warm.

3. In a medium frying pan, melt remaining 2 tablespoons butter over medium-high heat. Add mushrooms and cook, stirring occasionally, until tender, 3 to 4 minutes. Season with salt and pepper.

4. Prepare Hollandaise sauce according to package directions.

5. To serve, spoon equal amounts of mushrooms onto muffin halves. Top with a poached egg. Cover with Hollandaise and sprinkle with bacon bits. Serve hot.

280　TASTY EGG FOO YUNG

Prep: 10 minutes　Cook: 16 to 20 minutes　Serves: 4

For many Chinese food aficionados, egg foo yung ranks on a par with so-called comfort foods. Oyster sauce is a Chinese condiment available in the Asian foods section of most supermarkets and in Asian markets.

5 eggs
1 cup bean sprouts
4 scallions, chopped
1 cup sliced mushrooms
2 celery ribs, finely diced
¼ cup soy sauce or tamari

2 tablespoons oyster sauce
1 teaspoon Asian sesame oil
¼ teaspoon pepper
¼ cup vegetable oil
3 tablespoons rice wine
   vinegar

1. In a large bowl, beat eggs lightly. Stir in bean sprouts, scallions, mushrooms, celery, 1 tablespoon soy sauce, oyster sauce, sesame oil, and pepper until well blended.

2. In a large frying pan, heat vegetable oil over medium heat. With a measuring cup, pour batter by cupfuls into pan to make patties 4 to 5 inches in diameter. Cook patties 2 at a time, flipping carefully with 2 spatulas, until golden brown, 4 to 5 minutes on each side. Transfer to a serving platter.

3. In a small bowl, mix remaining 3 tablespoons soy sauce with rice wine vinegar. Sprinkle over egg foo yung before serving. Serve with steamed rice.

281 CHEESY PUDDING SHELL
Prep: 10 minutes   Cook: 25 minutes   Serves: 4

You can use this fully baked poppy seed–studded shell as an edible bowl for all sorts of fillings, such as ratatouille, Waldorf salad, or creamed spinach.

2 **eggs**	1 **teaspoon poppy seeds**
½ **cup flour**	½ **cup shredded Swiss cheese**
1 **cup milk**	1 **tablespoon butter**

1. Preheat oven to 425°F. In a large bowl, whisk together eggs, flour, and milk until smooth. Add poppy seeds and cheese.

2. Use butter to grease a 10-inch pie pan. Pour in batter and bake 10 minutes. Reduce oven temperature to 350°F and bake 15 minutes longer, or until shell is puffy and golden brown.

282 EGGS WITH TOMATOES AND ROASTED PEPPERS
Prep: 15 minutes   Cook: 18 to 24 minutes   Serves: 2 to 4

2 **red bell peppers**	1 **teaspoon ground cumin**
2 **green bell peppers**	4 **eggs**
1 **tablespoon olive oil**	**Salt and freshly ground**
1 **tablespoon butter**	**pepper**
1 **medium onion, finely diced**	
3 **medium tomatoes, peeled, seeded, and coarsely chopped**	

1. Preheat broiler. Set peppers on a baking sheet and broil as close to heat as possible, turning peppers with tongs, until lightly charred, 5 to 7 minutes. Place peppers inside a paper bag and seal. Let stand 10 minutes.

2. When peppers are cool, peel and seed under running water. Cut into 1-inch strips. Set in a colander to drain.

3. In a large frying pan, heat olive oil and butter. Add onion and cook over medium heat, stirring occasionally, until softened, 2 to 3 minutes. Add peppers, tomatoes, and cumin. Cook until most of liquid evaporates, 8 to 10 minutes.

4. With back of a large spoon, hollow out 4 nests among vegetables. Break an egg inside each nest. Season with salt and pepper. Cover and cook until white is set and yolk is partially set, 3 to 4 minutes. Separate portions with a spatula and serve immediately.

283 CURRIED CAULIFLOWER SOUFFLÉ
Prep: 25 minutes   Cook: 58 to 66 minutes   Serves: 4

This is a firm soufflé. When served cold, it makes a wonderful sandwich filling.

1 **medium head of cauliflower, broken up into small florets**	1 **cup shredded sharp provolone cheese**
2 **tablespoons butter**	1 **teaspoon curry powder**
1 **tablespoon flour**	3 **eggs, separated**
1 **cup milk**	½ **teaspoon salt**

1. Preheat oven to 400°F. In a large saucepan of lightly salted boiling water, cook cauliflower florets until soft, about 10 to 12 minutes. Drain and let cool slightly. With a potato masher or in a food processor, mash cauliflower.

2. In a medium saucepan, melt butter over medium heat. Whisk in flour and cook, stirring, 1 minute. Add milk and bring to a boil, whisking until sauce thickens, 2 to 3 minutes. Stir in cheese and curry powder; remove from heat. Let cool slightly, then beat in egg yolks, one at a time. Add mashed cauliflower.

3. In a large bowl, beat egg whites with salt until stiff peaks form. Fold gently into cauliflower mixture.

4. Heavily butter a 2-quart soufflé dish. Fill with cauliflower mixture. Bake 45 to 50 minutes, until soufflé feels fairly firm. Serve immediately from baking dish.

284 BAKED EGGS WITH RATATOUILLE
Prep: 10 minutes   Cook: 10 to 12 minutes   Serves: 4

This is a terrific way to use up any leftover ratatouille. For best results, reheat ratatouille, simmering down until most of liquid has evaporated. Serve with rice or crusty French bread.

3 **cups ratatouille (page 187) or store-bought**	4 **eggs** **Paprika**

1. Preheat oven to 400°F. Spread ratatouille over bottom of an 8-inch square baking dish or shallow 1½-quart ovenproof casserole. With back of a large spoon, make 4 hollow nests in ratatouille. One at a time, gently crack eggs and slip into a nest.

2. Dust eggs with paprika. Cover with foil and bake 10 to 12 minutes, until whites are set and yolks are partially set.

285   OWEN'S EGGS SARDOU

Prep: 20 minutes   Cook: 8 to 13 minutes   Serves: 4

This is my husband Owen's adaptation of his favorite brunch dish: the famous eggs Sardou served at Antoine's Restaurant in New Orleans. There are several brands of dry Hollandaise mixes on the market.

1 pound asparagus spears	1 tablespoon lemon juice
4 tablespoons butter	2 drops of Tabasco
1 garlic clove, minced	1 teaspoon distilled white
1 (17¾-ounce) can artichoke	vinegar
bottoms, drained	4 eggs
½ teaspoon salt	2 teaspoons chopped fresh
¼ teaspoon pepper	tarragon or parsley
1 (0.9-ounce) envelope	
Hollandaise sauce mix	

1. Snap off tough ends of asparagus spears. In a large saucepan filled with boiling water, cook asparagus until crisp-tender, 3 to 5 minutes. Drain and set aside.

2. In a large frying pan, melt 2 tablespoons butter over medium-high heat. Add garlic and artichoke bottoms and cook, stirring occasionally, until heated through, 2 to 3 minutes. Season with salt and pepper. With a slotted spoon, transfer to a dish and cover to keep warm.

3. Meanwhile, prepare Hollandaise sauce according to package directions. Season with lemon juice and Tabasco.

4. In a large saucepan of simmering water and vinegar, or in an egg poacher, poach eggs until white is firm, 3 to 5 minutes. Drain well.

5. To serve, arrange equal amounts of asparagus spears on 4 individual plates. Top with artichoke bottoms. Place a poached egg in each nest of artichoke bottoms. Cover with Hollandaise sauce and garnish with chopped tarragon. Serve immediately.

286 CUMIN ZUCCHINI FLAN
Prep: 20 minutes   Cook: 23 to 30 minutes   Serves: 4

My friend Andrea Peterson has devised numerous delicious ways to take advantage of the bounty of her garden. This is one of them.

2 pounds zucchini, scrubbed and cut into 3-inch chunks	½ to 1 teaspoon hot pepper sauce, to taste
3 eggs	1 cup milk
1 tablespoon ground cumin	½ cup shredded Cheddar cheese
½ teaspoon salt	⅓ cup fresh bread crumbs

1. Preheat oven to 325°F. In a large saucepan of lightly salted boiling water, cook zucchini until barely tender, 3 to 5 minutes; drain. Let stand until cool enough to handle. Then cut zucchini pieces in half lengthwise. With a spoon, scoop out zucchini into a small bowl, leaving a ⅜-inch shell. Set zucchini shells, cut-sides down, around edge of a lightly oiled 9-inch pie pan, like spokes of wheels.

2. Coarsely chop reserved zucchini. In a medium bowl, beat eggs, add chopped zucchini, cumin, salt, hot sauce, milk, shredded cheese, and bread crumbs. Mix well. Pour carefully over zucchini shells.

3. Bake flan 20 to 25 minutes, until set.

287 EGG TOASTS
Prep: 10 minutes   Cook: 28 to 35 minutes   Serves: 4

My mother often prepares these flavorful egg toasts smothered in fresh tomato sauce for a brunch or a light dinner.

1 tablespoon olive oil	½ teaspoon salt
1 small onion, chopped	½ teaspoon pepper
1 pound ripe tomatoes, peeled, seeded, and coarsely chopped	8 slices of sourdough bread, cut 1 inch thick
2 teaspoons dried basil	1 stick (4 ounces) butter
1 teaspoon sugar	8 eggs

1. In a medium saucepan, heat olive oil over medium-high heat. Add onion and cook, stirring occasionally, until soft, about 3 minutes. Add tomatoes, basil, sugar, salt, and pepper. Reduce heat to low. Cover and simmer 20 to 25 minutes, until sauce is slightly thickened.

2. Meanwhile, with a spoon, dig out a small cavity from center of each bread slice.

3. In a large frying pan, melt butter over medium-high heat. Add bread slices, cut-sides down, and cook until golden, 2 to 3 minutes. Turn over and break 1 egg into each cavity. Cook until white is set, 3 to 4 minutes.

4. With a spatula, transfer toasts to individual serving plates. Top with hot tomato sauce. Serve immediately.

288 WATERCRESS MACHACA
Prep: 15 minutes   Cook: 17 to 26 minutes   Serves: 4

Machaca is the Mexican version of scrambled eggs, and it's usually chock-full of all sorts of tidbits, from chile peppers to diced potato. This meatless machaca was inspired by watercress grower Linda Sadon, who cooks her watercress stems and all. The peppery flavor adds excitement to plain scrambled eggs. For a more substantial dish, as suggested here, the machaca is rolled up in a warm tortilla and served with a dollop of sour cream or fresh salsa on the side.

8 (8-inch) flour tortillas	8 eggs, well beaten
2 tablespoons olive oil	½ teaspoon salt
½ large red bell pepper, finely diced	¼ teaspoon pepper
1 small onion, finely diced	½ cup grated sharp Cheddar cheese
1 small bunch of watercress, chopped	Sour cream or Mexican salsa, for garnish

1. Wrap tortillas in aluminum foil and warm in a 200°F oven until heated through, 10 to 15 minutes. Or place tortillas between 2 double layers of moistened paper towels and microwave on High until heated through, 1½ to 2 minutes.

2. Meanwhile, in a large frying pan, heat olive oil over medium-high heat. Add pepper and onion and cook, stirring occasionally, until soft, 2 to 3 minutes. Add watercress and stir-fry until wilted, about 2 minutes.

3. Stir in eggs, salt, pepper, and cheese. Cook, stirring constantly, until cheese melts and eggs are set, 3 to 4 minutes. Remove from heat.

4. To serve, wrap up a spoonful of egg mixture, burrito style, in a warm tortilla. Serve with sour cream or salsa on the side.

Chapter 11

Super Sandwiches without Meat

Centuries after the Earl of Sandwich requested something to eat between two slices of bread so he wouldn't interrupt his game playing, his namesake food has gone far beyond the plain white bread stage. For the best sandwiches, I favor freshly baked whole-grain loaves. Thick slices of nut-filled bread also get my vote, as do hard-crusted rolls. These have acquired multicultural ties in recent years, whether petits pains from France or panini from Italy. Soft, herb-flavored cheeses and spreads also make delightful substitutes for the usual butter, mayonnaise, or mustard.

Whether open-faced, like Chuck's Open-Faced Mushroom Madness, or wrapped in a warm tortilla, like Fresh Vegetable Burrito, sandwiches can often double as meals unto themselves. The same applies to overstuffed pita pockets brimming with vegetables, sprouts, and nuts, like Crispy Falafel with Tahini Sauce, a Middle Eastern import topped with a healthful, sesame-based sauce. Some sandwiches don't even require bread at all. The Eggplant Sandwich, for instance, uses eggplant slices as a substitute for bread. Sesame Sandwich Ring not only tastes wonderful but looks smashing on a buffet table. So do Pineapple Curry Roll-Ups and Goat Cheese and Grilled Eggplant Tortilla Roll-Ups, which provide tasty mouthfuls when sliced into colorful little wheels. Hot sandwiches such as Apple Reuben Sandwich or California Welsh Rabbit are good to keep in mind for a light supper. Southwestern Fry Bread, an American original, will, like its pizza counterpart, satisfy the heartiest of appetites. As for me, thick slices of fresh bread encasing a generous layer of Apple-Nut with Watercress and Tangerine Mayonnaise rank as highly as a slice of chocolate cake.

289   APPLE REUBEN SANDWICH
Prep: 10 minutes   Cook: 16 to 22 minutes   Serves: 4

6 to 8 tablespoons butter, softened
2 medium apples, peeled and sliced
1 (16-ounce) package fresh sauerkraut
1 tablespoon brown sugar
1 tablespoon Worcestershire sauce
2 tablespoons grainy mustard
8 slices of fresh rye bread
½ pound sharp Cheddar cheese, thinly sliced

1. In a large frying pan, melt 2 tablespoons butter over medium heat. Add apples, cover, and cook, stirring occasionally, until tender, 6 to 8 minutes. Meanwhile, drain sauerkraut into a colander. Rinse under cold running water and drain again.

2. Add brown sugar and Worcestershire sauce to skillet. Cook, stirring to blend, until brown sugar dissolves, 1 to 2 minutes. Stir in sauerkraut. Cook uncovered, stirring occasionally, until heated through, 3 to 5 minutes. Remove from heat.

3. To assemble sandwich, generously spread mustard on inside of 8 bread slices. Set equal amounts of Cheddar cheese on 4 bottom slices. Spoon sauerkraut mixture over cheese. Cover with second layer of Cheddar cheese and second slice of bread. Generously butter outside of bread slices with about 2 tablespoons butter total.

4. In a large nonstick frying pan, melt 2 tablespoons butter over medium heat. Add sandwiches and cook until golden brown on bottom, pressing down with spatula to flatten, 3 to 4 minutes. Turn, add remaining butter to pan if needed, and cook until golden brown on second side, about 3 minutes. Cut sandwiches on the diagonal and serve hot.

290   APPLE-NUT SANDWICH WITH WATERCRESS AND TANGERINE MAYONNAISE
Prep: 15 minutes   Cook: none   Serves: 4

½ cup mayonnaise
½ cup sour cream
Grated zest of 1 tangerine
¼ cup fresh tangerine juice or 2 tablespoons frozen concentrate
½ teaspoon dried tarragon
¼ teaspoon pepper
1 tablespoon creamy horseradish sauce
2 tart apples, peeled, cored, and diced
2 celery ribs, thinly sliced
½ cup raisins
½ cup dry-roasted peanuts, coarsely chopped
8 thick slices of whole wheat bread
1 bunch of watercress

1. In a small bowl, combine mayonnaise, sour cream, tangerine zest, tangerine juice, tarragon, pepper, and horseradish. Blend well.

2. In a medium bowl, combine diced apples, celery, raisins, and peanuts. Add tangerine dressing and stir to blend well.

3. Spoon equal amounts of filling atop 4 slices of whole wheat bread. Top with sprigs of watercress. Cover with second slice of bread. Cut sandwiches in half on a diagonal and serve immediately.

---

291   MEXICAN BEAN BOLILLOS

Prep: 15 minutes   Stand: 1½ hours   Cook: 17 to 20 minutes
Makes: 12

These dense little rolls are filled with a tasty refried bean mixture.

2 (¼-ounce) envelopes Rapid Rise yeast
½ cup warm water (105°F to 115°F)
2 teaspoons sugar
3½ cups unbleached flour
2 cups plus 2 tablespoons yellow cornmeal
2 teaspoons salt
1 cup buttermilk, at room temperature

2 sticks (8 ounces) butter, melted
1½ cups shredded hot pepper Jack cheese
2 tablespoons vegetable oil
½ cup canned refried beans
3 scallions, chopped
1 teaspoon ground cumin

1. In a small bowl, dissolve yeast in water with sugar. Let stand until mixture bubbles, about 10 minutes.

2. Meanwhile, in a large mixing bowl, combine 1 cup flour, 1 cup cornmeal, and salt. Make a well in center and add yeast mixture. Knead with dough hooks of electric mixer, scraping dough from side of bowl with spatula, until blended, 2 to 3 minutes. Or knead by hand 4 to 5 minutes. Slowly mix in buttermilk, remaining 2½ cups flour and 1 cup cornmeal, and ¾ cup melted butter. Keep kneading until dough feels elastic to the touch, 10 to 12 minutes. Add shredded cheese and knead until just blended, 1 to 2 minutes.

3. Transfer dough to a lightly oiled bowl and cover with a clean cloth. Place in a warm, dry place until dough doubles in size, about 1½ hours.

4. Preheat oven to 400°F. Lightly grease a baking sheet and sprinkle lightly with 2 tablespoons cornmeal. In a small bowl, mix refried beans with scallions and cumin.

5. Punch down dough and separate into 12 balls of equal size. With a knife, slit center of each ball and fill with about 2 teaspoons bean filling. Pinch dough together to seal well. Set rolls on prepared baking sheet.

6. Paint rolls with remaining melted butter. Bake 12 to 15 minutes, until crust is golden brown. Turn rolls upside down and bake 5 minutes longer. Set on a rack to cool.

292   GARLIC BREAD WITH PARMESAN CHEESE
Prep: 15 minutes   Cook: 10 to 12 minutes   Serves: 4 to 6

10   garlic cloves, crushed
¼   cup extra-virgin olive oil
2   tablespoons chopped fresh
      parsley
1   teaspoon dried basil
1   teaspoon dried thyme leaves

¼   to ½ teaspoon crushed hot
      red pepper, to taste
¼   cup grated Parmesan cheese
1   (1-pound) loaf of Italian
      bread

1. Preheat oven to 350°F. In a blender or food processor, puree garlic, olive oil, parsley, basil, thyme, hot pepper, and Parmesan cheese until fairly smooth.

2. Slice bread loaf in half horizontally. Spread garlic filling over each half. Set 2 halves separately on baking sheet, cut-sides up.

3. Bake until nice and crusty, 10 to 12 minutes. Cut into thick pieces and serve warm.

293   CASTROVILLE SPECIAL
Prep: 10 minutes   Cook: 10 to 15 minutes   Serves: 4

Castroville, a couple of hours south of San Francisco, is the self-appointed artichoke capital of the world. Needless to say, artichokes play a major role in local kitchens. This sandwich showcases the area's claim to fame.

1   (6-ounce) jar marinated
      artichokes
4   crusty rolls, split in half
2   medium tomatoes, sliced
1   sweet onion, thinly sliced

¼   pound mushrooms, sliced
½   pound mozzarella cheese,
      thinly sliced
⅛   teaspoon crushed hot red
      pepper

1. Preheat oven to 375°F. Drain artichoke hearts over a small bowl, reserving marinade. Coarsely chop artichokes.

2. With a spoon, spread some marinade on bottom half of each roll. Place equal amounts of chopped artichoke hearts, tomatoes, onion, mushrooms, and mozzarella inside each roll. Sprinkle with hot pepper.

3. Wrap each sandwich in foil. Bake until cheese melts and sandwich is heated through, 10 to 15 minutes.

294   CHIPOTLE CORNBREAD
Prep: 10 minutes   Cook: 40 to 45 minutes   Serves: 4 to 6

Chipotle, fiery little Mexican peppers that are actually smoked jalapeños, are commonly available canned. Puree the whole chipotles in the blender, diluting them with a little water or broth to lessen their impact. Bottles of chipotle in adobo sauce can also be found in the Mexican foods section of supermarkets.

1 cup plus 1 tablespoon cornmeal	¾ cup buttermilk
½ teaspoon baking soda	1 cup shredded hot pepper Jack cheese
1 (17-ounce) can cream-style corn	2 eggs
½ medium onion, chopped	½ teaspoon chipotle in adobo sauce
2 tablespoons imitation bacon bits (optional)	

1. Preheat oven to 375°F. In a large bowl, combine 1 cup cornmeal, baking soda, cream-style corn, onion, bacon bits, buttermilk, cheese, eggs, and chipotle sauce. Mix well to blend.

2. Generously grease a 10-inch square baking pan. Sprinkle bottom and sides with remaining cornmeal. Pour batter into pan.

3. Bake 40 to 45 minutes, until a toothpick inserted in center comes out clean. Cut bread into squares and serve warm.

295   BRAIDED ONION-MUSHROOM LOAF WITH PISTACHIO NUTS
Prep: 15 minutes   Cook: 29 to 36 minutes   Serves: 4

1 stick (4 ounces) butter	2 tablespoons grated Parmesan cheese
½ medium onion, chopped	1 (8-ounce) loaf of frozen bread dough, thawed
½ cup chopped mushrooms	
1 garlic clove, minced	1 egg, lightly beaten
½ cup pistachio nuts, crushed	

1. Preheat oven to 375°F. In a medium frying pan, melt butter over medium heat. Add onion and cook, stirring occasionally, until soft, 2 to 3 minutes. Add mushrooms, garlic, and pistachio nuts and cook, stirring, until mushrooms give up their juices, 2 to 3 minutes. With a slotted spoon, transfer to a small bowl. Mix with Parmesan cheese.

2. Cut loaf lengthwise into 3 equal strips. Slit each piece down the center; flatten lightly. Place equal amounts of filling inside each slit. Seal edges closed.

3. Braid strands, making sure ends are well sealed together. Brush loaf with beaten egg.

4. Bake 25 to 30 minutes, until brown.

296   EGGPLANT SANDWICH

Prep: 20 minutes   Stand: 15 minutes   Cook: 16 to 22 minutes
Serves: 4

In summer, when eggplant is plentiful, you can prepare several of these sandwiches and freeze them. To quick-fry the eggplant slices, I use as little oil as I can in a nonstick frying pan. It is best to use the widest part of the eggplant to obtain the largest sandwich-size slices. Reserve the rest to make a ratatouille, for instance.

1 medium eggplant	8 ounces mushrooms, sliced
2 teaspoons salt	1 garlic clove, minced
1 cup bread crumbs	8 thin slices of sharp
3 egg whites, beaten until	provolone cheese
frothy	1 cup spaghetti sauce
¼ cup vegetable oil	
2 cups loosely packed and	
torn-up fresh spinach	
leaves	

1. Preheat oven to 400°F. Peel eggplant. Cut crosswise through widest part of eggplant to obtain 8 slices of approximately the same size. Sprinkle each slice with a little salt. On a flat surface lined with paper towels, let slices drain for 5 to 7 minutes on each side. Rinse quickly and pat dry.

2. Place bread crumbs on a shallow plate. Place beaten egg whites in a small bowl.

3. In a large nonstick frying pan, heat 2 tablespoons of oil over medium heat. With a fork, dip 4 eggplant slices into egg white, dredge in bread crumbs, and dip again in egg white. Let excess egg white drip off. Fry, turning once, until golden outside and tender, 1 to 2 minutes on each side. Drain on paper towels. Repeat with remaining slices, adding additional oil if needed.

4. Wipe frying pan clean with paper towels. In same pan, heat remaining 2 tablespoons oil over medium heat. Add spinach, mushrooms, and garlic and cook until spinach leaves are limp, 2 to 3 minutes. Remove from heat.

5. To assemble eggplant sandwiches, place 4 fried eggplant slices on bottom of a 7 x 11-inch baking dish. Cover with 1 slice cheese. Mound equal amounts of spinach mixture on each slice. Cover with second slice of cheese. Top with second eggplant slice. Press down lightly. Spread 2 tablespoons spaghetti sauce over top of each slice.

6. Bake until cheese is melted and sandwiches are heated through, 12 to 15 minutes. Serve hot or at room temperature. When cool, these sandwiches (without the sauce) can be wrapped in foil and frozen for up to 2 months.

297   CRISPY FALAFEL WITH TAHINI SAUCE
Prep: 20 minutes   Cook: 6 to 8 minutes   Serves: 4

Falafel, a flour made from ground garbanzo beans, is a staple of Middle Eastern cuisine. This sandwich is traditionally served with tahini, a sauce made from ground sesame seeds, which is also popular in that region. Falafel mix is available in bulk in health food stores or else packaged on supermarket shelves in the section featuring Jewish foods. So is canned tahini.

1 cup falafel mix	4 pita breads
1 tablespoon minced onion	Tahini Sauce (recipe
½ teaspoon ground cumin	follows)
½ teaspoon salt	1 cup shredded lettuce
¼ teaspoon pepper	2 medium tomatoes, diced
¼ cup vegetable oil	

1. In a medium bowl, mix falafel mix with ¾ cup water until thoroughly moistened. Add onion, cumin, salt, and pepper. With your hands, fashion 4 large or 8 small patties.

2. In a medium frying pan, heat oil over medium heat. Fry patties until brown, turning over with spatula, 3 to 4 minutes on each side. Drain on paper towels.

3. Fill each pita with 1 large or 2 small falafel patties.

4. To serve, spoon tahini sauce over falafel and top with shredded lettuce and diced tomato.

TAHINI SAUCE
Prep: 10 minutes   Cook: none   Makes: about 1 cup

⅓ cup tahini	3 garlic cloves, crushed
¼ to ⅓ cup lemon juice	through a press
½ teaspoon salt	1 teaspoon paprika

1. In a small bowl, combine tahini with ¼ cup lemon juice. Stir until well blended. Add ¼ cup cold water, salt, and garlic. Stir briskly until smooth. Add remaining lemon juice if needed and a little extra water if sauce is too thick.

2. Serve in a shallow dish, with paprika sprinkled on top.

298   PANINI NIÇOISE
Prep: 15 minutes   Cook: 9 to 11 minutes   Serves: 6

Panini are the crusty little Italian bread rolls that you can find in super-markets and, more often, in Italian bakeries.

½   pound green beans, cut into
         2-inch pieces
1   stick (4 ounces) unsalted
         butter, softened
6   garlic cloves, crushed
         through a press
¼   cup finely chopped parsley
6   freshly baked panini
¼   cup oil-cured black olives
1   (2-ounce) jar diced
         pimientos, drained

2   hard-boiled eggs, chopped
4   ounces feta cheese,
         crumbled
⅓   cup bottled vinaigrette
         dressing
2   medium tomatoes, thinly
         sliced
1   medium sweet onion, very
         thinly sliced

1. Preheat oven to 300°F. In a medium saucepan of boiling salted water, cook beans until tender, 4 to 6 minutes. Drain, rinse under cold running water, and drain well. In a small bowl, mix butter, garlic, and parsley. Set garlic butter aside.

2. Cut open panini and remove most of soft dough inside. Butter inside of each roll generously with garlic butter. Place on a baking sheet. Heat in oven 5 minutes.

3. Meanwhile, in a medium bowl, mix cooked green beans with olives, diced pimientos, hard-boiled eggs, feta cheese, and vinaigrette dressing. Toss to mix.

4. Remove rolls from oven. Fill bottom halves with equal amounts of green bean mixture. Top each sandwich with sliced tomato and sliced onion. Close with top half. Serve immediately.

299   GOAT CHEESE AND GRILLED EGGPLANT TORTILLA ROLL-UPS
Prep: 35 minutes   Cook: 2 to 4 minutes   Chill: 2 hours
Makes: about 48

These roll-ups make delicious hors d'oeuvres.

4   Asian eggplants or
         1 medium eggplant
1   cup sour cream
1   (1½-ounce) envelope dry
         fines herbes soup mix
¾   cup cream cheese, softened
8   ounces herbed goat cheese

1   tablespoon chopped sun-
         dried tomatoes
¼   cup olive oil
4   (10-inch) flour tortillas
1   cup marinated green olives,
         pitted and sliced
1   cup walnuts, crushed

1. Peel eggplant(s). Cut crosswise in half; cut each half lengthwise into ½-inch slices. Cut slices lengthwise into ½-inch strips.

2. In a medium bowl, using a hand-held electric mixer, beat sour cream, soup mix, and cream cheese together until smooth. With a spoon, stir in goat cheese and sun-dried tomatoes.

3. Preheat broiler. Line a baking sheet with foil. Spread eggplant strips in a single layer on sheet. Paint lightly with olive oil. Broil, turning with tongs, until lightly browned, 1 to 2 minutes on each side.

4. On a flat surface, unwrap tortillas. Spread evenly with sour cream mixture. Set eggplant strips down center of tortilla. Sprinkle whole surface with some sliced olives and some crushed walnuts. Roll up tortilla, jelly-roll style, fairly tightly without letting filling squeeze out. Proceed in same manner with remaining tortillas. Place on a platter, wrap in plastic wrap, and refrigerate for 2 hours or overnight.

5. To serve, cut roll-ups into slices ¾ to 1 inch thick.

---

300   OLIVE FOCACCIA
Prep: 15 minutes   Stand: 1 hour 20 minutes
Cook: 28 to 35 minutes   Serves: 6 to 8

My neighbor Ed uses this delicious Italian bread to make sandwiches or as an accompaniment to soups and stews.

2 **(8-ounce) loaves of frozen bread dough, thawed**	1 **tablespoon finely diced sun-dried tomatoes**
3 **tablespoons extra-virgin olive oil**	12 **oil-cured olives, halved and pitted**
⅓ **cup finely chopped onion**	1 **teaspoon dried thyme leaves**

1. Slice off half of 1 bread loaf and reserve for later use. In a lightly oiled 9 x 13-inch baking dish, stretch out remaining dough to cover bottom of pan evenly. Cover with a clean cloth. Let rise in a warm place until double in size, about 1 hour.

2. Preheat oven to 375°F. With fingers, poke holes all over risen bread dough. Sprinkle with 2 tablespoons olive oil. Let rise in warm place 20 minutes longer.

3. Meanwhile, in a small frying pan, melt remaining 1 tablespoon oil over medium heat. Add onion and cook, stirring occasionally, until golden, 2 to 3 minutes. Stir in sun-dried tomatoes and cook, stirring, 1 to 2 minutes. Remove from heat.

4. To assemble focaccia, spread onion mixture evenly over surface of dough. Lightly press in olives to form decorative pattern. Sprinkle with thyme leaves.

5. Bake 25 to 30 minutes, until focaccia is puffy and brown. Serve hot or warm.

301   CALIFORNIA WELSH RABBIT

Prep: 10 minutes   Cook: 12 to 17 minutes   Serves: 4

Diced green chiles give this classic Welsh rabbit a California twist.

2 cups shredded extra-sharp
   Cheddar cheese
2 teaspoons cornstarch
½ cup beer
4 ounces Velveeta cheese
2 teaspoons sweet-hot
   mustard

½ teaspoon chili powder
2 tablespoons diced green
   chiles
1 hard-boiled egg, chopped
4 tablespoons butter
8 thick slices of sourdough or
   rye bread

1. Preheat broiler. In a small bowl, toss Cheddar cheese with cornstarch.

2. In a small saucepan, bring beer to a simmer over medium heat. Add
Cheddar cheese mixture and Velveeta cheese. Cook, stirring, until cheeses
melt, about 3 minutes. Stir in mustard, chili powder, diced green chiles, and
chopped egg. Remove from heat.

3. In a large frying pan, melt 2 tablespoons butter over high heat. Lightly fry
4 slices of bread until golden, 2 to 3 minutes on each side. Repeat with
remaining butter and bread. Transfer slices to a 9 x 13-inch baking dish.

4. Spoon equal amounts of cheese sauce over bread slices. Broil until puffy
and brown, 1 to 2 minutes. Serve immediately.

302   MEDITERRANEAN HERO WITH GRILLED EGGPLANT AND ZUCCHINI

Prep: 5 minutes   Cook: 9 to 12 minutes   Serves: 4

1 red bell pepper
1 medium eggplant, peeled
   and cut lengthwise into
   ¼-inch-thick slices
2 zucchini, peeled and cut
   lengthwise into ¼-inch-
   thick slices
¼ cup olive oil

2 garlic cloves, minced
1 (4-ounce) package whipped
   herb cheese, softened
2 tablespoons plain yogurt
½ teaspoon salt
4 crusty rolls
1 tablespoon capers, drained

1. Preheat broiler. Broil red pepper as close to heat as possible, turning, until
skin blisters evenly, 8 to 10 minutes. Or roast directly over a gas flame about
5 minutes. Seal in a paper bag and let steam 10 minutes.

2. Meanwhile, in a medium bowl, toss eggplant and zucchini slices with
olive oil and garlic. Set vegetable slices in a single layer on a large baking
sheet. Broil until slices are soft and golden, 1 to 2 minutes on each side.
Remove from oven.

3. Peel and seed red pepper under running water. In a blender or food processor, puree roasted pepper with cream cheese and yogurt until smooth. Season with salt.

4. Spread rolls with red pepper mixture and fill with equal amounts of broiled vegetables and capers.

---

303   PINEAPPLE CURRY ROLL-UPS
Prep: 30 minutes   Cook: none   Chill: 2 hours
Makes: about 48

These roll-ups are always a hit at parties. They are traditionally made with *lavash*, a soft unleavened bread of Middle Eastern origin. I've substituted jumbo flour tortillas, which are more readily available. The rolls are easier to cut if you wrap them in plastic wrap and refrigerate them for a few hours before slicing them.

1 **(8-ounce) package whipped cream cheese, at room temperature**	½ **cup chopped raisins**
1½ **cups sour cream**	4 **scallions, finely diced**
½ **cup mayonnaise**	4 **(10-inch) flour tortillas**
2 **teaspoons curry powder**	1 **cup imitation bacon bits**
1 **tablespoon soy sauce or tamari**	1 **(7-ounce) can crushed pineapple, drained**
¼ **cup finely diced crystallized ginger**	4 **ounces alfalfa sprouts**

1. In a medium bowl, with a hand-held electric mixer, beat together cream cheese, sour cream, mayonnaise, curry powder, and soy sauce until smooth. With a spoon, stir in diced ginger, raisins, and scallions.

2. On a flat surface, unwrap tortillas. With a spatula, evenly spread one-fourth of cream cheese mixture over 1 tortilla. Sprinkle with ¼ cup bacon bits. Top with about 2 tablespoons pineapple. Spread a layer of one-fourth of alfalfa sprouts evenly over whole surface. Roll up jelly-roll style, fairly tightly, without letting filling squeeze out. Wrap in plastic wrap and refrigerate for 2 hours or overnight. Proceed in same manner with remaining tortillas and filling. To serve, cut rolls into slices ¾ to 1 inch thick.

304   CHUCK'S OPEN-FACED MUSHROOM MADNESS

Prep: 15 minutes   Cook: 6 to 8 minutes   Serves: 6

1 pound mushrooms, sliced	¼ cup olive oil
2 small tomatoes, diced	2 tablespoons lemon juice
1 ripe avocado, diced	1½ cups shredded sharp
2 garlic cloves, minced	provolone cheese
¼ cup crushed walnuts	6 thick slices of whole-grain
2 teaspoons dried oregano	peasant or French bread

1. Preheat oven to 375°F. In a large bowl, toss sliced mushrooms with tomatoes, avocado, garlic, walnuts, oregano, olive oil, and lemon juice. Stir in half of shredded cheese.

2. Set slices of bread on a baking sheet. Mound equal amounts of mushroom mixture on each slice. Top with remaining cheese.

3. Bake 6 to 8 minutes, until cheese melts. Serve at once.

305   INDIVIDUAL PISSALADIÈRES

Prep: 15 minutes   Cook: 15 to 20 minutes   Serves: 6

Pissaladière is the French version of pizza. The dough is usually thin, and the topping traditionally consists of onions, anchovies, and olives.

1 (10-ounce) package frozen patty shells (6), thawed	1 teaspoon salt
2 tablespoons Dijon mustard	1 teaspoon pepper
6 medium tomatoes, sliced	2 tablespoons herbes de Provence
1 cup kalamata olives, halved and pitted	2 cups shredded Swiss cheese

1. Preheat oven to 375°F. On a floured surface, roll out each patty shell into a circle 5 inches in diameter. Transfer circles to lightly oiled baking sheets.

2. Paint each circle of dough with mustard. Arrange tomato slices on dough circles and top with a few olives. Sprinkle with equal amounts of salt, pepper, and herbes de Provence. Cover with Swiss cheese.

3. Bake 15 to 20 minutes, until puff pastry is puffy and brown. Serve hot.

306   PITACADO
Prep: 15 minutes   Cook: none   Serves: 4

4 pita pockets
½ cup plain yogurt
2 tablespoons creamy
   horseradish sauce
1 teaspoon dried dill
1 small cucumber, peeled,
   seeded, and diced
12 slices of sharp Cheddar
   cheese (about 5 ounces)

2 ounces alfalfa sprouts
2 medium tomatoes, seeded
   and diced
2 avocados, cubed
1 sweet onion, thinly sliced
2 tablespoons imitation bacon
   bits

1. Split open pita pockets. In a small bowl, combine yogurt, horseradish, dill, and diced cucumber. Stir to mix dressing well.

2. Stuff pita pockets with equal amounts of cheese, sprouts, tomatoes, avocados, and onion slices. Spoon dressing over top and garnish with bacon bits.

307   HOT ROQUEFORT AND AVOCADO SANDWICHES
Prep: 10 minutes   Cook: 5 to 6 minutes   Serves: 4

4 ounces Roquefort cheese
1½ cups sour cream
1 tablespoon port wine
⅛ teaspoon Tabasco
2 ripe avocados, diced

1½ tablespoons lemon juice
4 thick slices of Italian
   country-style bread
½ cup walnut pieces

1. In top of a double boiler over simmering water, crumble Roquefort into sour cream. Add port and Tabasco and stir until Roquefort melts, 5 to 6 minutes. Remove from heat and set aside.

2. In a small bowl, toss avocado with lemon juice.

3. Place equal amounts of avocado on each slice of bread. Cover with warm Roquefort sauce. Sprinkle with walnuts. Serve at once, with a knife and fork.

308   SESAME SANDWICH RING
Prep: 15 minutes   Cook: 30 minutes   Serves: 6 to 8

1 (8-ounce) loaf of frozen
  bread dough, thawed
4 tablespoons butter, melted
2 teaspoons sesame seeds
1 (8-ounce) container
  whipped cream cheese
  with herbs

1 cup pecans, crushed
1 medium carrot, shredded
1 cup golden raisins
4 ounces alfalfa sprouts

1. Preheat oven to 375°F. Generously oil a 6-cup ring mold. Lightly dust with flour. Carefully stretch bread dough to fill mold evenly. Paint top of dough with melted butter and sprinkle with sesame seeds. Pat gently to help seeds adhere.

2. Bake 30 minutes, or until bread is crusty and golden. Invert bread onto a rack and let cool 10 minutes. When bread is cool, with a sharp knife, carefully slice it in half horizontally.

3. In a medium bowl, mix cream cheese with pecans, carrot, and raisins.

4. To assemble sandwich ring, generously cover bottom half of bread with cream cheese spread. Top with alfalfa sprouts. Cover second half with remaining spread and set atop bottom to form a complete ring. Wrap and refrigerate until ready to serve. To serve, cut into slices.

309   FRESH TOMATO TAPENADE ROLLS
Prep: 15 minutes   Cook: none   Serves: 4

Use this olive-and-caper-based tapenade as a spread for sandwiches or as a topping for pasta.

1 cup pitted black olives
1 stick (4 ounces) butter, at
  room temperature
4 garlic cloves, minced
2 tablespoons extra-virgin
  olive oil
2 tablespoons minced parsley
¼ teaspoon freshly ground
  pepper

2 tablespoons capers, drained
4 hard French rolls, split in
  half and toasted
2 large ripe tomatoes, thinly
  sliced
1 medium sweet onion, very
  thinly sliced
8 thin slices of mozzarella
  cheese (about 4 ounces)

1. To make tapenade, in a blender or food processor, combine olives, butter, garlic, olive oil, parsley, pepper, and capers. Puree to a smooth paste.

2. Spread tapenade over both cut sides of rolls. Divide tomatoes, onion rings, and mozzarella slices equally among rolls.

310   QUICK WHOLE WHEAT PITA PIZZAS
Prep: 10 minutes   Cook: 6 to 8 minutes   Serves: 2

2 whole wheat pita pockets,
   split in half horizontally
¼ pound Asiago cheese, thinly
   sliced
1 large ripe tomato, thinly
   sliced

6 Greek olives, pitted and
   sliced
1 teaspoon dried thyme leaves

1. Preheat oven to 375°F. Set 4 pita halves on baking sheet. Cover with cheese slices. Top with tomato slices and olives. Sprinkle on thyme leaves.

2. Bake 6 to 8 minutes, until cheese melts. Serve hot.

311   NUTTY PATTIES WITH CUCUMBER RAITA
Prep: 20 minutes   Cook: 20 to 25 minutes   Serves: 6

1 small onion, quartered
2 eggs
1 cup plain bread crumbs
1 cup walnut pieces, finely
   ground
2 garlic cloves, minced
½ teaspoon salt
¼ teaspoon pepper

2 tablespoons mayonnaise
1 tablespoon soy sauce or
   tamari
6 onion-flavored pita pockets
1 cup shredded lettuce
½ cup diced tomato
   Cucumber Yogurt Sauce
   (page 69)

1. Preheat oven to 350°F. In a blender or food processor, process onion with eggs until chopped.

2. Transfer mixture to a medium bowl. Add bread crumbs, ground walnuts, garlic, salt, pepper, mayonnaise, and soy sauce. Stir until mixture is moistened.

3. With your hands, fashion into patties 2 inches in diameter. Set on a lightly oiled baking sheet.

4. Bake until patties turn crusty, 20 to 25 minutes.

5. Fill each pita with 2 or 3 patties. Top with lettuce and tomato. Serve with Cucumber Yogurt Sauce on the side.

312 THE ULTIMATE SPROUTBURGER
Prep: 10 minutes   Cook: 10 to 12 minutes   Serves: 4

This is the ultimate veggie burger. Sprouted peas and lentils are generally available in the produce section of supermarkets and in health food stores.

2 cups fresh mixed sprouted peas and lentils
2 eggs, lightly beaten
1 small onion, quartered
½ teaspoon salt
¼ teaspoon pepper
1 garlic clove, crushed through a press
2 tablespoons Worcestershire sauce

2 tablespoons seasoned bread crumbs
¼ pound mushrooms, chopped
1 tablespoon olive oil
4 hamburger buns
2 tablespoons Dijon mustard
1 Bermuda onion, thinly sliced
1 tomato, thinly sliced

1. In a blender or food processor, combine sprouts with eggs. Process until fairly smooth. Add onion and process until blended. Add salt, pepper, garlic, and Worcestershire. Blend well. Transfer mixture to a bowl. Stir in bread crumbs and mushrooms. Let stand 5 minutes.

2. In a large nonstick frying pan, heat olive oil over medium heat. Spoon sprout mixture into pan to form 4 patties of equal size, flattening each one with back of a spoon. Fry until patties are golden, turning over with spatula, 5 to 6 minutes on each side.

3. Toast buns and spread with Dijon mustard. Top with a sproutburger. Garnish with onion and tomato slices.

313 GRILLED VEGETABLE CLUB
Prep: 10 minutes   Cook: 4 to 6 minutes   Serves: 2

1 medium eggplant
1 apple, peeled, cored, and sliced
2 medium tomatoes
2 medium onions

2 tablespoons olive oil
6 slices of whole-grain bread
2 tablespoons honey mustard
¼ pound Jarlsberg cheese, thinly sliced

1. Preheat broiler. Cut eggplant lengthwise into ¼-inch-thick slices. Cut tomatoes and onions into ¼-inch slices.

2. Line a baking sheet with foil. Set eggplant, tomato, and onion slices in a single layer on baking sheet. Paint lightly with olive oil. Broil vegetables, turning over carefully with tongs, 2 to 3 minutes on each side. Watch carefully to prevent scorching.

3. To assemble double-decker sandwiches, spread 2 bread slices with mustard. Top with equal amounts of grilled vegetables and then with 2 more slices of bread. Spread bread with mustard and cover with cheese slices, dividing equally. Top with remaining bread. Cut sandwiches into quarters and serve.

314   VEGETABLE SANDWICH LOAF

Prep: 30 minutes   Stand: 1 hour 10 minutes   Cook: 35 to 42 minutes
Makes: 1 loaf

A mosaic of diced vegetables dot this festive loaf of bread. Just spread with your favorite topping and enjoy.

1 (¼-ounce) envelope active
   dry yeast
½ cup warm water (105°F to
   110°F)
1 teaspoon sugar
1 tablespoon olive oil
1 medium onion, chopped
1 cup frozen diced vegetables,
   thawed
1 tablespoon fines herbes

1 cup plus 2 tablespoons
   warm milk
1 teaspoon salt
2 tablespoons vegetable oil
   About 4 cups all-purpose
   flour
½ cup shredded Parmesan
   cheese
1 egg, lightly beaten

1. In a small bowl, mix yeast, warm water, and sugar. Set aside until mixture starts to bubble, 10 to 12 minutes.

2. Meanwhile, in a large nonstick frying pan, heat olive oil over medium heat. Add onion and cook, stirring occasionally, until soft, 2 to 3 minutes. Add diced vegetables and cook, stirring, until barely tender, 3 to 4 minutes. Stir in fines herbes and set aside.

3. Combine softened yeast, milk, salt, and vegetable oil in a large mixing bowl. Beat in 3 cups flour and shredded cheese. Add additional flour, ½ cup at a time, to form a medium dough. Knead by hand or using an electric mixer with a dough hook, scraping dough from sides of bowl with a rubber spatula, until dough feels elastic to the touch, about 8 minutes. Add vegetables and continue kneading until they are incorporated, 2 to 3 minutes.

4. Lightly oil a baking sheet. Rub a little oil on your hands. Remove dough from bowl and form an oval loaf, about 12 x 6 inches. Place on baking sheet. Cover with a clean towel and set in a warm place to rise for 1 hour.

5. Preheat oven to 350°F. Paint loaf with beaten egg, taking care not to let it drip onto the pan. Bake 30 to 35 minutes, or until loaf is golden brown and sounds hollow when tapped. Remove from baking sheet and cool on a rack.

315   FRESH VEGETABLE BURRITO
Prep: 10 minutes   Cook: 18 to 25 minutes   Serves: 4

8 (10-inch) flour tortillas
1 tablespoon butter
½ medium onion, sliced
½ medium green pepper,
   diced
¼ pound green beans, cut into
   ½-inch pieces

1 cup broccoli florets
2 celery ribs, diced
1 cup shredded Swiss cheese
1 cup prepared salsa

1. Preheat oven to 325°F. Wrap tortillas in aluminum foil and bake until heated through, 10 to 15 minutes. (Or place tortillas in 2 batches between 2 double layers of moistened paper towels and microwave on High until hot, 45 to 60 seconds.)

2. In a large frying pan, melt butter over medium heat and cook onion and pepper, stirring occasionally, until pepper softens, 4 to 5 minutes.

3. Add green beans, broccoli, and celery. Cover and cook until broccoli is crisp-tender, 4 to 5 minutes.

4. Fill each tortilla with equal amounts of vegetables. Sprinkle with cheese, fold up sides, and roll in shape of burrito.

5. Serve immediately with salsa on the side.

316   ZUCCHINI QUESADILLAS
Prep: 10 minutes   Cook: 7 to 10 minutes   Serves: 4

2 tablespoons olive oil
4 scallions, chopped
1 medium zucchini, shredded
2 medium tomatoes, seeded
   and diced
½ teaspoon dried oregano
¼ teaspoon pepper

½ teaspoon salt
8 (7-inch) flour tortillas,
   preferably whole wheat
1 cup shredded Monterey Jack
   cheese
¼ cup sour cream

1. Preheat oven to 400°F. In a medium frying pan, heat olive oil over medium heat and cook scallions, stirring occasionally, until soft, 2 to 3 minutes. Add zucchini, diced tomatoes, oregano, pepper, and salt. Cook, stirring occasionally, until most of the liquid evaporates, 2 to 3 minutes. Remove from heat.

2. Place tortillas in a single layer on 2 large baking sheets. Top each tortilla with equal amounts of cooked vegetables and shredded cheese. Bake until cheese melts, 3 to 4 minutes.

3. Serve immediately, with a dollop of sour cream on top.

317   SOUTHWESTERN FRY BREAD
Prep: 30 minutes   Stand: 15 minutes   Cook: 16 to 32 minutes
Serves: 8

Whenever a Native American tribe holds a powwow in the San Diego area, one of the most popular booths at the gathering is the one featuring fry bread. The crisp, flat bread is usually topped with refried beans, shredded lettuce, grated cheese, and sour cream. This is my adaptation of that memorable snack.

2 tablespoons dry onion flakes	2 (15-ounce) cans refried beans, heated through
1½ cups warm water	4 cups shredded lettuce
3 cups all-purpose flour	2 cups diced tomatoes
1 cup whole wheat flour	2 cups shredded Monterey Jack cheese
1 tablespoon baking powder	Sour cream (optional)
2 teaspoons garlic salt	
Vegetable oil, for frying	

1. In a small bowl, combine onion flakes with warm water. Soak until soft, about 5 minutes. In a large mixing bowl, combine all-purpose and whole wheat flours, baking powder, and garlic salt. Make a well in center and add onion flakes and water. Stir to combine thoroughly.

2. Knead, using a mixer with a dough hook or by hand, until dough feels elastic to the touch, 10 to 12 minutes. Cover with a kitchen towel. Set aside for at least 15 minutes or up to 2 hours.

3. In a large frying pan, heat 1 inch of oil over medium heat. Break off a piece of dough the size of a golf ball. On a flat, lightly floured surface, roll out dough to 7 inches in diameter. Stretch gently with your fingers. Poke a hole in center of dough so bread fries evenly. Carefully set flattened dough in hot oil. Fry, turning over with tongs, until golden, 1 to 2 minutes on each side. Transfer to paper towels to drain.

4. To serve, top hot fry bread with equal amounts of refried beans, lettuce, and tomatoes. Sprinkle with grated cheese. Top with a dollop of sour cream, if desired.

318   NUTTY TOFU BURGERS
Prep: 10 minutes   Cook: 4 to 6 minutes   Serves: 6

Tofu and Chinese hot chili paste are generally available in supermarkets and in Asian markets. You can find nutritional yeast in bulk in health food stores.

1   (10½-ounce) package soft
       tofu, drained
1   medium onion, sliced, plus
       ½ onion, chopped
1   cup seasoned bread crumbs
¾   cup chopped walnuts
2   teaspoons soy sauce or
       tamari
½   teaspoon Asian sesame oil

⅛   teaspoon Chinese chili paste
       or Tabasco
1   garlic clove, minced
3   eggs, lightly beaten
1   tablespoon nutritional yeast
2   tablespoons peanut oil
6   hamburger buns
2   tablespoons mustard
1   large tomato, sliced

1. In a large bowl, coarsely mash tofu with a fork. Add chopped onion, bread crumbs, walnuts, soy sauce, sesame oil, chili paste, and garlic. Add beaten eggs and nutritional yeast and blend well. Form into 6 patties about 4 inches in diameter.

2. In a large frying pan, heat oil over medium heat. Fry patties until nice and brown, turning carefully with a spatula, 2 to 3 minutes on each side. Drain on paper towels.

3. Heat hamburger buns and assemble tofu burgers with all the fixings.

Chapter 12

Simply Vegetables

To my mind, a plate lined with fresh vegetables is on equal footing with a decorative vase holding a fragrant bouquet: Both items provide a feast for the eyes as well as the senses. That is why, when I encounter "cooking block," you will find me browsing through the cornucopia of fresh fruits and vegetables in the supermarket produce section, looking for inspiration. Sometimes it will strike in the guise of Tomato and Cabbage Fricassee, or slender Japanese eggplant simply cooked as Garlicky Eggplant Sauté. As all cooks know, the beauty of cooking with the season's bounty is to enjoy the product at its peak.

Many specialty produce items, like kiwifruit, purple potatoes, or even tomatoes in varying shades of yellow, were virtually unknown in mainstream food stores a few years ago. One way to keep abreast of all these agricultural developments is to frequent a farmers' market. There, once or twice a week, a tempting kaleidoscope of seasonal produce may include anything from newly developed squash or lettuces to rediscovered heirloom varieties of apples.

Whether you purchased your produce at the supermarket or at a farmers' market, as a matter of course soak all raw vegetables in cold water before preparing them. This will get rid of any residual grit, dirt, or wax. Dry fruits and vegetables gently and thoroughly after cleaning. Most vegetables are best kept stored in plastic bags or in their original containers, in the crisper drawer of your refrigerator. Others, like tomatoes for instance, attain full flavor only at room temperature. Steaming, boiling, or sautéing vegetables remains a matter of individual taste. Some prefer vegetables crisp-tender; others like them well done. In general, the shorter time vegetables are cooked, however, the more essential vitamins and nutrients they retain.

Several dishes in this section are meant as meals-in-a-dish, such as Grilled Vegetables with Eggless Basil Mayonnaise. Many dishes listed belong to the side-dish category, well suited to complement grains or pasta: Black-Eyed Succotash, Curried Onion Bake, and Jardinière de Légumes are a case in point. Tomatoes Provençale, the simplest of broiled vegetable side dishes, ranks high on my list of favorites when made with vine-ripened tomatoes. Other dishes offer out-of-the-ordinary combinations, such as Ragout of Eggplant and Artichoke Hearts, Honeyed Carrot and Prune Casserole, and Baked Sweet Squash Ring with Orange Sauce.

319   GREEK-STYLE ARTICHOKE AND POTATOES

Prep: 10 minutes   Cook: 30 to 35 minutes   Serves: 4 to 6

In Greece, this dish is made with tiny, tender cocktail artichokes, which can be cooked and eaten whole. Small new potatoes work best for this dish. If the potatoes are larger, quarter them to be approximately the same size as the artichoke hearts. For convenience's sake, I have substituted canned artichokes, which I personally prefer to the frozen variety. This dish can be served hot or at room temperature.

1 pound small red or white potatoes (about 1½ inches in diameter), peeled	2 garlic cloves, minced
	½ teaspoon dried rosemary
	2 tablespoons fresh lemon juice
1 (16-ounce) can pearl onions, drained	1 (14½-ounce) can artichoke hearts, drained
1 cup vegetable broth or reduced-sodium chicken broth	½ teaspoon salt
	½ teaspoon pepper
3 tablespoons extra-virgin olive oil	2 tablespoons chopped parsley

1. In a large saucepan, combine potatoes, pearl onions, broth, olive oil, garlic, and rosemary. Bring to a simmer, reduce heat to medium-low, cover, and cook until potatoes are almost tender, about 20 minutes.

2. Add lemon juice and artichoke hearts. Cook, uncovered, over medium-low heat until liquid has reduced by half, 10 to 15 minutes. Season with salt and pepper.

3. Transfer vegetables to a serving bowl and garnish with chopped parsley.

---

320   BROCCOLI ROMANA

Prep: 10 minutes   Cook: 11 to 14 minutes   Serves: 6

3 tablespoons olive oil	¾ teaspoon salt
2 garlic cloves, minced	½ teaspoon pepper
2 pounds broccoli, broken into small florets	½ cup grated Parmesan cheese
1 cup dry white wine	2 tablespoons Italian-seasoned bread crumbs

1. In a large frying pan, heat oil over medium heat. Add garlic and cook until soft, about 1 minute. Add broccoli and cook, stirring, about 1 minute to coat with oil. Add wine, salt, and pepper. Cover and cook, stirring once or twice, until broccoli is tender but not mushy, 8 to 10 minutes. Stir in Parmesan cheese. With a slotted spoon, transfer broccoli to a serving platter.

2. In the same pan, turn heat to high and bring juices to a boil, stirring and scraping sides of pan, 1 to 2 minutes. Pour sauce over broccoli. Sprinkle with bread crumbs and serve immediately.

321 FRICASSEE OF BRUSSELS SPROUTS AND PEARL ONIONS IN PESTO SAUCE

Prep: 10 minutes   Cook: 24 to 30 minutes   Serves: 4 to 6

1 pound Brussels sprouts, trimmed and cut in half	1 large carrot, cut into 1-inch chunks
4 tablespoons butter	2 tablespoons prepared pesto sauce
1 cup pearl onions, peeled	

1. In a large saucepan filled with lightly salted water, boil Brussels sprouts 5 minutes. Drain.

2. In a large saucepan, melt butter over medium heat. Add onions and carrot and cook, stirring occasionally, until onions turn golden, 4 to 5 minutes. Reduce heat to low and add Brussels sprouts.

3. Cover and cook, stirring occasionally to prevent vegetables from sticking to pan, until sprouts are very soft, 15 to 20 minutes. Add pesto sauce and stir to blend. Serve hot.

322 SESAME ASPARAGUS STIR-FRY WITH BLACK BEAN SAUCE

Prep: 10 minutes   Cook: 6 to 8 minutes   Serves: 4

Chinese black bean sauce is available in Asian markets or the Asian foods section of large supermarkets.

2 tablespoons dry sherry	1 cup vegetable broth or reduced-sodium chicken broth
1 tablespoon cornstarch	
¼ cup Chinese black bean sauce	2 tablespoons soy sauce or tamari
2 garlic cloves, minced	
1 teaspoon minced fresh ginger	3 scallions, cut into 2-inch pieces
1½ tablespoons vegetable oil	2 teaspoons Asian sesame oil
1½ pounds asparagus, cut into 3-inch pieces	1 tablespoon sesame seeds

1. In a small bowl, mix sherry with cornstarch until smooth. In another small bowl, mix black bean sauce with minced garlic and ginger.

2. In a wok or large frying pan, heat vegetable oil over high heat. Add asparagus and stir-fry 2 minutes. Add black bean mixture and cook, stirring constantly, for 1 minute. Add broth, soy sauce, and scallions. Cook, stirring, until asparagus is crisp-tender, 2 to 3 minutes.

3. With a slotted spoon, transfer vegetables to a serving platter. Reduce heat to medium. Add cornstarch mixture to wok and stir constantly until sauce boils and thickens, 1 to 2 minutes. Stir in sesame oil and remove from heat. Pour sauce over asparagus and sprinkle sesame seeds on top.

323   CASABLANCA CARROTS

Prep: 10 minutes   Cook: 14 to 20 minutes   Serves: 4

1 tablespoon olive oil
1½ pounds carrots, peeled
    and sliced
3 garlic cloves, minced
1 teaspoon ground cumin
1 teaspoon sweet paprika
¼ teaspoon ground cinnamon

⅛ teaspoon salt
1 tablespoon lemon juice
12 Mediterranean-style black
    olives, pitted and coarsely
    chopped
3 tablespoons chopped
    parsley

1. In a large nonstick frying pan, heat oil over medium heat. Add carrots, cover, and cook, stirring once or twice, until tender, 10 to 15 minutes. Reduce heat if carrots begin to brown.

2. Reduce heat to low. Add garlic, cumin, paprika, cinnamon, salt, and lemon juice. Cook uncovered, stirring occasionally to blend, 4 to 5 minutes. Transfer carrots to a serving bowl and sprinkle with olives and parsley.

324   ALSATIAN CABBAGE

Prep: 15 minutes   Cook: 42 to 45 minutes   Serves: 4

My friend Loretta Scott's ancestors hail from Alsace, where this dish is commonly served. This is an adaptation of one of her family recipes.

2 medium red potatoes
½ cup dried cranberries or
    raisins
2 tablespoons vegetable oil
2 medium onions, thinly
    sliced
1 small head of cabbage,
    shredded

2 tart apples, peeled, cored,
    and thinly sliced
1 garlic clove, minced
½ cup dry white wine
1 teaspoon salt
¼ teaspoon pepper
1 teaspoon Dijon mustard

1. In a medium saucepan of boiling water, cook potatoes until tender, about 20 minutes. Drain and let cool slightly. Peel potatoes and cut into ¼-inch slices.

2. Meanwhile, in a small bowl, soak cranberries in warm water for 15 minutes. Drain and set aside.

3. In a large flameproof casserole, heat oil over medium-high heat. Add onions and cook, stirring occasionally, until golden, about 5 minutes. Add cabbage and apples. Reduce heat to medium, cover, and cook, stirring occasionally, until cabbage is tender, 12 to 15 minutes.

4. Add potatoes, garlic, wine, salt, pepper, Dijon mustard, and dried cranberries. Cover and simmer 5 minutes. Serve hot or at room temperature.

325 HONEYED CARROT AND PRUNE CASSEROLE

Prep: 15 minutes   Cook: 1 hour 5 minutes to 1 hour 22 minutes
Serves: 4 to 6

This may sound like an unusual combination, but it is really delicious. Serve as a side dish or as a topping for cooked bulgur wheat or couscous.

2 tablespoons butter	1 cup vegetable broth or
1 (16-ounce) package frozen	reduced-sodium
baby onions (about 1 inch	chicken broth
in diameter), thawed	½ cup honey
1 cup pitted prunes	½ teaspoon ground cinnamon
1 (24-ounce) package fresh	2 garlic cloves, minced
peeled baby carrots	½ teaspoon salt
½ cup dry red wine	¼ teaspoon pepper

1. Preheat oven to 350°F. In a large flameproof casserole, melt butter over medium heat. Add onions and cook, stirring occasionally, until soft, 2 to 3 minutes. Add prunes and carrots. Cook, stirring, until carrots are lightly browned, 3 to 4 minutes.

2. Add wine, broth, honey, cinnamon, garlic, salt, and pepper. Stir to blend. Cover with foil and top with tight-fitting lid.

3. Bake until carrots are tender and caramelized, 1 to 1¼ hours.

326 BUTTERMILK CARROT FRITTERS

Prep: 15 minutes   Cook: 18 to 24 minutes   Serves: 4

For a complete meal, top these delicate fritters with fresh tomato sauce, Mexican salsa, or Cucumber Yogurt Sauce (page 69) and accompany with a tossed green salad.

1½ cups buttermilk	2 eggs
1 cup flour	½ teaspoon grated nutmeg
4 medium carrots, shredded	½ teaspoon salt
¼ cup chopped parsley	¼ teaspoon pepper
1 small onion, chopped	Vegetable oil, for frying
2 garlic cloves, minced	

1. Preheat oven to 250°F. In a large bowl, whisk buttermilk and flour until lumps dissolve. Add carrots, parsley, onion, garlic, eggs, nutmeg, salt, and pepper. Stir until mixture is well blended. Set batter aside.

2. Line a baking sheet with a double layer of paper towels. In a large frying pan, heat ½ inch of oil over medium heat to 375°F. Drop batter by ¼ cupfuls into hot oil. Fry in batches without crowding, pressing with back of a spoon to flatten and turning once, until fritters are golden brown, 3 to 4 minutes on each side. As they are done, transfer fritters to baking sheet to drain. Keep warm in oven while cooking remaining batter. Serve hot.

327 CAULIFLOWER MUSHROOM GRATIN

Prep: 20 minutes   Cook: 35 to 42 minutes   Serves: 6

1 medium head of cauliflower, broken into florets	2 tablespoons flour
½ lemon	1 cup milk
2 tablespoons bread crumbs	2 cups shredded Asiago cheese
2 tablespoons butter	⅛ teaspoon grated nutmeg
½ pound mushrooms, sliced	½ teaspoon salt
	¼ teaspoon pepper

1. Preheat oven to 375°F. In a large saucepan of boiling water, cook cauliflower with lemon half for 10 minutes. Discard lemon and drain cauliflower.

2. Dust bottom of an 8-inch-square baking dish with 1 tablespoon of bread crumbs. Cover with a single layer of cauliflower.

3. Meanwhile, in a large frying pan, melt butter over medium-high heat. Add mushrooms and cook, stirring, until they turn limp, 2 to 3 minutes. Sprinkle on flour and cook, stirring, 1 minute. Add milk and cook, stirring, until sauce boils and thickens, 2 to 3 minutes. Stir in 1½ cups of cheese, nutmeg, salt, and pepper.

4. Pour sauce over cauliflower. Sprinkle remaining 1 tablespoon bread crumbs and ½ cup cheese on top. Bake until topping is lightly browned and casserole is bubbly, 20 to 25 minutes.

328 GARLICKY EGGPLANT SAUTÉ

Prep: 10 minutes   Cook: 10 to 11 minutes   Serves: 4

I love to make this dish when the slender Japanese eggplant, also called oriental eggplant, are in season. You can usually find them in regular supermarkets or in Asian food stores. Serve this spicy dish over steamed white rice.

3 tablespoons vegetable oil	½ cup vegetable or reduced-sodium chicken broth
2 teaspoons peanut butter	
1 pound Japanese eggplant, quartered lengthwise	1 tablespoon soy sauce or tamari
5 garlic cloves, minced	½ teaspoon Chinese chili paste
1 teaspoon minced fresh ginger	

1. In a large frying pan, heat oil over medium heat. Stir in peanut butter until dissolved, taking care not to let it burn. Add eggplant, garlic, and ginger. Cook, stirring, 1 minute.

2. Reduce heat to low. Cover and cook, stirring occasionally, until eggplant is quite tender, 4 to 5 minutes.

3. In a small bowl, mix broth with soy sauce and chili paste. Pour over eggplant and simmer, covered, 5 minutes.

329 RAGOUT OF EGGPLANT AND ARTICHOKE HEARTS

Prep: 20 minutes   Cook: 22 to 28 minutes   Serves: 4

This light eggplant casserole can stand on its own, and it makes a delicious topping for pasta, rice, or couscous. If prepared ahead, the dish will keep well for several days in the refrigerator.

1 large eggplant, peeled and
  cut into ½-inch cubes
1 teaspoon salt
¼ cup olive oil
3 garlic cloves, minced
8 ounces mushrooms,
  coarsely chopped

1 (15½-ounce) can artichoke
  hearts, drained and cut
  into ½-inch dice
1 cup crushed tomatoes
1 teaspoon dried thyme leaves
½ teaspoon dried rosemary
¼ teaspoon pepper

1. Preheat oven to 400°F. In a large bowl, toss eggplant with salt. Place in a colander and let drain for 10 minutes. Pat dry.

2. In a large bowl, toss eggplant with 3 tablespoons oil and 2 minced garlic cloves. Spread eggplant in a single layer on a large baking sheet and roast, turning once or twice during cooking, 10 to 15 minutes, until tender.

3. Meanwhile, in a large frying pan, heat remaining 1 tablespoon olive oil over medium-high heat. Add mushrooms and cook, stirring occasionally, until they turn limp, 2 to 3 minutes. Stir in artichoke hearts. Remove from heat.

4. In a small bowl, combine crushed tomatoes with thyme, rosemary, and pepper.

5. In a medium flameproof casserole, alternate layers of eggplant, mushrooms, and artichokes at least twice until all vegetables are used. Top with tomato mixture. Cover and simmer over medium heat 10 minutes. Serve hot or at room temperature.

330   GREEK GREEN BEANS
Prep: 15 minutes   Cook: 14 to 18 minutes   Serves: 4

This simple dish is equally good served hot or at room temperature. The taste of the freshly ground pepper should be quite pronounced.

2   tablespoons olive oil
1   small onion, chopped
½   green bell pepper, diced
2   large tomatoes, peeled, seeded, and cut into 1-inch cubes

1   pound green beans, trimmed
2   garlic cloves, minced
¼   teaspoon salt
½   teaspoon freshly ground pepper

1. In a large frying pan, heat oil over medium heat. Add onion and green pepper and cook, stirring occasionally, until softened, 2 to 3 minutes.

2. Add tomatoes, green beans, and garlic. Cover and reduce heat to low. Cook until beans are tender, 12 to 15 minutes.

3. Season with salt and pepper. Serve hot or at room temperature.

331   CURRIED ONION BAKE
Prep: 15 minutes   Cook: 28 to 35 minutes   Serves: 4 to 6

4   tablespoons butter
2   cups coarsely crumbled soda crackers (about 30 crackers)
1½ teaspoons curry powder
¼   cup vegetable or reduced-sodium chicken broth
2   large onions, coarsely chopped

2   cups milk
1   egg
½   teaspoon salt
¼   teaspoon white pepper
¾   cup shredded Cheddar cheese
1   teaspoon paprika

1. Preheat oven to 375°F. In a medium ovenproof bowl, melt 2 tablespoons butter in oven or in microwave. Add soda crackers, curry powder, and broth and blend well.

2. In a large frying pan, melt remaining 2 tablespoons butter over medium heat. Add onions, cover, and cook, stirring occasionally until golden, 8 to 10 minutes.

3. In another medium bowl, beat milk with egg, salt, and pepper until blended. Spread half of cracker mixture over bottom of a generously buttered 8-inch square baking dish. Top with onions. Sprinkle on Cheddar cheese. Gently pour milk mixture over all. Cover dish evenly with remaining crumbled cracker mixture. Sprinkle paprika over top.

4. Bake 20 to 25 minutes, until hot and bubbly.

332 BRAISED ENDIVES

Prep: 10 minutes   Cook: 29 to 40 minutes   Serves: 4 to 6

This is an adaptation of a classic Belgian specialty. Don't confuse the delicate, flame-shaped Belgian endive with curly endive. Belgian endives have a slightly bitter taste, which brings out the flavors of salads and braised dishes such as this one.

8 white Belgian endives	1 cup shredded Gruyère cheese
1 stick (4 ounces) butter	¼ teaspoon salt
¼ pound mushrooms, sliced	⅛ teaspoon pepper
2 tablespoons lemon juice	⅛ teaspoon grated nutmeg
¼ cup flour	½ cup bread crumbs
1 cup milk	

1. Preheat oven to 375°F. Trim endives by slicing ¼ inch off root. Rinse endives quickly under running water and wipe dry. If endives are very plump, cut them in half lengthwise.

2. In a large frying pan, melt 4 tablespoons butter over medium heat. Add mushrooms and cook, stirring occasionally, until they are lightly browned, 4 to 5 minutes. With a slotted spoon, transfer to a small bowl. In same pan, set endives close together. Sprinkle with lemon juice. Cover and cook until endives are quite soft, 8 to 10 minutes.

3. With a slotted spoon, transfer endives to a lightly oiled shallow 1½-quart baking dish. Reserve pan juices.

4. Meanwhile, in a saucepan, melt remaining 4 tablespoons butter over medium heat. Whisk in flour and stir until lumps disappear, 3 to 5 minutes. Add milk and reserved endive juices and continue whisking until sauce thickens somewhat, 4 to 5 minutes. Add cheese and stir until melted. Season with salt, pepper, and nutmeg. Add mushrooms.

5. Spoon sauce over endives. Sprinkle with bread crumbs. Bake 10 to 15 minutes, until bubbly and golden brown.

333   POTATOES PAPRIKASH
Prep: 15 minutes   Cook: 33 to 40 minutes   Serves: 4 to 6

2 tablespoons vegetable oil
1 large onion, chopped
1 green pepper, cut into rings
4 medium red potatoes, peeled and sliced ¼ inch thick
1 tablespoon tomato paste

1 cup vegetable broth or reduced-sodium chicken broth
1 tablespoon imported sweet paprika
¼ teaspoon caraway seeds
¼ teaspoon salt
1 cup sour cream

1. In a large frying pan, heat oil over medium heat. Add onion and green pepper and cook, until softened, 3 to 5 minutes. Transfer mixture to a small bowl.

2. Cover bottom of frying pan with half of sliced potatoes. Spread onion and pepper mixture over potatoes and cover with remaining potato slices.

3. In a small bowl, mix tomato paste, broth, paprika, caraway seeds, and salt. Pour over potatoes. Cover tightly and cook over low heat until potatoes are tender, 30 to 35 minutes.

4. Remove from heat and spread sour cream over top. Let stand, covered, 5 minutes before serving.

334   MILWAUKEE-STYLE POTATOES
Prep: 15 minutes   Cook: 40 to 50 minutes   Serves: 6

2½ pounds small red potatoes, peeled and quartered
3 tablespoons flour
1 large onion, chopped

2 cups cubed smoked Gouda cheese
½ teaspoon salt
¼ teaspoon pepper
1½ cups beer

1. Preheat oven to 400°F. Place half of potatoes on bottom of a well-greased 2-quart casserole. Sprinkle with flour. Cover potatoes with diced onion and half of cheese. Season with half of salt and pepper. Cover with remaining potatoes. Top with remaining salt, pepper, and cheese. Pour beer down sides of dish.

2. Cover tightly with aluminum foil. Bake 35 to 40 minutes, until potatoes are very tender. Remove foil and bake 5 to 10 minutes longer, until bubbly and brown.

335 MÉMÉ'S GRATIN DAUPHINOIS

Prep: 20 minutes   Cook: 53 minutes to 1 hour   Serves: 4 to 6

My grandmother, who was born in France, always prepared this potato dish as a special treat. You can use russet baking potatoes or, better yet, buttery Yukon Gold potatoes. The tastiest part of this dish is the cheesy crust that forms around the potatoes.

2 **pounds Yukon Gold or russet potatoes, peeled and thinly sliced**	1 **egg**
	1 **stick (4 ounces) butter**
	1 **teaspoon salt**
1 **cup half-and-half**	¼ **teaspoon pepper**
1 **cup milk**	3 **cups shredded Swiss or Emmenthaler cheese**
2 **garlic cloves—1 minced, 1 cut in half**	

1. Preheat oven to 400°F. Soak sliced potatoes in a bowl filled with cold water for 10 minutes. Drain and pat dry.

2. In a medium saucepan, bring half-and-half and milk to a simmer. Remove from heat. Stir in minced garlic. When milk has cooled slightly, whisk in egg. Set aside.

3. Generously butter sides and bottom of an 8-inch square baking dish or other shallow 2-quart casserole. Rub bottom and sides of dish with cut garlic. Reserve remaining butter.

4. Layer half of potatoes in baking dish. Top with a few pats of butter. Season with half of salt and pepper. Add 1 cup shredded cheese. Layer remaining potatoes and 1 cup shredded cheese. Pour in milk mixture.

5. Cover tightly with foil. Bake until potatoes are tender and liquid is absorbed, 45 to 50 minutes. Remove foil. Sprinkle remaining cheese over top. Return to oven and bake, uncovered, 8 to 10 minutes, until top is nice and brown. Let stand 5 minutes before serving.

336 BLACK-EYED SUCCOTASH

Prep: 5 minutes   Cook: 12 to 15 minutes   Serves: 4

2 **tablespoons butter**	1 **cup heavy cream**
1 **small onion, chopped**	1 **teaspoon curry powder**
2 **cups frozen black-eyed peas**	**Grated zest of ½ lime**
2 **cups frozen corn kernels**	½ **teaspoon salt**

1. In a medium saucepan, melt butter over medium heat. Add onion and cook, stirring occasionally, until softened, 2 to 3 minutes.

2. Add black-eyed peas, corn, cream, curry powder, and lime zest. Cover and cook until black eyed-peas are tender, 10 to 12 minutes. Season with salt and serve.

337   OVEN-FRIED ACORN SQUASH
Prep: 10 minutes   Cook: 30 to 40 minutes   Serves: 4

3 tablespoons butter
1 medium acorn or golden
    acorn squash
2 eggs

1 cup seasoned bread crumbs
2 tablespoons grated Romano
    cheese

1. Preheat oven to 350°F. In oven, melt butter in a 9 x 13-inch baking dish. Set aside.

2. With a sharp knife, carefully cut acorn squash into wedges or rings. Scoop out filaments and seeds.

3. Break eggs into a shallow bowl and beat lightly. In another bowl, mix bread crumbs with Romano cheese.

4. Dip each squash piece in beaten egg. Dredge in coating mix. Set in buttered baking dish.

5. Bake until squash is tender and outside turns crispy brown, 25 to 30 minutes. Turn over with tongs and bake until second side is lightly browned, an additional 5 to 10 minutes. Serve hot.

338   SPAGHETTI SQUASH PRIMAVERA
Prep: 10 minutes   Cook: 1 hour to 1 hour 7 minutes   Serves: 4

1 (3-pound) spaghetti squash
3 tablespoons olive oil
2 garlic cloves, minced
½ cup sliced mushrooms
2 large tomatoes, coarsely
    chopped

2 teaspoons dried oregano
2 tablespoons chopped olives
2 tablespoons pine nuts
1 teaspoon salt
½ teaspoon pepper
1 cup shredded Romano
    cheese

1. Preheat oven to 375°F. Place spaghetti squash on a baking sheet. With point of a knife, poke several holes in squash. Bake until tender to center when pierced with a knife, 55 to 60 minutes. Cut squash open and let stand until cool enough to handle.

2. Meanwhile, in a large frying pan, heat 2 tablespoons olive oil over medium heat. Add garlic and mushrooms and cook until mushrooms turn limp, 2 to 3 minutes. Add tomatoes, oregano, olives, pine nuts, salt, and pepper. Cook, stirring occasionally, until most of liquid evaporates, 3 to 4 minutes. Set aside.

3. When squash is cool, discard seeds. With a fork, scoop out squash strands onto serving platter. Toss with remaining tablespoon of olive oil. Reheat sauce if necessary and pour over squash. Sprinkle cheese on top. Serve hot.

339 BAKED SWEET SQUASH RING WITH ORANGE SAUCE

Prep: 1 hour   Cook: 48 to 50 minutes   Serves: 8 to 10

Nothing beats the sweet taste of fresh winter squash, be it butternut, acorn, delicata, or golden acorn. To cook a whole squash, poke a few holes in the skin and bake it at 350°F for about an hour, until tender. Or microwave the squash on High for 6 to 10 minutes. Let it cool, discard the seeds, and scoop out the flesh. Or simply substitute 2½ cups solid-pack canned pumpkin for the fresh squash.

3 cups mashed cooked winter squash	3 eggs, separated
4 tablespoons butter	1 cup vegetable broth or reduced-sodium chicken broth
¼ cup cream	
1 tablespoon minced onion	1 teaspoon minced fresh ginger
½ teaspoon grated nutmeg	
⅔ cup bread crumbs	1 tablespoon brown sugar
2 teaspoons fines herbes	1 tablespoon soy sauce
Grated zest of 1 orange	⅔ cup orange juice
½ teaspoon salt	1 tablespoon cornstarch
¼ teaspoon pepper	

1. Preheat oven to 350°F. In a large bowl, combine squash with butter, cream, onion, nutmeg, bread crumbs, fines herbes, orange zest, salt, pepper, and egg yolks. Blend well.

2. In a medium bowl, beat egg whites until stiff. Carefully fold beaten whites into squash mixture.

3. Fill a 9 x 12-inch baking pan with 1 inch hot water. Generously grease a 6-cup ring mold. Set mold in baking pan. Spoon squash mixture evenly inside mold. Bake in warm water bath until set, 45 to 50 minutes. Let cool 10 minutes before unmolding.

4. Meanwhile, in a small saucepan, combine broth, ginger, brown sugar, and soy sauce. Bring to a boil over medium-high heat. In a small bowl, mix orange juice with cornstarch until smooth. Stir into boiling broth. Return to a boil and cook, stirring, until sauce thickens, about 2 minutes.

5. To serve, unmold ring onto a platter and spoon orange sauce over the top.

340   TOMATO AND CABBAGE FRICASSEE

Prep: 10 minutes   Cook: 35 to 42 minutes   Serves: 4

Serve this savory stew over steamed rice.

3 tablespoons vegetable oil
2 medium onions, coarsely
   chopped
1 (14-ounce) can Italian peeled
   tomatoes, drained and
   coarsely chopped
2 medium potatoes, peeled
   and cut into ½-inch dice
1 medium head of cabbage,
   coarsely chopped

1 tablespoon dried dill
1½ tablespoons cider vinegar
1 teaspoon salt
½ teaspoon pepper
⅓ cup chopped sun-dried
   tomatoes
1 cup sour cream

1. In a large nonreactive flameproof casserole, heat oil over medium heat. Add onions and cook, stirring occasionally, until softened, 2 to 3 minutes. Add tomatoes and cook until most of liquid evaporates, 3 to 4 minutes.

2. Add potatoes, cabbage, dill, and vinegar. Reduce heat to medium-low. Cover and cook until potatoes are tender, 30 to 35 minutes.

3. Add salt, pepper, and sun-dried tomatoes. Cook, stirring to blend, 1 minute. Remove from heat and stir in sour cream. Serve immediately.

341   BAKED SWEET POTATOES WITH CANDIED GINGER CREAM

Prep: 10 minutes   Cook: 55 minutes to 1 hour   Serves: 4

The first time I tasted a sweet potato *au naturel* was in China, where the vegetable is sold on street corners, much as roasted chestnuts are in other parts of the world. This is an adaptation of my Chinese gastronomic experience. Candied ginger is available in the gourmet or baking section of most supermarkets.

4 sweet potatoes or yams,
   scrubbed
4 tablespoons butter
½ teaspoon salt
¼ teaspoon pepper

1 cup sour cream
2 scallions, chopped
1 tablespoon candied ginger,
   finely diced

1. Preheat oven to 375°F. Wrap each potato in foil. With tines of a fork, poke several holes in flesh. Bake until knife easily penetrates potato, 55 minutes to 1 hour. Slice open. Insert butter and sprinkle with salt and pepper.

2. Meanwhile, in a small bowl, mix sour cream, scallions, and candied ginger. Serve on the side as a topping for the cooked yams.

342   JARDINIÈRE DE LÉGUMES
Prep: 20 minutes   Cook: 32 to 40 minutes   Serves: 4

Jardin means "garden" in French, and anything with the word *jardinière* in the title implies that it is made with garden-fresh vegetables.

6 tablespoons butter
2 medium turnips, peeled and diced (½ inch)
3 medium carrots, peeled and diced
1 large rutabaga, peeled and diced
½ pound red potatoes, peeled and diced
2 celery ribs, diced
1 cup vegetable broth or reduced-sodium chicken broth

½ pound fresh green beans, cut into 3-inch pieces
2 cups green peas
4 leaves of Boston or Bibb lettuce
1 tablespoon fines herbes
½ teaspoon dried mint
1 teaspoon salt
½ teaspoon pepper
½ cup heavy cream
2 tablespoons chopped chives

1. In a large flameproof casserole or a small Dutch oven, melt butter over medium heat. Add turnips, carrots, and rutabaga, cover, and cook until barely tender, 12 to 15 minutes.

2. Add potatoes, celery, and broth. Reduce heat to low. Add beans, peas, and lettuce leaves. Cook, covered, until potatoes are tender, 20 to 25 minutes.

3. Stir in fines herbes, mint, salt, pepper, and cream. Heat through. Transfer to a serving dish and sprinkle with chives.

343   TOMATOES PROVENÇALE
Prep: 10 minutes   Cook: 10 to 15 minutes   Serves: 4

This simple preparation is one of my favorite side dishes, especially when I have access to vine-ripened tomatoes.

4 large ripe tomatoes, cut in half
2 tablespoons olive oil
½ cup fine dry bread crumbs
4 garlic cloves, minced

¼ cup chopped parsley
½ teaspoon dried thyme leaves
½ teaspoon salt
¼ teaspoon pepper

1. Preheat oven to 450°F. Gently squeeze tomato halves to extrude most of seeds. Set, cut-side up, in small baking dish.

2. In a small bowl, mix olive oil, bread crumbs, garlic, parsley, thyme, salt, and pepper. Spoon bread crumb mixture over top of each tomato, dividing equally.

3. Bake 10 to 15 minutes, until topping turns light brown. Serve hot or at room temperature.

344 VEGETABLE KEBABS WITH PARSLEY BUTTER

Prep: 15 minutes   Stand: 30 minutes
Cook: 16 to 20 minutes   Serves: 6

12 small potatoes, 1 inch in diameter, or 6 larger potatoes, halved
2 medium carrots, cut into 1½- to 2-inch chunks
⅓ cup olive oil
½ teaspoon salt
1 teaspoon paprika
1 teaspoon dried marjoram
12 medium mushrooms, stemmed and wiped clean
12 cherry tomatoes

2 medium zucchini, peeled and cut into 2-inch chunks
12 pearl onions, peeled
1 green bell pepper, cut into 1½-inch squares
¼ cup chopped Italian parsley
1 stick (4 ounces) butter, softened
2 garlic cloves, crushed through a press
2 teaspoons lemon juice
2 teaspoons dry mustard

1. In a medium saucepan filled with boiling water, cook potatoes and carrots until barely tender, 8 to 10 minutes. Drain and let cool 5 minutes. Peel potatoes, if desired.

2. In a medium bowl, mix olive oil with salt, paprika, and marjoram. Add potatoes, carrots, mushroom caps, tomatoes, zucchini, pearl onions, and green pepper. Stir to coat vegetables. Marinate 30 minutes to 2 hours.

3. Preheat broiler or prepare a medium-hot fire in a barbecue grill. Thread equal amounts of vegetables on 6 skewers. Set on a baking sheet. Broil kebabs about 4 inches from heat, or grill, turning occasionally, until tender and lightly browned all over, 8 to 10 minutes.

4. Meanwhile, in a small bowl, blend parsley with butter, garlic, lemon juice, and mustard. Serve kebabs hot, with parsley butter on the side.

345   GRILLED VEGETABLES WITH EGGLESS BASIL MAYONNAISE

Prep: 20 minutes   Cook: 12 to 14 minutes   Serves: 4 to 6

Grilling vegetables under a broiler is not only a healthful way to cook, but also allows for a stunning table presentation.

½ cup olive oil
2 garlic cloves, minced
½ teaspoon dried thyme leaves
½ teaspoon dried marjoram
¼ teaspoon pepper
2 sweet potatoes, peeled and cut into ½-inch slices
1 medium eggplant, sliced ½ inch thick on an angle
3 yellow crookneck squash, sliced ½ inch thick on an angle

2 large zucchini, sliced ½ inch thick on an angle
2 medium onions, cut in ½-inch rings
1 green bell pepper, halved
1 red bell pepper, halved
4 small tomatoes, halved
Eggless Basil Mayonnaise (recipe follows)

1. Preheat broiler. In a small bowl, mix olive oil, garlic, thyme, marjoram, and pepper. Paint sweet potatoes with seasoned olive oil and set in a single layer on a large baking sheet. Broil about 4 inches from heat, turning once, until potatoes are tender and lightly browned, 4 to 5 minutes on each side.

2. Transfer potatoes to a serving dish and cover to keep warm. On same baking sheet, place eggplant, crookneck squash, zucchini, onion, green and red peppers, and tomato halves, cut-sides down. Paint vegetables lightly with olive oil. Broil, turning over with tongs, about 2 minutes on each side, until just tender.

3. Arrange grilled vegetables attractively on a serving platter. Serve with Eggless Basil Mayonnaise on the side.

346   EGGLESS BASIL MAYONNAISE

Prep: 10 minutes   Cook: none   Makes: about 1¼ cups

You can use this mayonnaise as a dressing or as a topping for sandwiches.

6 ounces soft tofu, drained
¼ cup vegetable oil
¼ cup walnut oil
1 cup fresh basil leaves

1 garlic clove, minced
1 teaspoon Dijon mustard
½ teaspoon salt

In a blender or food processor, puree tofu briefly. With machine on, gradually add vegetable and walnut oils and puree until smooth. Add basil, garlic, mustard, and salt; blend well. Transfer to a small bowl. Cover and refrigerate until serving time.

347   VEGETABLES EN PAPILLOTE
Prep: 20 minutes   Cook: 35 to 40 minutes   Serves: 4

Opening a *papillote*, the French culinary term for a small pouch made of parchment paper or aluminum foil, is like opening a surprise gift encased in a fragrant puff of steam. Best of all, the cooking process can guarantee a practically fat-free dish.

2 medium red potatoes, peeled and sliced ¼ inch thick
8 scallions, halved lengthwise and cut into 2-inch pieces
2 medium carrots, cut into 2 x ½-inch sticks
2 medium zucchini, cut into 2 x ½-inch sticks

1 cup frozen baby lima beans
4 small turnips, peeled and quartered
¼ pound sugar snap peas
4 slices of fresh ginger
2 tablespoons plus 2 teaspoons soy sauce or tamari
1 teaspoon pepper

1. Preheat oven to 400°F. Tear off four 12-inch squares of aluminum foil.

2. On each foil square, layer equal amounts of potatoes, scallions, carrots, zucchini, lima beans, turnips, snap peas, and ginger. Season each pouch with 2 teaspoons soy sauce and ¼ teaspoon pepper. Seal each packet tightly by crimping sides. Set on a baking sheet.

3. Bake 35 to 40 minutes, until vegetables are tender. Serve vegetables in their own packets to savor all the juices.

Chapter 13

Adding Pizzazz

I think of sauces, dips, and marinades as exclamation points. Often, an unusual sauce is all that is needed to transform a mundane dish into a memorable one.

The fact that chips and dip often translates as chips and salsa, and that sales of that multipurpose Mexican condiment have surpassed that of ketchup in the United States, is no coincidence. Sometimes it seems that this popular combination has become almost as American as apple pie and ice cream. Simply substituting freshly cut vegetables for chips turns a bowl of salsa into a virtually calorie-free snack. Tomatillo Salsa, a sauce made from the small green, tomatolike fruit known as Mexican husk tomato, and Pico de Gallo, another Mexican specialty made of fresh, diced vegetables, are well suited to a similar purpose.

Many savory blends, such as the garlic-scented garbanzo mixture known as Hummus in parts of the Middle East, belong to a nation's culinary repertoire. In Morocco, for instance, Chermoula, a cumin-accented marinade, is also used as a topping for cooked vegetables. Mexican food is practically synonymous with the creamy avocado blend featured here as My Favorite Guacamole. In India, chutneys such as Quick Banana Chutney go hand in hand with curry dishes. Apple Fuyu Persimmon Chutney, an American version inspired by persimmon growers in San Diego County, becomes an instant hors d'oeuvre when spread over a block of cream cheese and garnished with crackers.

Pasta or rice calls for toppings of a heartier nature, such as a rich Olive Marinara Sauce. Tasty and light, Hungarian Onion, Pepper, and Tomato Relish will jazz up not only cooked grains or pasta but also scrambled eggs. For the ultimate in *picante* flavor, a dash of fiery Sauce Guadeloupe is definitely in order.

348   QUICK BANANA CHUTNEY

Prep: 10 minutes   Cook: 9 to 14 minutes   Makes: about 3 cups

This chutney makes a good accompaniment to a rice curry dish. Garam masala, a blend of Indian spices, is available in some supermarkets, at Indian specialty markets, or wherever exotic spices are sold.

2 **tablespoons vegetable oil**	½ **teaspoon paprika**
2 **medium onions, chopped**	6 **ripe bananas, sliced**
4 **garlic cloves, minced**	¼ **teaspoon salt**
2 **teaspoons ground coriander**	¼ **cup plain yogurt**
1 **teaspoon garam masala**	¼ **cup chopped cilantro**
½ **teaspoon turmeric**	**(optional but desirable)**

1. In a large frying pan, heat oil over medium-high heat. Add onions and cook, stirring occasionally, until golden, 3 to 5 minutes. Add garlic and cook until softened and fragrant, 1 to 2 minutes longer.

2. Add coriander, garam masala, turmeric, and paprika. Cook, stirring to blend, 1 to 2 minutes to toast spices. Add bananas, salt, and ¼ cup water. Cook, mashing gently with a fork, until bananas are quite soft, 4 to 5 minutes. Remove from heat.

3. Transfer to a serving bowl and stir in yogurt and cilantro.

349   CORN RELISH

Prep: 10 minutes   Cook: 8 to 12 minutes   Makes: about 3 cups

4 **ears of fresh corn, husked**	4 **plum tomatoes, seeded and**
2 **tablespoons olive oil**	**finely diced**
1 **small Bermuda onion, finely**	2 **tablespoons chopped**
diced	**cilantro or parsley**
2 **garlic cloves, minced**	1 **tablespoon balsamic vinegar**
1 **serrano pepper, seeded and**	½ **teaspoon salt**
minced	⅛ **teaspoon cayenne**
1 **small red bell pepper, finely**	
diced	

1. In a large saucepan of lightly salted boiling water, cook corn until kernels are tender, 4 to 6 minutes. Drain and let cool. With a large sharp knife, cut kernels off cob and place in a medium bowl.

2. In a medium frying pan, heat olive oil. Add onion and cook over medium heat, stirring occasionally, until golden, 2 to 3 minutes. Add serrano and bell peppers. Cook, stirring, until peppers are soft, 2 to 3 minutes. Add to corn.

3. Add tomatoes, cilantro, vinegar, salt, and cayenne. Toss to mix. Serve chilled.

350   MY FAVORITE GUACAMOLE

Prep: 10 minutes   Cook: none   Makes: about 2 cups

To prevent the guacamole from turning brown, sprinkle with lemon juice. If guacamole is to be consumed more than 1 hour after it is prepared, cover with plastic wrap placed directly on the surface to prevent it from coming in contact with the air.

4 ripe avocados
1 tablespoon lemon juice
2 garlic cloves, minced
1 tablespoon minced onion

1 small tomato, seeded and cubed
1 tablespoon chopped cilantro
½ teaspoon salt

1. Cut avocados in half all around. Rotate 2 halves in opposite directions to separate. Remove and discard pits. Scoop out avocado into a medium bowl.

2. With a fork, coarsely mash avocado. Add lemon juice, garlic, onion, tomato, cilantro, and salt. Mix well.

351   APPLE FUYU PERSIMMON CHUTNEY

Prep: 30 minutes   Cook: 1 hour 35 minutes to 2 hours 7 minutes
Makes: about 8 cups

This is a wonderful way to make use of the Fuyu persimmon, a sweet variety which can be eaten out of hand, like an apple. If you prefer a chutney of a more liquid consistency, just reduce the cooking time. This one is cooked to the consistency of thick jam.

1 pint cider vinegar
1 pound plus 1 cup firmly packed brown sugar
1 tablespoon minced fresh ginger
1 teaspoon allspice
½ teaspoon ground cloves
1 teaspoon salt
1 large onion, chopped
2 green bell peppers, finely diced

1 cup dried cranberries or raisins
1½ pounds tart apples, peeled, cored, and coarsely diced
1½ pounds Fuyu persimmons, peeled and coarsely diced
1 jalapeño pepper, seeded and minced, or ⅛ teaspoon cayenne

1. In a large nonaluminum stockpot, combine vinegar, brown sugar, ginger, allspice, cloves, and salt. Bring to a boil. Reduce heat to medium-low and cook, stirring occasionally, until brown sugar is completely dissolved, 5 to 7 minutes.

2. Add onion, bell peppers, dried cranberries, apples, persimmons, and jalapeño pepper. Cover and reduce heat to low. Cook, stirring occasionally, until mixture is thick, 1½ to 2 hours.

3. Chutney will keep for 2 to 3 weeks refrigerated in an airtight container.

352 CURRIED FRUIT

Prep: 5 minutes   Cook: 53 to 60 minutes   Serves: 4 to 6

Served as a condiment or side dish, this perks up rice and grains.

1 (1-pound 13-ounce) can pear halves, drained
1 (1-pound 13-ounce) can peaches, drained
1 (1-pound 4-ounce) can unsweetened pineapple chunks, drained

12 maraschino cherries, cut in half
4 tablespoons butter
1 cup packed brown sugar
1 tablespoon curry powder

1. Preheat oven to 325°F. Place pears, peaches, pineapple, and cherries in a well-oiled 2-quart casserole. Stir fruit to mix.

2. In a small saucepan, melt butter. Add sugar and curry powder. Cook, stirring constantly, over medium heat until brown sugar is dissolved, 3 to 4 minutes. Pour butter mixture over fruit.

3. Bake 50 to 55 minutes, until top is bubbly and brown. Serve hot or at room temperature.

353 HUNGARIAN ONION, PEPPER, AND TOMATO RELISH

Prep: 10 minutes   Cook: 27 to 33 minutes   Makes: about 1 cup

Hungarians use this simple stewed green pepper and tomato mixture, called *lecso*, as a base for many of their dishes. You can use it on its own spooned over an omelet or scrambled eggs, over stuffed peppers, or as a topping for pasta. The dish keeps for several days in an airtight container in the refrigerator.

2 tablespoons vegetable oil
1 medium onion, thinly sliced
2 teaspoons imported sweet paprika
2 large tomatoes, peeled and coarsely diced

2 green bell peppers, cut into 3-inch strips
2 red bell peppers, cut into 3-inch strips
½ teaspoon salt

1. In a large frying pan, heat oil over medium heat. Add onion and cook, stirring occasionally, until golden, 2 to 3 minutes.

2. Stir in paprika, tomatoes, and pepper strips. Reduce heat to low. Cover and cook until thick, 25 to 30 minutes. Season with salt. Refrigerate until ready to use.

354   OLIVE MARINARA SAUCE
Prep: 10 minutes   Cook: 28 to 35 minutes   Makes: about 6 cups

This recipe makes a good amount of sauce, but it can be frozen for later use.

2 tablespoons olive oil
1 small onion, finely chopped
1 medium green pepper, diced
2 garlic cloves, minced
2 celery ribs, diced
1 (28-ounce) can Italian peeled tomatoes, drained and coarsely chopped

⅓ cup chopped parsley
½ cup dry red wine
2 teaspoons sugar
1 (6-ounce) can tomato paste
1 (2-ounce) can sliced black olives
1 teaspoon oregano
1 teaspoon salt
½ teaspoon pepper

1. In a large nonreactive saucepan, heat oil over medium heat. Add onion, green pepper, garlic, and celery. Cook, stirring occasionally, until vegetables soften, 3 to 5 minutes.

2. Add tomatoes, parsley, wine, and sugar. Reduce heat to medium-low. Partially cover and simmer 10 minutes.

3. Reduce heat to low. Stir in tomato paste, olives, oregano, salt, and pepper. Continue to cook, partially covered, stirring occasionally, until sauce thickens, 15 to 20 minutes. Serve immediately or reserve for later use.

355   MOROCCAN CHERMOULA
Prep: 10 minutes   Cook: 23 to 30 minutes   Makes: about 2 cups

In Morocco, this popular sauce is often used as a topping for cooked vegetables, such as green beans, cauliflower, or carrots. It tastes just as delicious served hot or at room temperature.

1 tablespoon olive oil
4 large very ripe tomatoes, peeled and cubed
2 teaspoons paprika
2 teaspoons ground cumin
2 garlic cloves, minced

¼ cup chopped cilantro
½ cup chopped parsley
½ teaspoon salt
¼ teaspoon pepper
1 tablespoon rice wine vinegar

1. In a medium nonreactive saucepan, heat oil over medium heat. Add tomatoes, paprika, and cumin. Mashing tomatoes down with a fork, cook, stirring occasionally, 4 to 5 minutes.

2. Add garlic, cilantro, and parsley. Reduce heat to low. Cover and cook until most of liquid evaporates, 15 to 20 minutes. Stir in salt, pepper, and vinegar. Cover and cook until heated through, 4 to 5 minutes longer.

356 SAUCE GUADELOUPE

Prep: 15 minutes   Cook: 5 minutes   Makes: about 1½ cups

Every cook on the Caribbean islands of Martinique and Guadeloupe has his or her own recipe for this spicy dip, called *sauce chien*, or "dog sauce." I don't know where the name comes from, but I can tell you it will set your palate afire, thanks to the inclusion of a fearsome pepper called a scotch bonnet, or *habañero* chile, reputed to be one of the hottest peppers known to man. When seeding a habañero pepper, be sure to wear rubber gloves to protect your hands. If habañeros are not available, substitute a jalapeño or serrano pepper or a dash of your favorite bottled hot sauce. Serve the sauce over rice, vegetable fritters, or grilled sandwiches.

1 habañero pepper, seeded and minced	¼ teaspoon salt
1 tablespoon chopped chives	¼ cup fresh lime juice
2 garlic cloves, minced	1 tablespoon coarsely chopped fresh cilantro
¼ cup chopped parsley	2 tablespoons peanut oil
⅛ teaspoon dried thyme leaves	

1. In a small saucepan, combine habañero pepper, chives, garlic, parsley, thyme, salt, and 1 cup water. Bring to a boil over medium-high heat. Reduce heat to medium-low and simmer 5 minutes. Remove from heat and let cool slightly.

2. Transfer to a serving bowl. Stir in lime juice, cilantro leaves, and peanut oil. Cover and refrigerate until serving time.

357 SALSA MEXICANA

Prep: 15 minutes   Cook: 10 seconds   Makes: about 1½ cups

To add more fire to this mild-tasting salsa, add a little finely diced jalapeño pepper.

4 medium tomatoes	½ teaspoon marjoram
2 tablespoons chopped cilantro	¼ teaspoon salt
1 tablespoon grated onion	⅛ teaspoon sugar
2 teaspoons lemon juice	1 or 2 drops Tabasco

1. Peel tomatoes by first blanching them in a large saucepan of boiling water for about 10 seconds to loosen skins. Transfer to a colander and rinse under cold running water. Slip off skins. Cut out stems and cut tomatoes crosswise in half. Squeeze gently to remove seeds. Chop tomatoes and set in a colander to drain, about 10 minutes.

2. In a medium bowl, mix tomatoes with cilantro, onion, lemon juice, marjoram, salt, sugar, and tabasco. Serve at room temperature or chilled.

358   TOMATILLO SALSA
Prep: 10 minutes   Cook: 8 to 10 minutes   Makes: about 2 cups

1 pound fresh tomatillos, husks removed, quartered
1 medium white onion, diced
1 cup vegetable broth or reduced-sodium chicken broth

4 garlic cloves, minced
½ jalapeño or serrano pepper, seeded and minced
¼ cup chopped cilantro
1 tablespoon lemon juice

1. In a medium nonreactive saucepan, combine tomatillos, onion, broth, garlic, and jalapeño pepper. Cook over medium-low heat, stirring, until tomatillos soften, 8 to 10 minutes. Remove from heat and let cool 5 minutes.

2. In a blender or food processor, puree cooked sauce until smooth. Stir in cilantro and lemon juice. Serve chilled.

359   URUGUAYAN ROASTED PEPPER SALSA
Prep: 10 minutes   Cook: none   Makes: about 2 cups

If time is of the essence, substitute canned green chiles for the freshly roasted pepper. Serve this over grilled vegetables or as a dip.

1 green bell pepper
1 bunch of scallions, coarsely chopped
1 large tomato, peeled, seeded, and coarsely chopped
½ cup cilantro
1 garlic clove, minced

¼ cup vegetable oil
1½ tablespoons fresh lemon juice
1 teaspoon salt
½ teaspoon pepper
3 drops of Tabasco, or more to taste

1. Roast pepper under a broiler as close to heat as possible or directly over a gas flame, turning until skin is charred all over, 5 to 8 minutes. Place in a paper bag and let stand 5 minutes. Peel off skin. Cut in half and remove stem, seeds, and inner white membranes.

2. In a blender or food processor, combine roasted pepper, scallions, tomato, cilantro, garlic, vegetable oil, lemon juice, salt, and pepper. Chop until fairly smooth. Transfer to a medium bowl. Stir in ¼ cup water and Tabasco. Serve chilled.

360 BASIL PESTO
Prep: 15 minutes   Cook: none   Makes: about 1½ cups

I like to make my pesto with almonds instead of the pine nuts called for in the classic recipe. Make sure the basil leaves are completely dry before using them.

2 cups loosely packed basil leaves, washed and patted dry	4 garlic cloves, minced
½ cup slivered almonds	1 cup freshly grated Romano cheese
¾ cup extra-virgin olive oil	¼ teaspoon pepper

In a blender or food processor, combine basil, almonds, olive oil, and garlic. Puree until fairly smooth. Add grated cheese and pepper and process until well blended.

361 GREEN CHILE-CILANTRO PESTO
Prep: 10 minutes   Cook: none   Makes: about 1½ cups

You can use this chile pesto as a topping for Mexican foods or as a dip with corn chips. It is simple to prepare, but is best made shortly before serving, because the distinctive taste of cilantro fades rapidly.

2 (4-ounce) cans diced green chiles	⅓ cup olive oil
1 cup loosely packed cilantro	3 tablespoons fresh lemon juice
2 garlic cloves, minced	½ teaspoon pepper
¼ cup pine nuts	

In a blender or food processor, combine chiles, cilantro, garlic, pine nuts, olive oil, lemon juice, and pepper. Puree until smooth.

362 GREEN TOFU MAYONNAISE
Prep: 10 minutes   Cook: none   Makes: about 1¼ cups

You can use this eggless mayonnaise as a dressing or as a spread for sandwiches. Make sure the tofu is well drained before using it.

6 ounces soft tofu, drained	2 tablespoons plus 1 teaspoon fresh lemon juice
½ cup extra-virgin olive oil	1 teaspoon Dijon mustard
1 cup fresh parsley	
4 garlic cloves, minced	

1. Puree tofu in a blender or food processor. With machine on, gradually add olive oil, blending until smooth.

2. Add parsley, garlic, lemon juice, and mustard and puree until mixture is completely smooth. Transfer to a serving bowl. Cover and refrigerate until serving time.

363   PICO DE GALLO
Prep: 15 minutes   Cook: none   Makes: about 3 cups

This traditional Mexican relish is best made with vine-ripened tomatoes. You will obtain the most flavorful results by dicing the vegetables very fine. Omit the jalapeño if spicy is not to your taste; substitute instead a small green or red bell pepper. Use pico de gallo as a topping for sandwiches or nachos, or as a dip with chips.

4 large ripe tomatoes, seeded
    and diced
1 small cucumber, seeded
    and finely diced
3 radishes, finely diced
4 scallions, finely chopped
1 fresh jalapeño pepper,
    seeded and minced

½ cup minced cilantro
2 garlic cloves, minced
½ teaspoon salt
¼ teaspoon sugar
3 tablespoons fresh
    lemon juice

In a medium bowl, combine all ingredients. Stir to mix well. Serve chilled.

364   HUMMUS
Prep: 10 minutes   Cook: none   Makes: about 1½ cups

Serve as a dip with potato chips or toasted wedges of pita bread.

1 (15¾-ounce) can garbanzo
    beans, liquid reserved
2 garlic cloves, minced
3 tablespoons lemon juice

2 teaspoons ground cumin
⅛ teaspoon cayenne
¼ cup plain yogurt
1 teaspoon paprika

1. In a blender or food processor, combine garbanzo beans with their liquid, garlic, lemon juice, cumin, cayenne, and yogurt. Puree until smooth.

2. Transfer hummus to a plate or shallow bowl and sprinkle with paprika.

365   YOGURT PESTO DIP
Prep: 15 minutes   Cook: none   Makes: 1⅔ cups

2 cups fresh basil leaves,
    loosely packed
1 cup plain yogurt
½ cup grated Romano cheese

4 garlic cloves, minced
½ teaspoon salt
¼ teaspoon dried thyme leaves

1. In a blender or food processor, combine basil and yogurt. Process until coarsely chopped.

2. Add cheese, garlic, salt, and thyme. Process until fairly smooth. Transfer to a small bowl. Cover and refrigerate until ready to use.

Index